T0330844

THE LEGACY
OF THE GOLDEN AGE

THE LEGACY
OF THE GOLDEN AGE

The 1960s and their economic consequences

Edited by
Frances Cairncross
and
Alec Cairncross

London and New York

First published 1992
by Routledge
2 Park Square, Milton Park, Abingdon, Oxon, OX14 4RN

Simultaneously published in the USA and Canada
by Routledge
a division of Routledge, Chapman and Hall, Inc.
270 Madison Ave, New York NY 10016

Reprinted in 1999, 2001

Transferred to Digital Printing 2005

Routledge is an imprint of the Taylor & Francis Group

Typeset in Baskerville by
Pat and Anne Murphy, Highcliffe-on-Sea, Dorset

British Library Cataloguing in Publication Data
A catalogue reference for this book is available from the
British Library.
ISBN 0-415-07154-2

Library of Congress Cataloging in Publication Data
The Legacy of the golden age: the 1960s and their economic
consequences/[edited by] Frances and Alec Cairncross.
p.   cm.
Based on papers from a conference held at Glasgow University,
Apr. 1991.
Includes bibliographical references and index.
ISBN 0-415-07154-2
1. Great Britain – Economic conditions – 1945 – Congresses.
2. Great Britain – Economic Policy – 1945 – Congresses.
3. Economic history – 1945-1971 – Congresses.
I. Cairncross, Frances. II. Cairncross, Alec, Sir,
1911-
HC256.5.L42   1992   330.941'0856-dc20
91-33651 CIP

CONTENTS

PREFACE

This book is based on a conference held at Glasgow University early in April 1991 to celebrate the 80th birthday of my father, Sir Alec Cairncross, who was Economic Adviser to Her Majesty's Government from 1961 to 1964 and Head of the Government Economic Service from 1964 to the end of 1968.

The aim of the conference was to review economic policy in the 1960s, and to ask whether errors in that decade contributed to the inflation that broke out in the 1970s. The participants included a number of the key actors who helped to shape economic policy in the 1960s either in a political or an official capacity. Among them were Lord O'Brien, Governor of the Bank of England from 1966 to 1973 and two former Chancellors of the Exchequer under whom Sir Alec served: Lord Callaghan, who acted as chairman of the conference and contributed greatly to its relaxed and friendly atmosphere, and Lord Jenkins, who took the chair in the second session and introduced the discussion of Sir Ralph Dahrendorf's paper in the fifth session.

While discussions inevitably had a predominantly British flavour, an international perspective was added by a number of distinguished American and European participants. Unfortunately, two of those who had originally agreed to speak, Signor Carli, the Italian Finance Minister, and Alexandre Lamfalussy, Economic Adviser of the Bank for International Settlements, were unable to attend and their places were taken at short notice by John Williamson and Sir Alec Cairncross.

In some cases, those who delivered papers stuck closely to their draft when introducing them. In others, new points were brought in, which have been presented here as amplifications. The conference was planned, and the discussions transcribed and edited, mainly by my father himself.

PREFACE

The conference was funded partly by the Scottish clearing banks and partly by Glasgow University, of which my father is Chancellor. Arrangements in Glasgow were admirably directed by Professor Andrew Skinner. The generosity of the university and the warmth of all its staff made it a truly memorable occasion.

Frances Cairncross

INTRODUCTION: THE 1960s

Seen in retrospect, in the glow of the 'Golden Age' that stretched from the Second World War to the first oil shock in 1973, the 1960s in Britain were a kind of economic apogee, the high point reached before the descent to the tribulations that followed. The national income grew faster than ever before – nearly half as fast again as in the 1950s when the Prime Minister thought we had 'never had it so good'. Unemployment remained below 2.5 per cent of the labour force and for most of the time was under 2 per cent – far below the levels of the next two decades. Inflation, although a cause for serious concern, averaged under 4 per cent for most of the decade, only rising to 5–6 per cent in the last two years. Even the current balance of payments, the abiding problem of the post-war years, was close to balance for the decade as a whole and ended in healthy surplus after the devaluation of 1967 had had time to take effect.

From another point of view, the 1960s was a decade of experiment in economic and social policy. In Britain the innovations included the introduction of a seemingly endless succession of departures in fiscal policy: the tax regulator, a capital gains tax, corporation tax, the selective employment tax and, on the other side of the ledger, the regional employment premium and investment grants. An attempt was made to accelerate economic growth through the National Economic Development Council and the National Plan; to curb inflation through a long succession of experiments in incomes policy; to fashion new ways of operating on the balance of payments, notably through the temporary import surcharge and the provision for the surrender of 25 per cent of the premium on investment currency; and to restructure industry through the Industrial Reconstruction Corporation. Other initiatives had a broader purpose: the efforts to join the European Community; the founding of many new universities,

1

including the Open University; and the relaxations in the law that came to be labelled 'permissiveness'.

Yet the survivors of that decade do not look back on it as a resounding success. As Lord Jenkins pointed out, 'those who presided over the Golden Age did not feel at the time that they were singularly blessed and carried in a golden coach'. People are more likely to remember the decade as one of repeated crises – particularly balance-of-payments crises. There were currency uncertainties almost throughout; a long-deferred devaluation in 1967; and in 1968, so far from devaluation putting an end to balance-of-payments difficulties, there was a general sense of catastrophe ahead. And if they think back to the experiments of the 1960s, they may reflect on how many were later abandoned.

Perhaps the reappearance of balance-of-payments difficulties in the 1990s may revive interest in the crises and experiments of those years. With a rate of exchange fixed within fairly narrow limits in the European Monetary System and an enormous external deficit, there is a strong inclination to ponder what would be gained or lost by a new depreciation and an equally strong temptation to turn again to incomes policy as an alternative to devaluation in restoring Britain's competitive power. The situation in the 1990s may be very different from that of thirty years ago but the events of the past have some bearing on the dilemmas of the present.

Although the discussion at the conference tended to focus on the United Kingdom, it was not possible to disregard what was going on elsewhere in the world. The problems of the United Kingdom have to be seen in the light of developments in other countries; the experience of any one industrial country is affected by what is thought elsewhere and what happens elsewhere. The problems experienced by the United Kingdom in the 1960s were also in some measure the problems of other industrial countries.

The continental countries grew faster than the United Kingdom but, unlike the United Kingdom, less fast than in the 1950s. Nearly all of them had their troubles. The French franc was devalued a year after the pound sterling and again at the end of the decade; earlier in 1968 the riots in Paris were followed by a general strike that came near to bringing down the government. Germany also changed the value of its currency, at the beginning and again at the end of the decade, but upwards, not downwards, and suffered higher inflation in 1969–70 than at any time since the war. Italy, although growing faster than Germany and enlarging her share of world trade in manufactures, faced rapid inflation in the early 1960s. The United States enjoyed falling unemployment throughout the decade and with it a steady rise in gross national product (GNP) at an average rate of 4.5 per cent per annum between 1960 and 1969. But the American balance of payments on current account deteriorated after 1964 and the reserves of gold and foreign exchange fell slowly over the decade by about 20 per cent in total. By 1968 the gold pool had become a two-tier gold market, low priced for central banks, with fluctuating but higher prices for other buyers.

The first question discussed at the conference was why the Golden Age lasted so long. But there was a prior question. Why did it occur in the first place? There had been no 'golden age' after the First World War: only a short re-stocking boom followed by a plunge into depression in 1921. Some countries, notably the United States, had recovered quickly and enjoyed renewed prosperity throughout the 1920s. But others, particularly in Europe, had floundered throughout a decade of underemployment only to sink still deeper in the Great Depression of the 1930s. Yet the circumstances after the two World Wars were not so very different. There had been the same wholesale destruction of capital, even if it was by no means as extensive in the two cases; the same accumulation, year after year, of arrears of repair, maintenance and replacement; the same setting aside till after the war of the innovations becoming available as the war progressed; and the same widening gap between developing American industrial practice and the backward technology of war-time Europe.

It is arguable that what made the difference was not superior knowledge and economic skill but quite simply the Marshall Plan: the willingness of the United States to supply a bridge of Marshall Aid across the depression threatened by the dollar shortage and so allow Europe to maintain the pressure of demand without a series of balance-of-payments setbacks. Once employment was maintained long enough for output to recover to beyond the pre-war level, and for exports and fixed investment to take up the running, there was no immediate danger of a relapse. After Marshall Aid had ceased, the United States kept pumping out dollars all through the 1950s so that there was no major threat from external imbalance; and arrears of all kinds sustained investment and removed the immediate threat of internal imbalance. The process was helped by the gradual liberalization of trade, the revival of international investment and the equilibrating influence of the European Payments Union and other international institutions, in an atmosphere of active international co-operation totally different from that of the inter-war years. At the same time the rising level of employment and productivity, by generating additional income and demand, was constantly renewing the need for more capacity and higher investment, and so in turn maintaining the pressure on resources. It was of particular importance that the pivot of the system, the United States, was unexpectedly successful in achieving a high level of employment that might not be altogether stable but was subject to only minor fluctuations. The accumulation of arrears of investment and innovation throughout the 1930s and war-time in the early 1940s no doubt contributed to this result.

But was the process one that could go on indefinitely? Would investment demand continue to renew itself? A variety of dangers was discussed. The Golden Age might be just one more Kondratieff cycle, whatever the cause of such cycles. Not much importance was attached to this if the cycle itself went unexplained. But was it not to be expected that economic growth would slow down once the urgent needs and opportunities of post-war reconstruction were over? Professor Malinvaud admitted that while he had thought so up to the middle 1960s, he had changed his mind when rapid growth continued or even accelerated. Others no doubt had a similar experience.

In some places there was unmistakable evidence of a slowing down of economic growth. As Professor Matthews pointed out, Germany provided a clear example with the growth in gross domestic product (GDP) falling cycle by cycle from an average of 8.1 per cent per annum in 1952–7 to 6.6 per cent in 1957–60, 5.0 per cent in 1960–5, 4.1 per cent in 1965–73, 2.2 per cent in 1973–80 and 1.9 per cent in 1980–9. For the European members of the OECD, the growth of GDP at an average of 6.6 per cent per annum between 1948 and 1954 compared with 5.1 per cent between 1954 and 1960 and 4.8 per cent in the 1960s. But the big slowdown came later. In OECD Europe the growth in GDP dropped to 3.1 per cent in the 1970s and to 1.8 per cent in the 1980s.

So far as output growth was concerned the break came suddenly in 1974–5 after the first oil shock. In that sense the Golden Age was brought to an end by the events of 1973: not just the quadrupling of the price of oil but also the world economic boom that preceded it and drove up commodity prices through a synchronization of expansion in all the industrial countries. But as James Meade pointed out, there were two elements to the Golden Age: full employment and rising productivity. That there was a turning point in employment in 1973 is plain enough: unemployment in industrial countries had been rising gently for some years but it was only after 1973 that a sharp break occurred. Unemployment began to rise steadily, year after year, to a peak of over 10 per cent in OECD Europe in 1984–5 and to a somewhat higher average level than before in the United States and Japan in the later 1970s and 1980s.

It is more difficult to pinpoint a change in the upward trend of productivity. Professor Solow suggested 1969 as the watershed in the United States. On the European continent the trend had been downwards from the 1950s. In the British case there was no mistaking the abrupt change after 1973. But a comparison between rates of growth in total factor productivity in the years between 1950 and 1973 and the decade or so after 1973 shows a large drop all over the industrial world (Chapter 6, table 6.8). It was this drop, more even than the failure to maintain full employment, that spelt the end of the Golden Age.

But were the two things unconnected? Did a less buoyant business outlook and rising unemployment have no effect on the growth of productivity? Some economists would expect a more rapidly expanding market to yield more rapidly growing productivity and would be able to point to a marked short-term, cyclical relationship of this kind (Okun's law). A similar long-term relationship has been suggested on various grounds by Allyn Young, Lauchlin Currie, P.J. Verdoorn, Lord Kaldor and others. One line of reasoning would be that if innovations are set aside in periods of depression like the 1930s to be brought forward again in more prosperous times like the 1950s, may not some of the slowdown in productivity since 1973 be traceable to similar forces? Quite apart from any dampening of venturesomeness, is it not usual for a less rapidly expanding market to reduce the scope for economies of scale and raise obstacles to readjustments that would raise efficiency? In any event the more rapid growth of productivity once unemployment began to fall in the mid-1980s is a reminder that if the pace has slowed it can still quicken in favourable circumstances.

On another view, the Golden Age did not so much end as fade away. This view laid stress, not on particular events in any one decade, but on a long-continuing slowdown in productivity growth. This it interpreted as reflecting a gradual catching up on American levels of productivity, ending in a rate of growth similar to the American rate of growth once advantage had been taken of the full quiver of American technology and managerial knowhow. It could be shown that by 1984 output per hour worked (but not per head per annum) was almost identical with the American rate in France, Sweden and the Netherlands and only slightly lower in Germany and Belgium, with the United Kingdom and Italy further, and Japan much further, behind. On this view, a period of depression might delay but not arrest the process of convergence. Curiously enough a diametrically opposite point of view was sometimes expressed in the days of the dollar shortage after the war when it was argued that America's advantage was cumulative and that, so far from overtaking American levels of productivity, other industrial countries would fall further and further behind.

It was also doubted whether sustained high pressure made for faster growth. David Worswick hesitated to decide whether high pressure was favourable or unfavourable to rapid growth and was sceptical of its contribution. This raised a second major question discussed in the second session of the conference: why was it that mounting inflation did not bring the Golden Age to an earlier end? Why, when the pressure was so intense and unemployment so low, was there so little acceleration in wage settlements? If it was inflation that produced the break in 1973 why did it not happen earlier?

But first, was it true, David Worswick asked, that there was little or no acceleration? The economics profession still talks glibly of Phillips curves and non-accelerating inflation rates of unemployment (NAIRUS) as if there were some evident functional relationship between the level of unemployment and the magnitude of wage increases. No one doubts that there is such a relationship over the cycle in the same way as all prices show some response to rising demand. But as Henry Phelps Brown pointed out many years ago, the issue is not whether workers are less exigent in their demands when they see their mates being sacked. It is rather whether a sustained lower level of unemployment is likely to be accompanied by a succession of higher wage settlements; or a higher, continuing level of unemployment by a move to lower wage settlements. In addressing these questions one has to be mindful of many other factors: changes in import prices, the level of previous settlements, the trend in profits, the political climate and so on. At one extreme the pressure can become intense for a limited supply of labour while at the other extreme the labour may be so abundant that it loses all bargaining power. But between these extremes there is a wide area of uncertainty and indeterminacy. It is simply not possible by looking at the level of unemployment (and nothing else) to know where wages will settle in any given year.

What David Worswick demonstrated was that, whether one considered the United Kingdom, OECD Europe or the United States, there was no convincing evidence of acceleration in wages or prices before the mid-1960s or indeed before 1968 in the case of the United Kingdom. The rise in consumer prices touched 4.5 per cent in 1956 and then, after dipping below 1 per cent in 1959 and 1960, rose again to 4.5 per cent in 1965. It was not until the last two years of the decade, after the devaluation of 1967, that prices rose by more than 4.5 per cent. Similarly, if one takes hourly wage rates the increase fluctuated around 6 per cent throughout the decade, with a low increase of under 4 per cent in 1963 and 1967 and a high increase of just under 7 per cent in 1966 and 1968. It was not until the 1970s that wages accelerated.

The story for other countries is not fundamentally different. In OECD Europe consumer prices had risen after 1952 at an average of under 3 per cent and during the period 1960–9 the average was still no more than 3.5 per cent. What one can point to is some acceleration at the end of the decade and a failure of the United States (discussed later) to curtail excess demand by raising taxes. But even in the United States the annual rise in consumer prices was never more than 5.4 per cent (in 1969) and averaged only 2.3 per cent over the decade.

Whatever we may now think of the rate of inflation in the 1960s it was taken sufficiently seriously to make governments adopt measures to reduce it. These were of several kinds. Governments might use fiscal or monetary policy to check the growth of demand in the hope that some of the check would be to the rise in prices. This could be a costly method since it involved a loss in output and momentum: in Britain it was known as 'stop–go' because the check was liable to halt the expansion of output instead of merely reducing the rate of increase. Two other possibilities were the subject of experiments. One was planning; the other was incomes policy.

In Britain the aim of economic planning was primarily to engage the support of employers and workers (particularly the trade union representatives of the workers) in measures to accelerate growth. It was hoped that setting targets consistent with faster growth would make it easier to induce all parties to take the necessary action and help avoid the stops that were made necessary by inflation. Some economists argued that if only everybody would agree to pursue faster growth and carry out their part in the plan, faster growth would automatically result. Unfortunately, faster growth in an economy starting from full employment can be achieved only by raising productivity which does not result automatically from concerted action. What is only too likely to happen is a burst of inflation when the higher output that should come from higher productivity is sought instead from higher employment. If the pressure does increase then the other object of regulating wage settlements and keeping down costs is correspondingly jeopardized. Whatever might have happened under the National Plan, it was never put into action. It assumed that the balance-of-payments difficulties would be resolved – presumably by devaluation – when the government belatedly opted for deflation.

The National Plan's one lasting effect was on government expenditure. It could not in any real sense commit employers or workers but it could and did commit the government. The government committed itself to a 4.25 per cent annual increase in public expenditure: in fact public expenditure up to devaluation never increased by as little as 4.25 per cent and by 1967, when it mattered most, the increase (in real terms) had reached 13 per cent.

As Sir Donald MacDougall pointed out, Ministers have difficulty in dealing with complex economic programmes involving rates of change in productivity. It may be, as he suggested, that there would have been little point in a plan aiming at less than 4 per cent growth per annum. But the French, whose example we thought we were following, did not pick growth rates higher than they had ever achieved. And as Sir Donald reminded the conference, Selwyn Lloyd was only with difficulty dissuaded from setting a target of 5 per cent growth (which later Chancellors would have had difficulty in revising downwards).

The second method of attempting to control inflation was incomes policy. More effort was put into incomes policy in Britain than any other element in high policy. The 1960s did not herald the beginning of efforts to limit wage increases nor were the efforts made in the 1960s the most successful: the agreement with the Trades Union Congress (TUC) following the devaluation of 1949 was much more effective. But a more continuous effort was made from the beginning to the end of the decade to exert influence on wage settlements than in any similar period. These efforts were recalled by Lord Croham in his paper, drawing on his recollections of a long association with incomes policy.

In July 1961 Selwyn Lloyd had announced a pay 'pause' which lasted until about the end of the year. A year later came the National Incomes Commission which heard few cases, had little influence and was abolished by the Labour Government in 1964. A fresh attempt to establish a voluntary policy was made by George Brown but in 1965 wages rose faster than before. A wage-freeze in July 1966 was successful in holding the position for a time and was succeeded by a statutory policy with a norm fixed by the government. In 1969, however, Ministers gave precedence to a different target and prepared to introduce legislation restricting the powers of trade unions. This was successfully resisted by the TUC with the support of Lord Callaghan, while in the meantime incomes policy was abandoned.

These events were extensively discussed in the third session of the conference, in particular by Lord Callaghan, who was then Home Secretary, and by Lord Jenkins, at that time Chancellor of the Exchequer. Lord Jenkins agreed that the Labour Government had taken a deliberate decision to back the policy in the White Paper *In Place of Strife* rather than maintain a stringent incomes policy. But he regarded it as unthinkable that no attempt should have been made to curb trade union power, even if it meant relaxing incomes policy. In this he had the support of Lord Callaghan who had felt at the time that it was not for a Labour Government to invoke the law as a means of reforming the trade unions but had changed his mind after witnessing the behaviour of the unions in the 1970s.

The evidence of the 1960s showed the limits of incomes policy but also suggested its utility in some circumstances. Governments had tended to turn to incomes policy when the pressure in the labour market was at its highest and the power of trade unions (if so minded) to limit wage increases was least. When the pressure eased, on the other hand, wage settlements moderated almost automatically. Moreover, incomes policy raised all the difficulties of deciding on relativities which workers took more seriously than the level of pay. Hence a wage-freeze, which did not disturb relativities, was accepted much more willingly than a policy affecting individual settlements. The question remained, as put by Robert Solow at the end of his paper: 'can one imagine demand management and incomes policies working together and not in opposition?' He concluded: 'with some effort one can imagine that'.

The upshot of this part of the discussion was that governments were not faced until late in the decade with the kind of acceleration in inflation that was later to bring the Golden Age to an end. But neither had they succeeded in finding an antidote to inflation. In Britain incomes policy had been tried and abandoned. In the United States inflation was being stoked by the war in Vietnam. In France 'the events of June' had released new inflationary forces. Even in

Germany, as Professor Kloten explained, there had been a powerful reaction in the second half of 1969 to the earlier efforts of the government to limit wage increases and in 1970 hourly wages in manufacturing were rising at over 13 per cent per annum.

By the end of the 1960s there was widespread concern over the power of the unions to accelerate inflation. Wage inflation had reached 14 per cent with unemployment at 2.5 per cent and rising gently. In Frank Blackaby's survey of the literature on incomes policy, Arthur Lewis is quoted as arguing that 'it is merely a matter of time before the unions are deprived of their collective bargaining functions in Western Europe and North America' and Henry Phelps Brown as warning that 'to persist with collective bargaining as it is working now is to commit ourselves to a South American future' (Blackaby, 1971). This was well before the world economic boom of 1973 and the first oil shock.

What produced this apparent change in wage inflation at the end of the 1960s? In the United States, in contrast with Western Europe, the rise in wages, as David Worswick points out, mirrored the fall in unemployment over the decade and continued until it reached a peak of 9 per cent in 1975. In Britain and other European countries there may have been a delayed reaction, as there had been in Germany, to efforts to limit wage increases. Henry Phelps Brown has suggested that the fading of memories of the inter-war years may also have played a part. Younger workers coming to power in the unions set less store by job security, had higher expectations and were more disposed to a militant use of their bargaining power. Whatever the explanation, labour attitudes left Europe ill prepared for the stresses of 1973 that put an end to the Golden Age.

If it was inflation that put an end to the Golden Age does that exonerate the policies of the 1960s? It was the inflation of the 1970s, not the 1960s, that went beyond the level of tolerance and made policy-makers attach a priority to the control of inflation that was fatal to full employment. But what of that extra wage-push at the end of the 1960s and the rise in inflation in the United States from 1.5 to 5 per cent, with its repercussions on countries linked to the dollar under the Bretton Woods system? Could these have been absorbed, as David Worswick argued, in the absence of the first oil shock? Or did they herald progressively higher rates of inflation even without the oil shock? Faster inflation in America was enough to bring down the Bretton Woods system well before the first oil shock; and the two-tier gold market went further back. Inflation in America may have been modest by European standards, but it was accompanied by an external deficit which in some ways is a form of concealed inflation, and even modest inflation in a reserve currency can be damaging to the entire system. As for the move from 4 to 6 per cent in Britain it must be doubtful whether once the rate started moving up it would not move higher – as indeed it did in 1970–2.

If the situation deteriorated in the 1960s, could that be blamed on a lack of instruments, as was discussed in the second session of the conference, or on inadequate international co-operation, as the fourth session was asked to consider? Many instruments of policy involving the use of direct controls had been abandoned by the 1960s, but many of the most powerful remained and quite a number of new devices, as we have seen, were introduced. Indeed, the 1960s stand out as the period of maximum fertility in instrument-making in the post-war period. It is true that the government would have liked a more effective instrument for controlling prices. But if incomes policy was of limited help it was partly because too much was asked of it and partly because of the lack of public understanding and support. The government also hankered after instruments for promoting faster growth. But whether industrial governments can do much to raise productivity (which is what faster growth implies at full employment) must be very doubtful.

When discussion turned to international co-ordination, it was with a sense of the intellectual effort that had gone into devising a framework for the international economic system during and after the Second World War. The Bretton Woods arrangements had been a compromise that leaned strongly towards the American position and had worked in the immediate post-war situation only because the United States made it work by helping to restore international balance. Indeed it could be said that it was not until the establishment of convertibility at the end of 1958 that the system was in full working order and by 1971 it had broken down. It had been on the international side that the imbalances of later years had begun to assume serious proportions and it had been in the 1960s that the trouble began.

The Bretton Woods arrangements were intended to be symmetrical and rule-based and there were those like John Williamson who strongly favoured such arrangements. On the other hand, the system after the war was far from symmetrical and later ceased to be rule based. Professor Kindleberger doubted whether rule-based systems were ever symmetrical: the Bretton Woods system was essentially a

11

dollar system, money evolved in a Darwinian way and evolution did not conform to strict rules.

Much of the argument was about the causes of the breakdown of the Bretton Woods Agreement. John Williamson gave three possible explanations. The first was the inadequacy of the policy instruments: there was insufficient exchange rate flexibility (e.g. the use of a crawling peg) and incomes policy did not succeed in reconciling full employment with low inflation. A second explanation was the inadequacy of the intellectual framework: there had been no accelerationist theory of inflation and it had been allowed to build up to a fatal extent. The third explanation was that maybe it was only a fortunate accident and sheer coincidence that kept the system in balance in the 1960s. Andrew Crockett agreed that it was inability to deal with inflation and divergences in inflation rates that caused the system to break down, but doubted whether, if this crucial weakness could be rectified, it would allow a return to a rule-based system. He pointed in particular to the growth of capital movements which could overwhelm the efforts of central banks to control exchange rates.

A second form of co-ordination, supplementing the rules of the Bretton Woods system, took the form of meetings of Ministers (e.g. at various summits) and officials (usually at Working Party 3 of the OECD). Officials, as John Williamson explained, were largely engaged in a kind of peer review of each other's policies, whilst Ministers might bargain with one another on the modification of existing policies. This part of the discussion was relatively brief and ignored co-ordination between central banks at meetings in Basle, organized financial assistance to countries in balance-of-payments difficulties such as the United Kingdom from 1964 to 1969 and France in 1968–9 the Kennedy Round and other forms of co-operation on international economic policy.

The final session of the conference discussed the question underlying the earlier topics. Were the troubles of the 1970s brought on or intensified by errors and failures in the previous decade? Professor Solow's answer was 'not very much'.

It was not possible to put all the blame on OPEC, given the turbulence of the early 1970s and the explosiveness of the world-wide boom of 1973 – already past its peak before the first big rise in oil prices. One obvious error, on which there was general agreement, was the failure of the American government to raise taxes to finance the Vietnam War. That had pushed up inflation from 3 per cent to 6 per cent between 1967 to 1970 and had helped to lever up prices in other countries, more perhaps through the overflow of excess demand and the outflow of funds than through the direct impact on foreign prices. The main error, both in America and Europe, had been to give way too readily to inflation.

In some cases, notably Great Britain, this took the form of putting too much faith in incomes policy. This had encouraged the belief that when full employment was pursued to the point of greatly increased pressure, a voluntary or, if need be, a statutory incomes policy would moderate wage increases and keep inflation within limits. But in circumstances of excess demand, incomes policy was of limited help. What had prevented wages from accelerating until the late 1960s had been 'stop–go' (including the 'stop' of 1966) rather than incomes policy. It is arguable that the most serious error of the 1960s in Britain was the failure to apply in 1964 the measures that were taken too late in 1966.

Britain's experience of inflation in the late 1960s, however, was not fundamentally different from that of other countries. If, as argued in the third session, inflation speeded up because of the arrival of new and more thrusting wage bargainers and the fading of memories of unemployment in the 1930s, then the speeding up cannot so easily be attributed to errors of policy. Similarly, if slower growth in productivity in the 1970s had little to do with the reduction in pressure in industrial countries or with the anti-inflationary policies causing the reduction, the policy-makers may escape blame. But if the two things were connected and slower growth made it harder to contain the rise in wages, then increased importance is attached to the source of the acceleration in inflation at the end of the 1960s. At the end of the day, governments in the last years of the 1960s failed to counter what had become a more serious wage inflation than any since the Korean War and allowed inflationary expectations to develop that proved increasingly difficult to extinguish.

REFERENCE

Blackaby, F.T. (1971) 'Incomes policy and inflation', *National Institute Economic Review*, November.

OPENING THE CONFERENCE

Lord Callaghan, opening the conference, said that not everyone would have chosen an economic seminar as a birthday present. It was an unusual choice by an unusual man who had advised the government on everything from anthrax and crofting to the Channel Tunnel as well as all kinds of other things. Like the Queen's Birthday the event did not coincide with a real birthday but was an official affair, although he doubted whether those who took part could expect a holiday to go with it. Half a dozen countries were represented and all present were delighted to take part in the splendid surroundings of the University Senate Room. He hoped for plenty of cut and thrust in the discussion of the 1960s and was himself, as a practitioner in those days, in no mood to apologize for them, especially after having seen what happened in the 1970s and 1980s.

1

WHY DID THE GOLDEN AGE LAST SO LONG?

Charles Kindleberger

As the first speaker, it falls to my lot to welcome Sir Alec into the Club of Nonagenarians. Some of you may protest that he has become merely an octogenarian. I cling to the view that he is completing his eighth and entering into his ninth decade. Join the Club, Alec. Eighty is a good round number; 81, coming up, is a square number. If you regret leaving 79 which was a prime number, take comfort from the fact that when you reach 83 you will be in your prime again.

We met in 1943 or 1944 through the kindly office of Bill Salant, late brother of your friend and mine, Walter Salant. As intermediary, Bill invited me to lunch with you. With my present enfeebled faculties, I am unable to recall who, if anyone, produced trenchant or particularly witty remarks, but I have strongly in memory that it was a very pleasant occasion. And our friendship, started perhaps forty-eight years ago, goes on. We are currently engaged in a genial competition in hypergraphia, to see which of us, as aging over-achievers, will produce more acres of print. I cheat in one way, by publishing old letters and books. You enlist collaborators, such as Nita Watts and Barry Eichengreen. Nor do I know how to score edited books, such as your magnificent *Robert Hall Diaries*, volumes 1 and 2. Both of us count our medals back to the Second World War and its German aftermath. But if you will permit me a personal note, my father-in-law, a professor of English, once produced a paper for a small literary group on 'Shakespeare's Old Men', and irritated his white-haired auditors by emphasizing how cranky and tiresome Shakespeare's old men all were. You provide a brilliant counter-example.

The original programme for this happy occasion was entitled 'The Legacy of the 1960s', and this paper was to be on 'Why Did the Boom Last So Long?'. I apologize for taking the liberty of altering my title

15

to 'Why Did the Golden Age Last So Long?', and for leaving out any reference to the 1960s. I, for one, am glad to have seen the 1960s go. OPEC, that got us into so much trouble, was founded in 1960, although on my earlier showing that may belong to the 1950s. The 1960s themselves were a turbulent period socially, with the free-speech movement in Berkeley in 1963, the assassinations in the United States in 1963 and 1968, the Notting Hill Gate riots, the Vietnam War which drove President Johnson from office and the so-called 'events of May–June' in Paris which did the same for President de Gaulle, not to mention Woodstock in 1969.

Rather than limit myself to the 1960s, I propose to deal with what has been called the 'Golden Age', from around 1950 to 1973, a quarter century in economic history just as 1815 to 1914 was a century, not in the decimal system starting with the birth of Christ, but in the economic phenomena that interest our profession. The period was first called the golden age in 1944 in a discussion of post-war planning by Sir Richard Hopkins of the UK Treasury who urged the Chancellor of the Exchequer to concentrate his budget speech on the transitional period which 'is what matters to most people', with only brief remarks on the 'golden age' that might follow (Cairncross and Watts 1989: 86). The term has been adopted in the 1980s by that consummate statistical analyst of economic growth, Angus Maddison (1982: ch. 6) and by a group of leftist economists (Glyn *et al.* 1990) who are thought by one of their number to have originated the term (Singh 1990: 239). A somewhat more refined characterization is provided by Herman van der Wee, who calls the 1960s a 'golden age', but the 1950s a 'silver' one (1986: ch. 2). Gold and silver are both precious metals, and I adopt the Alfred Marshall programme of symmetalism, but inflate the name to 'golden'.

I might have entitled this talk 'Why did the Golden Age Come to an End?' When positive feedback, or a self-reinforcing mechanism which has lasted for a considerable period, comes to a halt, the question as readily arises why the virtuous circle broke down as why it was so virtuous over such a distance. It is difficult, perhaps impossible, to separate the two. *Pace* Alfred Marshall, Nature, at least in its social-science manifestation, seems to have made a jump, or at least suffered a fall.

How did the Golden Age happen to last for roughly 23 years? On one showing I could claim that the period was half of a Kondratieff cycle, and that these are 50 (or 55) years in length, and half of 50 is 25, which is more or less 23. I shall not do so. I come to the Kondratieff explanation later but not to accept it. A preferable explanation, in my judgement, runs in terms of a start, a self-reinforcing mechanism, and an end of the boom. I also propose to dwell to some extent on the height and the spread of the boom, as well as its length. An abundance of theories have been put forward on these issues, by no means virtually exclusive, and the analysis runs the risk of over-determination, with more equations than unknowns, of the sort that I have recently encountered dealing with the British economic crisis of 1621, where observers list causes running up to eight or more, and as many as eight remedies.

A preliminary word on the spread and the height. I confess to some surprise that Britons think of the 1950s and 1960s as a period of boom. My recollection of the time runs in terms of (1) league tables in which the United Kingdom (and the United States) stood at the bottom of the list; (2) stop–go, or more accurately go–stop, with the British authorities obliged to slam on the deflationary brakes every few years after the economy had picked up speed, in order to prevent the balance-of-payments deficit running up too sharply; and (3) books such as Lord (Nicholas) Kaldor's *Causes of the Slow Rate of Economic Growth of the United Kingdom* (1966) and Wilfred Beckerman's *Slow Growth in Britain* (1979). The reasons for focusing on slow growth then, and a golden age now, may well be a change in the field of vision, from comparison with other industrial countries in the immediate post-war period (Table 1.1) to that with the historical British performance later. Past United Kingdom figures – though the early numbers are somewhat shaky – show the 1950–73 British performance to have been an outstanding one (Table 1.2).

Table 1.1 Growth of output (GDP at constant prices) per head of population, 1950–73

Country	% Annual average compound growth rate
Japan	8.4
Germany	5.0
Italy	4.8
France	4.2
Canada	3.0
United Kingdom	2.5
United States	2.2

17

Table 1.2 Growth of United Kingdom output (GDP at constant prices)
per head of population 1700–1987

Period	% Annual average compound growth rate
1700–1820	0.4
1820–1870	1.5
1870–1913	1.0
1913–1950	0.9
1950–1973	2.5
1973–1979	1.3
1973–1987	1.5

Source: Maddison 1982: 44; figures for 1973–87, Maddison 1989: 35

Let me first attempt to dispose of the notion that the Golden Age
was simply the fourth Kondratieff downswing in prices (or in some
versions upswing in GDP) in a system that has been reproducing
itself since 1790 (Rostow 1978: ch. 10, especially pp. 109–10), or in
one version since 1495 (Goldstein 1988). In Rostow's formulation,
upswings (1790–1815, 1848–73, 1896–1920, 1935–51 and 1972
onward) occur when the population outgrows foodstuffs and raw
materials, especially energy, whereas downswings (1815–48,
1873–96 and 1920–35) are intervals when primary product prices are
falling along with interest rates. Rostow calls 1941–72 a downswing
but notes that it was a period of endemic inflation that shares some
but not all of the characteristics of previous downswings.

I find no persuasive explanation for the periodicity of complete
Kondratieff cycles of fifty to sixty years, or for upswings and downswings of roughly half that length. At first view the upswings seem to
occur in major wars – the Napoleonic Wars and the First and Second
World Wars, with perhaps the Crimean War, the American Civil
War and the Prussian Wars against Denmark, Austria and France
responsible for the upswing from 1848 to 1873. Such wars are
presumably extrinsic to economic behaviour, although Goldstein's
rather tortured model makes them endogenous. Maddison expresses
some sympathy with Rostow's characterization of the Golden Age as
part of a Kondratieff, though he is uncomfortable with calling it a
downswing (1982: 80), and finally rejects the Rostovian analysis on
the ground that prices are an inadequate substitute for an aggregate
such as GDP. Jay W. Forrester is also a follower of Kondratieff, but

with a different central driving force – industrial investment, rather than the relationship between population and resources.

I choose to dismiss the Kondratieff hypothesis without further treatment, believing with Samuelson that it is science fiction (Goldstein 1988: 21). Kitchin, Juglar and Kuznets cycles have intuitive explanations in inventories, industrial investment and housing respectively. Intuitive explanations for the fifty-five-year cycle are superabundant beyond the Rostow population–resources relationship and Forrester's long-term investment. They involve technological breakthroughs, including Fordism (Mensch 1979), and overshooting plus correction in capital markets (Berry 1991). Each is single-valued. None is persuasive. I proceed with the Golden Age of 1950–73 without the Procrustean bed furnished by the eminent Russian statistician.

Opposed to the notion that economic activity moves in repeating fifty-five-year cycles of which this golden age is a recent half is the leftist view that the golden age was a historical aberration (Singh 1990: 240), 'the product of a *unique economic regime*' (Glyn *et al.* 1990: 40; emphasis in the original). The regime arose from a mixture of four elements: (1) a macroeconomic structure in which wages followed productivity growth, profits held up and investment stood high along with consumption – a positive feedback mechanism ran from profits to investment to rising productivity to profits again; (2) a system of production emphasizing large-scale units, and labour satisfied because of an expectation of rising income; (3) co-ordination of domestic policies affecting wages, prices and governmental policies, both monetary and fiscal; and (4) a benign international monetary system under United States hegemony, with stable money, low trade barriers, progressively lowered still further, and trade growing faster than output (Glyn *et al.* 1990: 40ff.). All this began to unravel in the late 1960s before the first OPEC price hike of 1973. Wages kept on rising, but this time faster than productivity, prices underwent inflationary increases and the international system fell apart, beginning in 1968 when President Nixon closed the gold window, and very evidently in 1971 when the dollar was devalued, before being followed in 1974 by floating. The emphasis is on uniqueness on the one hand and the hint of underconsumption on the other. As far as it goes, the analysis carries conviction, though I think it leaves out one or two important elements.

Nor do mainstream economists lack a variety of explanations of the Golden Age, emphasizing real economic variables, sociological variables and policy choices. There is a wide difference of opinion between those who ascribe the boom to policy decisions and others who emphasize institutions and chance events. The span as a whole can be divided into the initial propulsive forces, the positive feedback mechanism and finally, though that word is too strong, the reversal. I will offer lists of theories and their authors, by no means mutually exclusive, before coming to my preferred combination. I hasten to add that I do not feel dogmatic about the list of factors, nor the weights that should be assigned to them, though I am made uneasy by those like the ambitious Edward Denison (1967) who try to disaggregate the various forces and measure their contributions exactly.

The main theories of the Golden Age divide somewhat along the following lines: initial recovery from war, followed by 'catching up' (Abramovitz 1986, 1990; Dumke 1990); governmental policies (Maddison 1964, 1982, 1989; Heller 1966); sociological theories (Postan 1967; Olson 1982); and eclectic theories (Denison 1967; Matthews *et al.* 1982; van der Wee 1986). A second group assume that the boom has somehow started – whether by catching up, governmental policy or other means – and concentrate on the feedback mechanisms. These include export-led growth as the boom in leading countries spills over into imports (Lamfalussy 1963) and elastic supplies of labour (Kindleberger 1967). On the forces that brought the Golden Age to an end there are exogenous factors like the Russian wheat crop failures of 1971 and 1972 that raised the cost of living, the OPEC shock of 1973, the breakdown of the Bretton Woods system, the exhaustion of positive stimuli under catching up and the exhaustion of the positive feedback mechanism.

Recovery can be said to have been achieved when economic output had reached the pre-war level. We need not deal with the contribution to that recovery of the Marshall Plan, monetary reform (in Germany), currency devaluation from overvalued levels and the like. Following Maddison (1982: 93) it can be said that recovery was complete by 1950. Catching up then begins and has to do with investment in productive capital – not housing – at the level of the most technologically advanced country. In discussing investment in the United Kingdom, Matthews takes the very high rate of investment in historical terms as 'exogenous', but it can be regarded, following Abramovitz and Dumke, as catching up to the United States level. A wide gap had resulted from the two World Wars in which American technology made rapid advances while that of Europe did not. Some catching up may have taken place in the 1920s, but little in the 1930s when technological progress, despite Schumpeter, was limited.

Catching-up theory postulates convergence, that levels of technological proficiency have an inherent tendency to reach the same point. Abramovitz notes that fifteen countries which, on the average, had levels of productivity about 45 per cent of that of the United States in 1950, had reached more than 65 per cent in 1963, and continued to advance to 75 per cent by 1979. Among the catching-up countries, convergence was demonstrated by the fact that the coefficient of variation among the fifteen declined from 0.37 in 1950 to 0.15 in 1973 (Abramovitz 1990: 3, Table 1). That the fifteen industrial countries caught up to the extent they did, while the less developed countries still lagged behind, is ascribed to his belief that to close a technological gap a country needs 'social capability'. This concept is unmeasurable, but a proxy for it may be found in years of popular education, or in political, commercial, industrial and financial institutions (Abramovitz 1986: 388).[1] Abramovitz asserts that economic catching up is self-limiting (1990: 9), although he notes the Matthews view that the closer one gets to the technological leader the easier it should be to close the gap. Indeed there is no necessary limit at full convergence since the country that is behind but rapidly advancing technically can, as Japan illustrated, surpass the level of the country originally serving as the standard. Abramovitz further notes that a theory postulating convergence as a normal tendency fails to explain the past century and a half when Britain opened up a wide gap from 1760 to 1850, and later was overtaken by Germany in a number of industries and overall by the United States.

Dumke's investigation of recovery and catching up for Germany presents a great deal of analysis and econometrics, on the latter of which I beg to be excused from comment. He shows a graph (Dumke 1990: 457, Figure 2) in which there is a sharp drop after the war from the 1930 trend, which trend is shortly regained. The recovery after the Second World War, however, was not matched after the First World War. On that occasion, long-run growth did not recover to the pre-war trend line, but moved parallel to it, at a lower level. I ascribe the difference in the two post-war recoveries to widely different social conditions, along lines noted by Mancur Olson.

Catching up goes a long way to explain why rates of investment were so high in the Golden Age, but surely not all the way, nor is the process helpful to our understanding of the end of the Golden Age. A technological gap remained in 1973, and there is no reason to think that Germany and Japan will cease to make technological progress at a rapid pace when they reach the general US level.

Government policy, and especially Keynesian control of demand, was a favourite explanation for the supergrowth of the 1950s at least, even if the model looks a little less robust in the following decade. In his earliest book Maddison (1964) looks almost exclusively to demand rather than supply. Two years later, Walter Heller's Godkin Lectures at Harvard proclaimed the arrival of a new look in economic policy and process, with the countercyclical focus of the 1950s discarded in favour of gap-closing and growth (1966: vii). In a passage verging on *chutzpah*, Heller asserted:

> The doubling of our growth rate in the last five years – moving it up from the bottom to the top of the ladder among advanced countries – has strengthened not only the dollar, but our strategic position in dealing with our free world partners. What a change from 1961 when President Kennedy 'ordered' me not to return from an international economic meeting in Paris until I had discovered the secret of European growth! What satisfaction he would have found in the 'reverse lend-lease' of ideas which now finds European nations studying and borrowing some of the techniques of what President Johnson has called 'the American economic miracle'.
>
> (1966: 11)

Pride went before a fall. American Keynesian economists recommended a tax increase in 1967 to reverse the reduction finally achieved in 1964 – to mop up the purchasing power that heated up the economy as the Vietnam War went on – but President Johnson was unwilling to present such a proposal to the Congress, lest his Vietnam policies be challenged. A bit later in Britain, Matthews (1968) denied that the high level of investment in Britain had been the result of demand policy manipulated by government, since the Britain budget on current account was in surplus practically all through the past decade, a conclusion that was subsequently challenged by an economist who called attention to the government's deficit on capital account. Matthews also rejected the possibility that the British economy had been stabilized by the balanced-budget multiplier, holding that the expansionary effect of high government taxation and spending was smaller than the restrictive bias of the current-account surplus. He admitted that the great investment boom was stimulated to a degree by tax policy, but claimed that its main cause was the scope for investment provided by the low level of the capital stock – catching up at the investment if not at the technological level – and not to government policy. Somewhat distinctly related to the balanced-budget multiplier is Minsky's (1986) view that the much larger role of government in the total economy dampens the business cycle because of built-in stabilizers, and thus permits continuous growth. But in this case the relationship of government spending and taxation to GDP cannot be ascribed to any particular policy to achieve growth.

Another government policy which requires mention is planning. French planning, pushed by Jean Monnet,[2] went back to 1947, when the first four-year plan set goals for a limited number of strategic sectors, and continued into the 1960s. At the height of enthusiasm for planning a spate of books appeared explaining how it worked (Hackett and Hackett 1963; Bauchet 1964). One enthusiast claimed that economic planning extended all over Europe, except for the United Kingdom, including even the Federal Republic of Germany where the emphasis on *sozialmarktwirtschaft* was on *sozial* rather than on *markt* (Shonfield 1966). In the United Kingdom, moreover, a start at planning was made in 1962 with the establishment of a National Economic Development Council that finally produced a plan in 1965. This never got off the ground, however, as a conservative government tried to convert it from growth into a means of restraining inflation against trade union pressure. In due course France lost its appetite for *planification* which gradually gave way to *déplanification*. Planning would not work, the alibi ran, in a single country bound with others in a Common Market; it was necessary to plan for all, and others would not go along. The real reason was that business firms preferred to be guided by profits rather than by government indication of the path to be followed.

One more possibility for government policy guiding economic growth rests in monetary policy – though Cairncross and Watts (1989: ch. 14) make clear that, at least before 1961, the Bank of England did not always see eye to eye on monetary policy with the economic section of the Cabinet or the Treasury. Maddison resists Harry Johnson's claim that well-behaved management of money will automatically produce full employment (Maddison 1982: 132). I suspect that if Harry were with us today he would decline to claim that monetary policy was responsible either for the boom when it was overshadowed by Keynesian fiscal policy or for the let-down after 1973 when monetary policy came into intellectual favour.

I now turn to sociological theories. The most ambitious relates to the spread of growth rates between Japan and Germany on the one hand and the United Kingdom and the United States on the other. Slow growth was blamed on what Mancur Olson called 'distributive coalitions', or, in more usual American parlance, vested interests. These protect their narrow welfare with ferocity without regard to the common weal. Each group seeks to ensure that it bears no or a minimal share of the burdens of society, whether from reconstruction or, in the 1920s German case, reparations, fending off taxes and raising prices to push inflation on others. Deadlocked distributional coalitions block the national agenda and slow down overall decisions. In Olson's view defeat in the Second World War destroyed the groups in Germany and Japan that had power to look after parochial concerns. An illuminating comparison lies between Germany after the First World War and West Germany after the Second World War. In the first case, Junkers, peasants, industrialists, trade unionists and civil servants all survived relatively intact to hold on to political power and to block action against them, with the result that reconstruction and reparations led to hyper-inflation. After the Second World War, these groups had been destroyed – trade unionists, peasants and civil servants during the Nazi rule, and Junkers by the loss of territory in the east – and while industry survived, its prestige did not. The way was cleared for a far-reaching monetary reform in 1948 to restore incentives to work and invest, a process aided by the fact that the country was governed by occupying powers which took responsibility for the necessary heroic measures. After the Marshall Plan had restocked the economy, the *Wirtschafts-wunder* took off. In Postan's (1967) analysis, most of Europe after the Second World War, but not the United Kingdom, was led by 'new men' in government and industry after the failures of occupation and defeat.

There is an important issue here as to whether it would have been possible to have the monetary reform of the Second World War after the First World War or whether it would have been blocked and resisted. To my mind there has not been enough discussion of the failures of monetary reform in France, where the question was raised but never properly discussed, and the weak monetary reform in a country like Belgium. The issue is very relevant to what is happening now in Eastern Europe.

A crucial aspect of the German experience was the fact that after having been cooped up in autarky during the 1930s and the war, businessmen looked abroad more and more, with the more vigorous among them choosing to sell in foreign markets. High rates of investment, first for recovery and then for catching up, drove up national income which then spilled abroad from the leaders in the league tables to other countries, not as import surpluses but as rapidly rising gross imports. West Germany and Japan in fact had strong export surpluses in a world of declining import barriers and discrimination. The openness of the world economy, fostered by the Bretton Woods institutions, the General Agreement on Tariffs and Trade (GATT), economic assistance – initially to Europe and later to the Third World – plus convertibility, made possible mutually supporting high growth for countries engaged in catching up.

How did the Golden Age last so long? My explanation runs in terms of positive feedback, much along the lines of Glyn *et al.* (1990), with profits leading to investment leading to increased productivity, higher wages, higher consumption, higher profits and so on. The process is self-reinforcing so long as wages do not squeeze profits by rising faster than productivity. Where I differ from Glyn *et al.* is in the mechanism that restrains wages to the rate of productivity increases. They emphasize labour's expectations of continued growth in real income, and presumably self-imposed restraint. That may have played a role in West Germany when it had a weak trade union movement, and perhaps even in French coal mining in the early 1950s when Communist unions, co-operating with the government, held wages down. I cling, however, to my old view that wages were held down by an elastic labour supply (Kindleberger 1967). West Germany was blessed by a steady inflow of expellees and refugees from the East – labour with high levels of 'social capability', to return to Abramovitz's phrase, easy to absorb because educated to more or less the same degree as the existing West German population, German speaking, and avid to restore their wealth, income and social status, and hence willing to work hard. Following the Germans from the East were the so-called 'guest workers', initially largely from Italy, then from Spain, Portugal, Yugoslavia and Turkey. These were at first readily absorbed, as they were mostly skilled, single, young and content to live in barracks, consume little and save a lot to remit to families at home. Later, when parts and whole families joined the movement, the economic benefits of immigration declined; it was necessary to provide more adequate housing and other social overhead capital, especially hospitals and schools.

The real limits to immigration, however, proved to be social, rather than economic. When foreign workers reached one-third of the Swiss labour force, the flow was cut off as the Swiss voters felt their Swiss identity threatened. Similar social unhappiness arose in West Germany, which closed off those urban areas where the guest workers and their families reached 12 per cent of the local population.

Let me say parenthetically that this positive feedback process (or Marxian or Lewis model of growth with unlimited supplies of labour) will probably not apply to the 1990–1 movement of ethnic Germans and others westward after the November 1989 collapse of the Wall. The original Lewis model helped the receiving country by holding wages down and profits up, *permitting*, but *not* inevitably leading to, high reinvestment of profits. At the same time, it stimulated growth in the country of emigration by draining off underemployed workers, raising the share of rent and bringing the marginal revenue product of remaining labour up to the point where it more nearly approximated the wage rate, thus stimulating investment there as well. In today's world I fear that westward European migration may inhibit growth in both sending and receiving countries: in the sending countries by leaving gaps in the balance of skills and making some towns and firms inefficient as they lose necessary professional and skilled workers; in the receiving countries in the West by diverting capital from productive uses to infrastructure, at a time when pressures on savings to provide aid and capital for reconstructing and cleaning up the environment in the East and buying off the Russians are already great.

I must not rely too heavily on the expellee–refugee stream plus the guest workers in the Golden Age. There were other sources of surplus labour: unemployment left over from the 1930s and the war; migrants from the countryside to the city, especially in countries like France and Italy with rapidly rising productivity in agriculture; natural population growth after emigration had been cut off, in a country such as the Netherlands, for example, which no longer shipped a stream of colonists to the East Indies. It is significant, however, that British agriculture was already efficient and had little surplus population to send to factories, and that British labour unions beat off the attempt of government to admit as immigrants Polish miners reluctant to return to their country. Miners were clearly needed in Britain after the war-time Bevin-boy experiment failed and when many of the soldiers from mine districts, like the Durham and Northumberland Light Infantry, failed to go back to the mines.[3] Britain did experience considerable immigration from former colonial possessions, directly or, in the case of some Indians and Pakistanis, via other former colonies. This supply was ultimately cut off because of social disturbances, but seemed meanwhile to have moved into service industries rather than mining or manufacturing. There may well have been a question about its social capability.

Britain had very low unemployment up to 1965, and even acute shortages of labour in the booms of 1960 and 1964, especially of skilled labour but to some extent of labour in general (Matthews *et al.* 1982: 85–93). This was partly because management treated labour as an overhead rather than a variable cost, preferring to shorten hours when demand slackened rather than lay workers off, for fear that in a recurring boom it would not be able to rehire (ibid.: 90, especially Figure 3.4).

The gilt of the Golden Age was beginning to wear thin in the late 1960s. The widespread notion that the boom was stopped by the price rise in all of OPEC in November 1973 overstates the matter considerably. This shock put punctuation to the Golden Age, perhaps as the *coup de grâce* to an already wounded boom that was slipping into stagflation. Various elements that earlier contributed to positive feedback were weakening. In the Netherlands wages had been held down and profits held up by a deliberate incomes policy that collapsed as early as 1961. A further inflationary element was the 'Dutch disease', a general rise in wages to match those in the Dutch North Sea gasfields. Productivity figures are on the whole crude, and calculated over long periods, such as the Golden Age as a whole rather than year by year (Maddison 1982: ch. 4; 1989: Tables 7.2 and 7.3). I nonetheless hazard a guess that US productivity increases slowed down with the outbreak of war in Vietnam and the programme of space exploration that followed the Soviet Union's launching of Sputnik in 1957 and the American landing on the moon in 1969. One student of technological history states that the break in American technological advance came in 1971 when the Congress refused to allocate funds for a supersonic transport proposed to match the Concorde (Gimpel 1976: 2).

It is generally recognized that military research in the Second World War stimulated civilian productivity increases, especially in airplanes, electronics and computers. More recent military and space research in the United States seems to have yielded fewer innovations of civilian importance, with teflon coming to the mind of most people looking for examples. With productivity slowing down and expectations of real-wage growth continuing, the United States slipped into an inflationary mode, compounded by failure to reverse the 1964 tax cut as the economy heated up. Depreciation of sterling in 1967 called for restrictive macroeconomic measures, which led to rising unemployment after the long years below 3 per cent, a level which had been regarded as 'full employment' during the post-war planning stages. When the French students rioted in May of 1968 they were joined by trade unionists at the Renault plant in Villancourt outside Paris, necessitating the Accord de Grenelle between the unions and the government. This raised wages sharply, much like the Accord de Matignon of June 1936 when the Blum government yielded to the strikes that brought the Popular Front to power.

There is perhaps no need for me to recite the gradual breakdown of the Bretton Woods Agreement, but I would like to make two or three points, with emphasis on my disagreement from the conventional opinion on particular matters. First, I disagree with Triffin (1960) who thought the dollar system was a disaster because he measured balance-of-payments disequilibrium on the liquidity definition, which I believe is appropriate for most countries in the world economy but not for one that acts like a world banker. Bankers are in the business of lending long and borrowing short, and doing so does not constitute disequilibrium. Second, the system was doomed by the fact that more and more individuals and national monetary authorities hoarded the base money of the system, borrowing dollars (or selling assets for them) and converting the dollars to gold, encouraged by the publicly lamented fears of US authorities from Eisenhower to Reagan about the so-called 'deficit'. Benign neglect was a mistake made later under President Reagan; it was a desirable policy in the 1960s. Third, a critical mistake was made in 1971, when the Federal Reserve System lowered interest rates in the United States at a time when the Bundesbank was trying to repel imported inflation by tightening. With the two capital markets joined through the Euro-currency system, the inconsistent policies poured dollars abroad, lowered world interest rates, set international banks looking for loans and started the wave of Third World borrowing that has produced such difficulty since 1982, this well before the OPEC price rise of November 1973. I used to call the Board's action 'the Crime of 1971'; now I prefer, with Talleyrand, to believe it was worse than a crime: it was a blunder.

I return to my subject: how did the Golden Age last so long? Which Golden Age: the British in comparison with a century and a half earlier, or the world's, largely the industrial countries, led by the miracles of Japan and Germany? For Britain, I would emphasize the growth of exports, catching up (investment) and, despite Matthews, government policy which time and again pulled back from impetuous forced-draft tactics. There were a number of economists at the time – I fear I have forgotten whom – who advocated pushing ahead when the balance of payments turned adverse, on the theory that more growth with economies of scale would lower costs, expand exports and right the balance of payments through growth. 'Damn the torpedoes: full speed ahead!' This may work on occasion but not, I think, with unemployment hovering around 1 per cent.

I do not know enough about Japan to pronounce on its economic miracle. Unemployment decreased from a high of 2.5 per cent of the labour force in 1955 to a steady 1.1–1.3 per cent through the 1960s (Maddison 1982: 208, Table C6(b)). Labour productivity per man hour in 1970 relative prices went up almost sixfold between 1950 and 1975 compared with only double or triple for most other advanced countries (ibid.: 212, Table C10). This was catching up, and surpassing with a vengeance.

When I started this paper I did not think I would find myself in agreement with Glyn *et al.* (1990) – in fact I did not know of the existence of their work. If they will allow me to incorporate in their analysis the Lewis model of growth with unlimited supplies of labour – and after all it derives from Marx – I will go along happily. Let us hope that future depression and war-time gaps do not open so widely again as to encourage a match-up process to start, nor that millions of people will be driven from their homes to depress wages where they are taken in.

Perhaps you will let me go beyond my brief. If I choose not to believe in the Kondratieff cycle, and hesitate to predict that a new Golden Age will never recur, I am committed to the S- or Gompertz curve as a general truth in economic life. Chaos theory suggests that growth movements begin as mutations which, if they take root, start slowly. Many wither. Those that grow do so slowly at first and may later pick up speed. In due course, however, they meet with some obstacle, decay in entropy, in any event slow down. If one fits a trend and plots deviations from it, the S-curve may be reduced to cycles, but the essence is in the S itself, not in the derivative, and there is no reason why the deviations should be of a given length. That catching up carries within it the seeds of its own levelling off or decline seems to me a general truth akin to the population of fruit flies in a jar, the life cycle of the individual and, I suspect, the life cycle of people in the aggregate or society. The S-curve is useless for prediction because new S-curves may emerge from others as new mutations occur. But the top of the long S-curves in British and American history may help explain why the United Kingdom and the United States were on the bottom of the league tables.

COMMENTS BY ROBIN MATTHEWS

Charles Kindleberger's paper is a fitting introduction to a grand occasion. I must limit my comments, however, to only a few of the many interesting points he has raised.

Which was the aberration: the Golden Age, or the ensuing time of troubles? Or were they perhaps both aberrations? These questions can be asked about each of the two respects in which the Golden Age was golden, namely the high growth rate and the high average rate of utilization of labour and capital. I shall speak only about the growth rate.

One approach is to look at the *trends* over long periods. A certain amount can be learnt in that way, even though the relevant periods are so long that a conclusive result may not be available even by the time of Alec's 100th Birthday Conference. The alternative approach, which Kindleberger mostly adopts, is to look at the various possible *causes* of the trends, and to consider whether they were by their nature transitory or permanent.

The most striking conclusion that comes out of the trends seems to me to be the difference between OECD Europe and Japan on the one hand and the United States on the other. These three blocs seem to me more appropriate units for comparison than the usual alphabetical list of countries, especially now that most European countries have much the same growth rates. OECD Europe and the United States are economies of roughly the same size as each other. Japan is about half that size, but still comparable. On the other hand the nation-states within the OECD vary in economic size by a factor of up to about 70, so they are not in the least comparable. Nation-states are the appropriate units of comparison only if one has decided in advance that the crucial variables are the policies of national governments. Consider, then, productivity trends in the three blocs.

In OECD Europe and in Japan the rate of growth of GDP per worker since 1973 has, of course, been lower than it was in the Golden Age. But it has remained higher than it was in the disturbed period 1913–50. Also, more surprisingly, it has remained rather higher than it was before 1913. This suggests that not *all* of the improvement in the Golden Age over earlier periods was aberrant.

Experience in the United States has been different. Productivity growth since 1973 has been very low: lower than in 1913–50, and lower even than before 1913. This suggests that the American golden age in productivity growth *was* an aberration, even though it was never such a golden age as in most other countries.

The foregoing contrast between the United States and the other regions takes us on to the question of possible causes and their transitoriness or otherwise. The regional contrast supports the catch-up hypothesis. Moreover it suggests that catch-up is still playing a part in Europe and Japan. There is room for it too: European productivity is still only about three-quarters of American, and (contrary to popular belief) Japanese productivity, reckoned per man hour, is lower than European.

Kindleberger points out that a catch-up theory would not provide a good explanation of why a golden age should suddenly turn into hard times. But, as he also points out, this is not a good description of what happened. There was a gradual slowdown well before 1973, and that *is* consistent with there having been a progressive decline in the amount of arrears to be caught up. The German case is perhaps the plainest. The growth rate between cycle peaks fell steadily from the beginning of the post-war period until the end of the 1980s (Table 1.3).

Table 1.3 Growth rate of GDP between cycle peaks in West Germany since 1952

Period	% Annual growth rate
1952–57	8.1
1957–60	6.6
1960–65	5.0
1965–73	4.1
1973–80	2.2
1980–89	1.9

As Kindleberger says, scope for catch-up may exist without being used. The requisite 'social capability' includes the will; and the will may be subject to the S-shaped process of growth and decay which Kindleberger follows Marshall in invoking. In the particular case of Continental Europe, especially Germany, the will was provided in the

first instance by extreme need. When that had been relieved, a new
stimulus was provided by the European ideal. It was perhaps because
that too had ceased to be exciting that Germans in the 1980s were
surprisingly content with what was really a rather poor performance
in real terms.

Will the absorption of migrants from the ex-communist areas
provide the basis for a new S? Kindleberger points out that this
migration differs considerably from the migration to northern Europe
that took place in the Golden Age, from Mediterranean countries, the
West Indies and Asia. He may be right that it is more liable to denude
the countries of origin of human capital. But in that it is not so unlike
much of the historic migration from Europe to the New World, and
for that matter not so unlike the historic migration from Scotland to
England. That migration, *pace* Lewis, was surely much more to the
advantage of the receiving country than of the country of origin, both
in the long run and in the medium-run inverse cycles to which Alec
introduced us in *Home and Foreign Investment 1870–1913*. The loss to
the countries of origin did not prevent the countries of destination
from gaining.

Another difference is that the ex-communists are mostly emigrating
without definite promises of work, as their predecessors did in the
nineteenth century, whereas the guest workers and their counterparts
in France and the United Kingdom usually took employment in
sectors where employers had been actively seeking them out, as
London Transport did in the West Indies in the 1950s. There are
advantages and disadvantages in both arrangements. The outcome is
likely to be determined largely by attitudes, the attitudes of both the
incumbents and the immigrants. In American history, 'economic
migrants' have proved to be better agents of economic change than
political refugees; and that at least is a favourable element in the
present situation.

I revert to other transitory and permanent factors in the Golden
Age.

1 Kindleberger's concluding remark about the S-pattern and the
  league tables is a version of the early start hypothesis, if I understand it aright. It makes good sense for the United States, but some
  complicating elements have to be introduced in order to make it
  apply to the United Kingdom. The difficulty is that the period
  when the United Kingdom was considered to be disgracing itself
  most conspicuously in the league tables was half a century or so

later than the period when the United Kingdom's growth rate was at its own historical minimum.

2 Feedback was part of the Golden Age, and feedback included an element of 'overdoing it' that was clearly transitory, manifested in many countries in a rate of capital accumulation that was too high to be compatible with stable profit rates. Governments were at least as carried away by this 'wave of optimism' as the private sector. As Lord Croham's paper (Chapter 3) reminds us, the British government began to talk seriously about increasing the growth rate at just about the time when the growth rate was actually about to decline.

3 I have elsewhere retreated somewhat from the scepticism I expressed in 1968 about policy's contribution to full employment in the United Kingdom, so there is no need to argue about that.[4] In so far as sensible public policy, national and international, contributed to making the Golden Age golden, and in so far as it did not depend on fooling people by creating money illusion, it falls into the class of improvements that are potentially permanent.

DISCUSSION

Opening the discussion, *Professor Katz* said that he would like to supplement the German story in a way relevant to the conference. Charles Kindleberger had described how Germany took off after restocking under the Marshall Plan and after the currency reform of 1948, one of the most important pieces of social engineering of all time. In the winter of 1950, however, it had looked as if the recovery might fail. The OEEC had sent a team to Germany consisting of Alec Cairncross and Per Jacobsson which made a survey of the situation and submitted recommendations outlining a programme on the basis of which Germany could be offered financial assistance. In effect the team had called on the OEEC to accept the risks involved in the programme and put their money behind it. This the OEEC did although they did not provide quite as much finance as was recommended. It was the first of the international rescue operations in the post-war period (international as distinct from International Monetary Fund (IMF) or institutional) and it turned out to be successful.

The sequel came in 1956 when the German surpluses had become so large that everybody wanted Germany to revalue. Revaluation became an intense political conflict in Germany. Chancellor Erhard was in favour of revaluation and publicly acknowledged that he had been outvoted by his colleagues. He was anxious that the German economy should not be excessively oriented toward exports. Emminger, who had just been appointed to the Bank deutscher Länder (BdL, the Central Bank), was also in favour of revaluation. The commercial bankers, however, and particularly Herman Abs, were opposed to it and they prevailed. Abs had recently negotiated the London Debt Agreement of 1953, regarded as a great triumph in Germany and a generous gesture in America, and was highly influential with Adenauer. He had the support of Vocke, the chairman of the BdL, and of Per Jacobsson. Indeed in 1961, when the Germans did revalue (by 5 per cent), Per Jacobsson had attacked Emminger when he came to see him in Washington, asking him 'What *have* you done, you scoundrel?' (Kaplan and Schleiminger, 1989). Professor Katz wondered, therefore, whether, if Alec Cairncross had been at the IMF instead of Per Jacobsson, the system of par values would have been allowed to rigidify and become one in which currency values for the major countries could not be changed except under market compulsion.

Lord Callaghan remarked that if Erhard said he had been outvoted by his colleagues he could only have meant that Adenauer was against revaluation, since there was at that time an understanding that if the Chancellor and the Minister of Finance were in agreement they could not be outvoted by the rest of the German Cabinet. This was an arrangement that Erhard had commended highly to Lord Callaghan when he was Chancellor. So he had put it to the Prime Minister what an improvement it would be if they were to adopt the same principle; but the most he could get from Harold Wilson was an invitation to sit beside him in Cabinet instead of sitting, as he then did, opposite him.

Sir Alec Cairncross, when asked what he thought of Sam Katz's counterfactual, said that he doubted whether anyone at the IMF could have prevailed on the German government against the strong view of Adenauer to the contrary.

Professor Katz, however, said that the end-result of this decision was to create a lop-sided evolution of the German economy marked by overdependence upon exports and a chronic export surplus which has lasted until the end of 1990.

Sir Alec Cairncross said that the issue raised by Charles Kindleberger's paper was whether the slowdown after the 1960s was inevitable and whether it could have been foreseen or prevented by action in the

1960s. It was hard to believe that it could have been predicted that there would be such a dramatic change in the rate of growth in output and productivity in the 1970s. It took everybody by surprise. There was no expectation of such a sharp change in trend – least of all in the European Community which Britain was so anxious to join – or of the vast increase in unemployment that accompanied it.

He had some difficulty with explanations of trends in growth in terms of convergence. Many of the less developed countries did not seem able to take advantage of the wide gaps that in theory offered them the opportunity of rapid progress. There was more to development than profiting from more advanced technology. It required capital which countries might not have and a process of adaptation and domestication of foreign practice that was not easy. As for Western European countries, there was surely nothing inevitable about the decline in Germany from a growth in productivity of over 8 per cent per annum to a rate less than a quarter of that. As Robin Matthews had said, it was extraordinary that Germany was content with a 2 per cent rate of growth. The slowing down of growth throughout Continental Europe in the 1970s and 1980s was not only unexpected but was associated with unusual circumstances that might have little to do with convergence. It was too easy to assume that it was only a matter of time before backward countries would take advantage of all the opportunities available to them of copying the leaders and begin to catch up with them. Countries making rapid progress, with plenty of momentum behind them, might carry on and take the lead without much of a slowdown. We knew very little about what governed the underlying rate of technical progress (or even the level of 'social capability').

Was it right in the 1960s to think that governments could accelerate growth or was growth in industrial countries something little influenced by governments? And could one ever predict that growth would be on a falling scale for the next twenty years?

Professor Meade asked what made an age 'golden'. In his view it was a combination of two interlinked elements which could, however, be discussed separately. One element was the good old-fashioned Keynesian side and the other was the real side, the growth of output per head.

He had abandoned real life in 1947 when he left Whitehall and devoted himself to economic theory, but by 1947 he was conscious of a major change from the pre-war era: the acceptance by government that it had a duty to maintain demand. It might be that what kept up demand, as Robin Matthews argued, had not been simply Keynesian doctrine but other things such as the need to rebuild and repair, and the fact was that it was now accepted that governments had a responsibility not to allow a collapse of demand. The intellectual atmosphere had changed and had an important influence on how people behaved.

The real side depended on quite a different set of things: training, the finance of research and development, social factors such as Mancur Olson (1982) discussed and so on. What was critical in the Golden Age was a coincidence between the two sides. The United Kingdom had been highly successful at first, with very little unemployment and low inflation. Why had that broken down? Surely it had to do with wage fixing. When the blame was put on OPEC, what had caused the trouble was that the change in the terms of trade could not be translated into a reduction in real wages. What had made the difference was a move from a world in which wage fixing did not require a fall in real wages to one in which it did.

During the Second World War he had been a member of a committee on reparations along with Keynes and Robbins. Members had proposed a variety of horrors and some had wanted to require Germany to remove tariff barriers and observe free trade. Keynes had expostulated: 'You're not going, are you, to impose on Germany the blessings of disarmament as well as free trade?' This was just what did happen to Germany (and to Japan); but how it affected their later growth he would leave to others to say.

Lord Jenkins pointed out that those who presided over the Golden Age did not feel at the time that they were singularly blessed and carried in a golden coach. He also deduced, from what was said by Robin Matthews and Charles Kindleberger, that the best time to be in charge of a country was when its growth rate was getting steadily worse. In the United States economic performance had deteriorated throughout its imperial age from 1941 onwards. Similarly with Germany: its growth rate was highest in the early 1950s when it was almost a pariah among nations and fell to its lowest level just when it was looked up to as a remarkable example of how a country should be run. The United Kingdom was not in that league but had been at its most influential at the end of the nineteenth century when growth was already falling fast.

It was also a mistake to be in power too long after the low point. If you wanted to be a successful head of state (or even foreign minister) the best course was to have a finance minister who would let the economy start to run down at exactly the time you were in power.

Finally, on James Meade's suggestion that the wage explosion accounted for the end of the Golden Age and the change from one kind of regime in the 1960s to a quite different one in the 1970s, was it not likely that the breakdown of the Bretton Woods Agreement and the move to violently fluctuating currencies also had something to do with the change?

Professor Tobin wanted to comment on the 'crime' or 'blunder' of 1971 blamed on Arthur Burns. It involved the distinctions drawn by James Meade between the demand side and the supply side, and between the monetary and the real forces at work. In 1971 the United States was recovering rather slowly from the recession that began in 1969. It was frustrating that unemployment did not recover more rapidly and that inflation fell off so slowly from what had inspired the anti-inflationary policy in the first place. It was this, in the context of the approaching election campaign, that led President Nixon to abandon the Bretton Woods Agreement. The episode linked with Sam Katz's point that the defect of Bretton Woods was the absence of pressure on surplus countries to appreciate. The other side of that defect was the impotence of the United States to depreciate. The constant charge in the 1960s that the United States was exporting inflation was ironic at a time when it did not have all that much inflation to export. It is frequently argued that it was the abandonment of the Bretton Woods Agreement that put an end to the Golden Age. But was it not more the asymmetry in the system – an asymmetry that worried Keynes when the system was created and Harry White had his way?

US unemployment had not been particularly low in 1971–2 in relation to the views of the 1960s on what constituted a reasonable target. Was it then a 'crime' in these circumstances to give the economy a boost in 1971 by lowering US interest rates? The Germans might be tightening policy but ought they not to have let the Deutschmark appreciate as the Americans maintained?

There was also a question as to the action that should have been taken by the Federal Reserve System and the Bank of England in the private gold market. The drain on gold through the market had already been sufficient by 1968 to lead to its closure. It was a drain that could be associated with a shortage of the base money needed by the system – a shortage that Triffin had wanted to remedy with paper gold that would have kept the official system going even if the metal was being removed. Perhaps Arthur Burns's policy wasn't so reprehensible after all.

Professor Kloten agreed with Charles Kindleberger that the Kondratieff long-wave approach threw no light on what happened in the 1950s and 1960s and was even less useful in explaining the next two decades. To understand the 1950s one had to be clear as to the unique circumstances of the time. Also the S-curve approach does not apply properly. This approach is a general device for the explanation of social developments and only appropriate under certain conditions. An explanation of post-war economic development could be given in terms of normal economic analysis.

The currency reform had been an Allied affair, not a German one. It had been a necessary, but not sufficient, condition for the German recovery. A second pillar of the recovery was the freeing of prices from control by Erhard. A third pillar was the fortunate absence of a German government and the weakness of the labour unions. This gave Erhard the time to convince Adenauer and others of the advantages of adopting the social market concept and using it as a slogan in the first post-war election (won by the Christian Democrats and Liberals by a narrow majority).

In 1951 there had come what the Germans called the Korea crisis and he recalled that the recommendations of the OEEC had been neither popular nor consistently applied, since they called for regulation of the economy when the government was wedded to policies of liberalization.

Later in the 1950s labour supply played a major role in German development. The combination of an abundant labour supply and the shortage of real capital meant that wages remained low while profits were high, but wages rose in step with the rapid growth in productivity, always lagging a little behind. Liberalization in Germany had been applied externally as well as internally, with early convertibility of the currency and rising imports as well as exports. There had been a strong terms of trade effect and the Deutschmark had remained consistently undervalued. Stabilization policy had been successful in marrying monetary and financial policy.

The over-supply of labour ceased at the end of the 1950s, especially after the building of the Berlin Wall. That was a political affair. Social factors played a bigger part at the end of the 1960s when an effort was made to stop the inflow of guest workers. In the 1950s there had been no business cycle but the shape of the cycle became increasingly distinct in the 1960s. It was referred to as 'the growth cycle' because growth rates were always positive except in 1976. Deviations from the trend showed the cyclical movement while the trend itself reflected the path of growth. Differences in the rate of capacity utilization indicated whether there was an upswing or a downswing.

One last comment on what was happening in the new German Länder and in other European countries: this could not be compared with what had happened earlier in Germany; nor could it be explained with normal economic analysis since there did not exist what might be called a theory of transformation. One should therefore be careful in drawing comparisons: for example between labour migration after the Second World War and from Eastern Europe after 1989.

John Williamson said that he found the idea of convergence one round which to organize his thoughts. It had to be coupled on the supply side with the idea of social capability – rather a vague phrase and not the subject of any theory of which he was aware. But what was undoubtedly relevant – and surprisingly had not been mentioned – was education and training. Any explanation of Japan's success in outgrowing other countries and reaching the frontier in many industries could not neglect this factor. Her success was clearly due to the great emphasis on education. Similarly, if Germany had done so well and shot ahead of the United Kingdom the reason lay in the training system. The same reasoning provided an explanation for the difficulty of many developing countries in growing faster and also for the success of some countries in East Asia. On the demand side he doubted whether, without Keynesian demand management, there would have been no growth in demand. In a well-functioning economy demand tended to grow so long as the economy was capable of producing what was required. But he would agree that demand management, which had been more sophisticated in the 1960s than later, had made a contribution to growth.

The inflation explosion at the end of the 1960s derived from failure to understand the accelerationist theory of inflation. Inflation was allowed to get out of hand and this coincided with the oil price increase in 1973 which interacted with the catching-up process and produced a sudden break in the growth rate instead of a more gentle deceleration that would otherwise have occurred.

In reply to a question from the Chairman, who pointed out that, in the days of Robbins, education could hardly be said to have been neglected, John Williamson said that much less emphasis had been placed by Britain on education (and training) than in competing countries. Robbins had been an exercise in catching up.

Lord O'Brien said he was the only simple central banker present in a cage full of the lions of the economic world. Montagu Norman, to whom he had once been private secretary, was said to have replied to someone asking him whether he ever took the advice of his economists: 'I don't go to them for advice; I go to them to tell me why I do the things I've decided to do.'

The Bretton Woods system, when established in the 1940s, had taken the form prescribed by Harry White rather than Keynes and so had followed American ideas. The great weakness of the system, as had been said, was that the strong currencies were not capable of being adequately disciplined. The strongest currency had been the US dollar and it remained the dominant currency until 1960. The gold market then functioned satisfactorily, with the London market the largest mainly because of the sale of South African output there. Later, the South Africans became disenchanted with arrangements and marketed some of their gold in Switzerland.

It was only in the 1960s, with the Vietnam War and other problems, that it became increasingly difficult to operate at the gold price of $35 an ounce. When the price rose above $35 in 1968 Secretary Dillon had rung Lord O'Brien (as Deputy Governor) to insist that a fresh transaction be put through the London market to re-establish the validity of that price. This was a ridiculous request, made in a rather bullying manner, and as an O'Brien he took it amiss. However, that was merely a stage and was succeeded by an increasing outflow of dollars which the Americans were unwilling to turn into gold at $35 an ounce. Instead they offered Roosa gold certificates which were bought by the Germans but by hardly anybody else. In the end, the whole system broke down.

When Lord O'Brien went to Washington after the closure of the gold market he did so (unsupported by the British government) in an effort to get the Americans to agree to raise the price of gold substantially. If they wanted to preserve the Bretton Woods system they would have to make the dollar convertible into gold at an agreed price and the world would have accepted a much increased price. Now there was a price ten times higher. He was not arguing that a higher price would have enabled the system to last very much longer but it was a sad refusal at that time.

Lord Callaghan said that de Gaulle had intended to bring down the dollar standard if he could but Giscard had a slightly different view: that the standard would decay of its own accord. *Lord O'Brien* agreed that, even if de Gaulle had not sought to embarrass the Americans by demanding gold for net dollar earnings, decay would ultimately have set in. No system relying on a key currency would last if the key currency did not live up to its reputation.

John Williamson argued that what really mattered had been inflation. The real value of the gold stock became too low to act as a monetary base so that either one had to build the Special Drawing Right (SDR) into the system or get rid of the monetary base, as did eventually happen.

Lord Jenkins said that the Bretton Woods system was based on the dollar being as good as gold and in 1968 this ceased to be so. It began to crack and cracked more severely in 1971.

Lord O'Brien reminded Lord Jenkins of how they had worked in Stockholm on a plan to let the SDR take the place of gold but it had never seen the light of day.

Lord Jenkins said that the only occasion when there had been any difference between himself and Lord O'Brien when he was Chancellor was over the Washington Conference in 1968 when the government line had been against a rise in the price of gold because the immediate benefit would be to three countries – South Africa, the Soviet Union and France – none of which the government wanted to benefit (France having just vetoed British entry to the European Community). This was a doubtful political view of an economic problem. Equally, given the international imbalance that had developed, he was doubtful whether letting the official price of gold rise along with the unofficial price in 1968 would have saved the system.

Lord O'Brien pointed out that there had also been a strong intellectual dislike for the use of gold as the base of the system and *Professor Katz* added that a rise in the gold price would have done nothing to readjust currency values. It might have afforded more time but contributed nothing to the fundamental problem of the overvaluation of the key currency.

Sir Donald MacDougall said that when he was in the OEEC in 1949 he was anxious to see a doubling of the price of gold. Trade was strangled by low reserves and the dollar shortage and these problems would have been alleviated by raising the price of gold which in real terms was only half its pre-war price. Admittedly much of the gold would have ended up in the United States and the main beneficiary would have been South Africa but there would have been some gain to all gold holders. He had failed to win the approval of the OEEC largely because of American opposition. This was not surprising but what *had* surprised him when he spoke later in Cambridge was to have his proposal denounced as immoral by one speaker after another.

Professor Solow, returning to the argument of the paper, said that the period of the 1950s and 1960s might have been quite special. If one looked at the movement of total factor productivity across a wide spectrum of large industrial countries (i.e. productivity purified of cyclical fluctuations and of the input of additional capital) it was increasing much more rapidly between 1950 and 1973 than it had between 1913 and 1950 or in the twenty years after 1970. Was this an endogenous factor or had it something exogenous about it? There was no possibility of verifying or refuting either possibility. In his view the Golden Age was special because for a long time before it improvements in science and technology had been put into cold storage and, with notable exceptions like the aircraft industry, not built into the capital of manufacturing industry during the depression of the 1930s or in the Second World War. So there was a chance that from 1950 onwards the world could draw on something like a twenty-year backlog of technological change. That might account for twenty to twenty-five years of rapid productivity increases.

If this was so, on any theory of inflation that rested on the reconciliation of competing claims to output, macroeconomic management was eased by the rapidity of growth. A semi-exogenous bonus from higher productivity made it easier in the same way as it was easier to keep the children from fighting just before Christmas.

NOTES

1 The case of Sweden in the middle of the nineteenth century may be cited as an illustration of 'social capability'. This was a country at a fairly low level of economic development, but with a high degree of literacy and the foundations of an efficient banking system. With the British repeal of the Corn Laws in 1846 and later the timber duties, exports of oats for British horses and lumber for building, carried in Norwegian and Swedish bottoms after the repeal of the Navigation Acts, produced very rapid export-led growth (Sandberg 1979).
2 Paul Streeten used to say that 'the love of Monnet is the root of all evil'. Let me also record his dictum that 'if Russian planning was imperative and French planning indicative, British planning was surely subjunctive'.
3 In many European countries, coal mining had been the lowest paid occupation in the inter-war period, but leaped to become one of the highest after the Second World War. What had been a non-competing group became assimilated into the total labour force, with the result that the

disagreeable character of the work required wage premia. A sociological parallel phenomenon occurred in France in the First World War. Before the war, the major coal mining areas of the Pas de Calais and the Nord had birthrates much higher than that of the rest of France, breeding, in fact, more or less like animals (Zola 1885). The First World War and the reconstruction of the northern battleground afterwards integrated the miners into the French labour force and brought the birthrate down to the national level (Ariès 1948: 202–63).

4 'Direct injections of demand by fiscal or monetary policy or public-sector investment were not responsible for the unusually high level of activity. . . . It is possible, however, that government policy in a broader sense did contribute to the high average level of activity, partly on account of the devaluations of 1949 and 1967, partly by the timing of fiscal and monetary measures, partly by effects on confidence. Within the post-war period there was a trend towards more expansionary policies up to the mid-1960s' (Matthews *et al.* 1982: 313).

REFERENCES

Abramovitz, M. (1986) 'Catching up, forging head, and falling behind', *Journal of Economic History* 17 (2) (June): 385–406.

——— (1990) 'The catch-up factor in postwar economic growth', *Economic Inquiry* 18 (January): 1–18.

Ariès, P. (1948) *Histoire des populations françaises et leurs attitudes devant la vie depuis le XVIIIe siècle*, Paris: Philippe Ariès.

Bauchet, P. (1964) *Economic Planning: The French Experience*, New York: Praeger.

Beckerman, W. (ed.) (1979) *Slow Growth in Britain*, Oxford: Oxford University Press.

Berry, B.J.O. (1991) *Long-Wave Rhythms in Economic Development and Behavior*, Baltimore, MD, and London: Johns Hopkins University Press.

Cairncross, A. (ed.) (1989, 1991) *The Robert Hall Diaries*, vol. 1, *1947–1953*; vol. 2, *1954–56*, London: Unwin & Hyman.

Cairncross, A. and Watts, N. (1989) *The Economic Section, 1939–1961: A Study in Economic Advising*, London and New York: Routledge.

Denison, E.F. (assisted by Poullier, J.-P.) (1967) *Why Growth Rates Differ*, Washington, DC: Brookings Institution.

Dumke, R.H. (1990) 'Reassessing the *Wirtschaftswunder*: reconstruction and postwar growth in West Germany in an international context', *Oxford Bulletin of Economics and Statistics* 52 (2): 51–91.

Gimpel, J. (1976) 'How to help the United States age gracefully', unpublished memorandum, pp. 1–24.

Glyn, A., Hughes, A., Lipietz, A. and Singh, A. (1990) 'The rise and fall of the Golden Age', in S.A. Marglin and J.B. Schor (eds) *The Golden Age and Capitalism: Reinterpreting the Postwar Experience*, Oxford: Clarendon Press.

Goldstein, J.H. (1988) *Long Cycles: Prosperity and War in the Modern Age*, New Haven, CT: Yale University Press.

Hackett, J. and Hackett, A.-M. (1963) *Economic Planning in France*, Cambridge MA: Harvard University Press.

Heller, W.W. (1966) *New Dimensions of Political Economy*, Cambridge, MA: Harvard University Press.

Kaldor, N. (1966) *Causes of the Slow Rate of Growth of the United Kingdom*, Cambridge: Cambridge University Press.

Kaplan, J.J. and Schleiminger G. (1989) *The European Payments Union*, Oxford: Clarendon Press.

Kindleberger, C.P. (1967) *Europe's Postwar Growth: The Role of the Labor Supply*, Cambridge, MA: Harvard University Press.

Lamfalussy, A. (1963) *The United Kingdom and the Six: An Essay on Economic Growth in Western Europe*, Homewood, IL: Irwin.

Lewis, W.A. (1954) 'Economic development with unlimited supplies of labour', *The Manchester School* (May).

Maddison, A. (1964) *Economic Growth in the West: Cooperative Experience in Europe and North America*, New York: Twentieth Century Fund.

—— (1982) *Phases of Capitalist Development*, Oxford, New York: Oxford University Press.

—— (1989) *The World Economy in the 20th Century*, Paris: OECD.

Matthews, R.C.O. (1968) 'Why has Britain had full employment since the war?', *Economic Journal* 77 (311) (September): 558–69.

Matthews, R.C.O., Feinstein, C.H. and Odling-Smee, J.C. (1982) *British Economic Growth, 1956–1963*, Oxford: Clarendon Press.

Mensch, G. (1979) *Stalemate in Technology*, Cambridge, MA: Ballinger.

Minsky, H. (1986) *Stabilizing an Unstable Economy*, New Haven, CT: Yale University Press.

Olson, M. (1982) *The Rise and Decline of Nations: Economic Growth, Stagflation and Social Rigidities*, New Haven, CT: Yale University Press.

Postan, M.M. (1967) *An Economic History of Western Europe, 1945–64*, London: Methuen.

Rostow, W.W. (1978) *The World Economy: History and Prospects*, Austin, TX: University of Texas Press.

Sandberg, L.C. (1979) 'The case of the impoverished sophisticate: human capital and Swedish economic growth before World War I', *Journal of Economic History* 39 (March): 225–41.

Shonfield, A. (1966) *Modern Capitalism: The Changing Balance of Public and Private Power*, New York: Oxford University Press.

Singh, A. (1990) 'Southern competition, labor standards and industrial development in the North and South', in Bureau of International Labor Affairs, US Department of Labor, *Labor Standards and Development in the Global Economy*, pp. 239–64, Washington, DC: US Department of Labor.

van der Wee, H. (1986) *Prosperity and Upheaval: The World Economy, 1945–1980*, Berkeley, CA: University of California Press.

Zola, E. (1885) *Germinal*, Harmondsworth: Penguin, 1954.

2

HOW WAS IT POSSIBLE TO RUN ECONOMIES AT SUCH HIGH PRESSURE WITHOUT ACCELERATING WAGE RATES?

David Worswick

INTRODUCTION

The question I was invited to address was posed with respect to the 1960s. Though not confined to Britain, particular interest was attached to the British case. I was also asked to bear in mind that an important objective of the conference was to establish whether policy mistakes were made in the 1960s which had adverse consequences later on, especially as regards inflation.

Before addressing the substantial question, it seemed to be prudent to ask an antecedent question – did we, in fact, have high pressure and non-accelerating wages? The first part of the paper provides some background data. It turns out that experience in different countries in the 1960s was more diverse than is implied by a simple 'high-pressure, non-acceleration' formula. When I turn to analysis, therefore, I concentrate on the cases of the United Kingdom and the United States, which appear to be towards the opposite ends of the spectrum. In the final section I take up the issue of policy mistakes.

DID WE, IN FACT, HAVE HIGH PRESSURE AND NON-ACCELERATING WAGES?

The British case

As a measure of 'pressure', I choose the unemployment rate.[1] It is not ideal, being in many cases a lagging indicator, but there are easily available data for many countries. For 'wage inflation' I have chosen

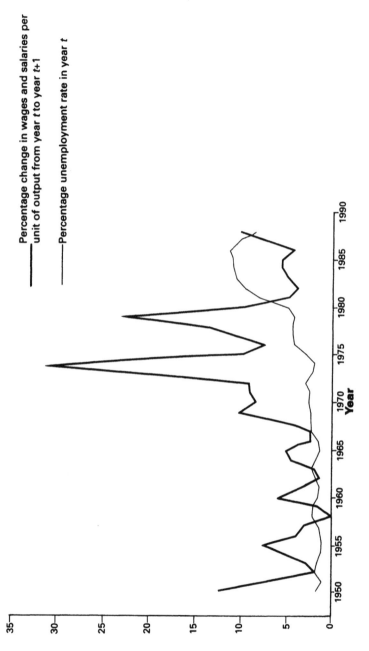

Percentage change in wages and salaries per
unit of output from year *t* to year *t*+1

Percentage unemployment rate in year *t*

Figure 2.1 Wage and salary costs per unit of output and unemployment in the United Kingdom, 1950–89.

the index of 'wages and salaries per unit of output for the whole economy', which is the only official series which covers the whole period since 1950.[2] I shall use a different indicator in the international comparisons. In Figure 2.1 I record the unemployment in each year t, matching it with the percentage increase in wages and salaries per unit of output from year t to year $t + 1$. This, in a crude way, is the Phillips direction of causality. The figure shows that unemployment was very low after the war, by previous and subsequent standards, that it had drifted up a little by 1970, took a sharp step up after 1974, and a sharper and larger step up after 1979, reaching 3 million in the mid-1980s, which is comparable with the Great Depression of the early 1930s. A closer examination of the movement within the 1960s exposes an abrupt jump in 1966, of over 0.5 per cent, to which I will refer later when discussing policy. A small question mark was thus being put against 'high pressure' at the end of the 1960s. Cost inflation, measured by our chosen indicator, oscillated between zero in 1959 – the *annus mirabilis* of Prime Minister Harold Macmillan, when we had 'never had it so good' – and 6 per cent, until near the end of the 1960s. Then there is an acceleration which, after a pause until 1973, is followed by further acceleration, peaking at over 30 per cent. All in all, we can say that in the first half of the 1960s, Britain was experiencing high pressure, with non-accelerating wage inflation, but that some clouds were beginning to appear on the horizon in the second half of the decade.

Other countries

Was the British experience of pressure and wage inflation typical? For 'pressure' I continue to use unemployment, and Table 2.1 gives unemployment rates for sixteen countries in the two decades between the First and Second World Wars and the four decades since the Second World War.[3] Among the countries included, unemployment rates were in most cases lower, and in one or two cases much lower, than in the preceding or following decades (the war years are excluded). In a few cases – the United States, Canada, Norway and the United Kingdom – unemployment in the 1950s had been even lower, though only by a decimal point or two. In all the countries unemployment was below the 1930s value, which, of course, included the Great Depression, but also in most cases, though not all, below the 1920s value. In particular, in the United States, the rates of the 1950s and 1960s were similar to those of the 1920s. All the figures are

Table 2.1 Average unemployment rates

	Australia	Austria	Belgium	Canada	Denmark	Finland	France	Germany	Italy	Japan	Netherlands	Norway	Sweden	Switzerland	United Kingdom	United States
1920s	5.6	6.0[1]	1.5[2]	3.5[2]	8.0	1.6	n.a.	3.8	n.a.	n.a.	2.3	5.6[2]	3.2	n.a.	7.5	4.8
1930s	13.5	12.8	8.7	13.3	10.9	4.1	n.a.	8.8	4.8[3]	n.a.	8.7	8.1	5.6	3.0	11.5	14.2
1950s	2.0	3.9	4.1	4.1	4.5	1.3	2.1	5.0	7.2	2.0	2.6	2.0	1.8	0.0	2.5	4.4
1960s	1.8	1.9	2.1	4.2	1.5	1.9	1.6	0.8	4.5	1.3	1.4	2.3	1.7	0.0	2.7	4.7
1970s	3.8	1.4	4.0	6.6	3.8	3.6	3.7	2.5	5.7	1.6	4.7	1.7	2.0	0.2	4.3	6.2
1980s	7.5	3.2	10.8	9.3	8.9	4.8	9.1	6.0	9.5	2.5	9.7	2.7	2.5	0.6	10.0	7.2

Sources: 1920–79, Maddison 1982; 1980–9, OECD Standardized Unemployment Rate

Notes: [1] 1924–9.
[2] 1921–9.
[3] Average of seven years.

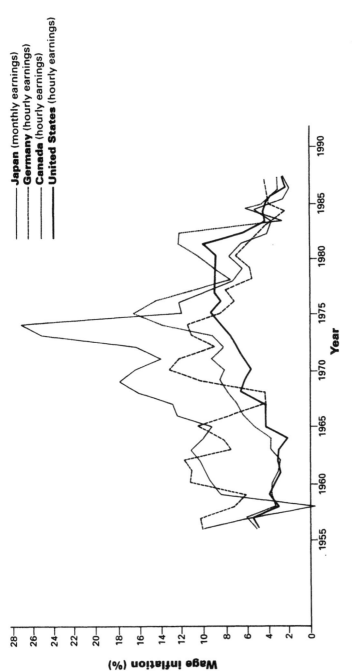

Figure 2.2 Wage inflation in manufacturing in Japan, Germany, Canada and the United States: year-to-year percentage change in hourly earnings and monthly earnings.

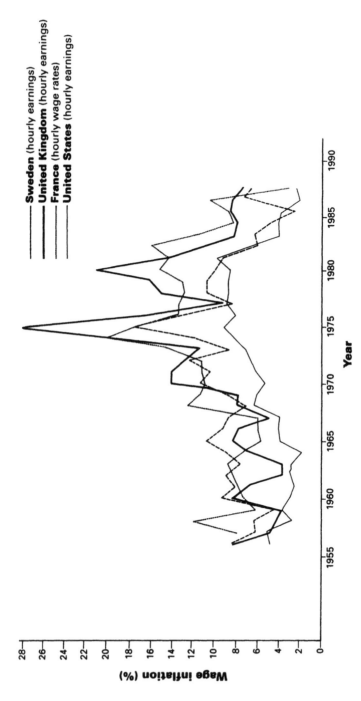

Figure 2.3 Wage inflation in manufacturing in France, the United Kingdom, Sweden and the United States: year-to-year percentage change in hourly earnings and hourly wage rates.

averages for the whole decades. There were different movements within the decade. One contrast is especially striking. Unemployment in the United Kingdom in 1961, at 1.3 per cent, was almost as low as in any year since the war; by 1969, at 2.4 per cent, it was at the top of the band for the post-war period so far. In the United States, on the other hand, the unemployment rate in 1961, at 6.7 per cent, was the second highest since the war, but it then fell to 3.4 per cent in 1969, which, though not the lowest since the war, was below the 4 per cent that many economists at that time thought to constitute 'full employment'.

Turning to wages, Figures 2.2 and 2.3 show what I call, with deliberate ambiguity, 'wage inflation in manufacturing' between 1956 and the 1980s, for seven industrial countries. Ideally, we would like precisely comparable series, but this is not possible. In five cases – the United States, Canada, Germany, Sweden and the United Kingdom – I chart year-to-year percentage changes in hourly earnings in manufacturing. For France, I give hourly wage rates, and for Japan, monthly earnings in manufacturing.[4] Unlike Figure 2.1, the changes in year t are measured from year $t - 1$ to year t.

The figures illustrate the variety of experience in the scale and timing of wage inflation in manufacturing in the seven countries. Over the whole period 1956–84 – for which we have data for all seven countries – hourly earnings in the United States rose nearly five times, at an annual average rate of 6 per cent. This was the lowest rate in the group. At the top were the United Kingdom (hourly earnings), Japan (monthly earnings) and France (wage rates), all averaging over 10 per cent a year. In between were Canada (7.5 per cent per annum) Germany (8.4 per cent per annum) and Sweden (9.3 per cent per annum). We should bear in mind that the figures refer to earnings or wage rates in manufacturing, and that their increases will normally be greater than rises in prices in general, for a variety of reasons, of which the most important is the growth of productivity in manufacturing. Thus, the average annual increases in the GDP deflator of the three largest economies, the United States, Germany and Japan, were 4.8, 4.2 and 4.0 per cent respectively, which are much closer together, and in the reverse order of average wage inflation.

Looking at Figures 2.2 and 2.3, can we discern any features which call for explanation, in particular common features?

1 There is a general impression of increasing rates of wage inflation between the mid-1950s and the mid-1970s – most graphs peaked

in 1974 or 1975, after which a decline set in, interrupted by a second, smaller, peak in 1980 or 1981, with a final return to the rates of the mid-1950s. The 'twin peaks' were most prominent for the United Kingdom and Canada, and barely perceptible in the United States. Germany does not fit into the general picture at all, having a peak in 1970, after which a gradual, and fluctuating, decline sets in.

2 We notice that the annual fluctuations in the United States are notably smaller than elsewhere. The United States also shows a clear, gentle, acceleration from the mid-1960s to the mid-1970s, which is not mirrored elsewhere except in Canada, which does, however, have much sharper peaks.

3 Focusing on the 1960s, we can say that the United Kingdom, Germany and France do not show any upward trend before 1967 or 1968, but can be seen to take an upward step in 1968 or 1969. This is followed in the United Kingdom and France by even steeper rises in the first half of the 1970s, when, however, Germany has started on its decline.[5] Sweden seems to lie between these cases and the United States. Japan starts a big leap earlier than the others.

Does the evidence we have presented support the view that the 1960s were a decade of high pressure and non-accelerating wage inflation? In the case of pressure, the generalization is not unreasonable. Nine out of sixteen countries included in Table 2.1 had, in the 1960s, the lowest average unemployment in any decade between 1920 and 1990, and others were not far from it. However, given its weight in the world economy, the exception of North America is an important one. In both the United States and Canada, unemployment was low by their own standards, but not exceptionally so. Moreover, in the United States unemployment had been high at the beginning of the 1960s but was falling fast during the decade. As to wage inflation, it seems that, prior to the late 1960s, we can accept that there was no upward trend beneath the year-to-year fluctuations. Once again North America is an exception, where a gradual and definite acceleration set in, starting from a low level in 1963 and climbing throughout the remainder of the 1960s until 1975. In the case of a number of European countries, 'non-acceleration' obtained until the late 1960s, at which point there was a distinct step up in the rate of inflation, leading on to the record rates of the mid-1970s. Once again, however, there is an exception: this time it is Germany, whose wage inflation peaked in 1970 and thereafter set out on a downward trend.

The diversity of experience, both in pressure and in wage inflation, poses a problem, as we attempt to explain the phenomena and to comment on policies taken, or not taken, to respond to adverse developments. The procedure I will adopt is to write in the first instance as though the generalization were valid, but when I need to focus more sharply on the 1960s and to discuss policies, I will draw illustrations from the United Kingdom and the United States, which appear, in many respects, to be towards opposite ends of the spectrum.

ANALYSIS – WITH SPECIAL REFERENCE TO THE UNITED KINGDOM AND THE UNITED STATES

Pressure

Why did many countries experience high pressure and low unemployment in the 1960s? Very simple, say some. With so much war damage, and such extensive dislocation of trade, once the basics of physical reconstruction had taken place, a post-war boom was inevitable. Add to that the desire of European countries to catch up with the higher productivity levels already achieved in the United States, and we have the ingredients of an unusual prolongation of high investment. But will such a simple explanation do? The decade of the 1960s began fifteen years after the end of the Second World War. Fifteen years after the First World War takes us to 1933, the bottom of the Great Depression. Yet much the same conditions of war damage and productivity differences existed in 1918 as in 1945. One could argue that there was more damage after the Second World War, or that productivity differences were not so obtrusive after the First World War, but not too convincingly. Similar conditions for a post-war boom were present on both occasions, but what followed was slow growth and high unemployment, to be followed by depression in the one case, and a golden age of full employment and exceptional productivity growth in the other. The big difference was, in my view, the emergence of government as the overall manager of the economy, paralleled by the creation by the Anglo-American alliance of effective international economic institutions such as IMF, GATT and OEEC (later OECD). Between the wars the ideas were developing about how economies might be managed, and some of the necessary instruments were being forged. Colin Clark's *National Income and Outlay* was published in 1937, and Britain's first official estimates came in 1941. There were similar developments in the

United States. The war economies themselves were better managed than in 1914–18. Controls and rationing were introduced earlier, and extended for longer after the war. In Britain, prices were pegged from 1941 to 1947.[6] The demand pent up during the war was not immediately dissipated in an inflationary splurge but released gradually, as resources grew, helping to put Britain onto a path of growth with high employment.

As controls were removed, 'global' demand management, which was explicitly aimed at maintaining a high level of employment, took over, and proved largely successful. It ought not to be forgotten that certain direct controls, over hire-purchase (consumer credit) and bank advances for example, were retained throughout the 1960s. After an uncertain start, Continental European countries, victor and vanquished alike, embarked on paths of expansion with the assistance of Marshall Aid. In this they were helped by the OEEC freeing trade and payments between them. The role of governments as overall managers of national economies and planners of international institutions was accepted as normal, in a manner which would have been inconceivable in 1913.

As the post-war period of high demand and low unemployment unfolded, business confidence grew and there was a continuing rise in the ratio of investment to output, which increased supply and helped to maintain demand. At the same time, the new international institutions worked well enough to permit a quite extraordinary growth in world trade, which appeared to be assisting in the maintenance of a high level of demand in many countries. Some will remember the perennial grumbles about British export delivery dates in the 1950s and 1960s. A partial exception to the high pressure story was the United States, which experienced unemployment of the order of 6 per cent in the late 1950s and early 1960s, well above the level then considered to constitute full employment. If the above brief explanation of the continuation of high pressure through the 1960s is correct, one has to ask why it should ever come to an end. Yet, by the mid-1970s, the pressure of demand was manifestly lower throughout the industrial world. But by then, inflation in most, though not all, countries had considerably accelerated. We shall have to look for the causes of this acceleration, and at the extent to which it brought about the rise in unemployment. But before we come to that, it is worth asking a preliminary, hypothetical, question. Were there *real* factors, other than inflation, which brought full employment to an end? Again, I will ask this question about the British economy. Suppose, that is to say, wage inflation (as measured by hourly earnings in manufacturing) had continued to run at between 4 and 8 per cent, with prices running between 3 and 5 per cent per annum, with no tendency to change, whatever was happening to the real economy.

One feature of the economy in the 1950s and 1960s, which was regarded at the time as encouraging, was the gradual rise in the share of the national income going to investment. One explanation offered for this, in the case of industrial investment, was the desire to catch up with superior American technology. Would not a point be ultimately reached when the capital stock would out-run the growth of income? As a matter of arithmetic, this was very likely. But, at the end of the 1960s, while we might have been catching up, there was still a long way to go. And if, eventually, the rate of return on private investment fell, could this not be offset by the appropriate adjustment of the balance of government expenditure and revenue? A common objection that this would entail inflation has here been ruled out by assumption. What about the decline in Britain's international competitiveness? Certainly, the British economy ran into frequent balance-of-payments deficits in the 1950s and 1960s. But the evidence is that the 1967 devaluation succeeded in correcting the current balance, at any given level of capacity utilization, for a number of years. The case against devaluation was, precisely, that it might be self-defeating through provoking more inflation. If that is ruled out by assumption, however, the case of rising unemployment through declining competitiveness can also be excluded. What about the breakdown of the Bretton Woods system? Let it not be forgotten that floating was advocated by many economists, not to mention the British Chancellor in 1972, as a liberation. Be that as it may, although floating has not lived up to expectations, it has not destroyed trade either. In the recession of the early 1980s, world trade in goods did drop a percentage point or two, but there was nothing like the plunge of the 1930s, and by 1985 normal business was resumed, with trade growing faster than production. I would not wish to argue that real factors may not have contributed to the rise in unemployment which actually occurred, but I do not know of any candidates which would produce such large effects. Nor, so long as we retain the assumption of 'invariant' inflation, would there be any reason why whatever deficiency of demand did occur could not have been offset by fiscal or monetary policy.

There is one qualification we ought to make. If we distinguish 'structural' unemployment from 'demand deficiency' unemployment, it could be that structural changes occurred which raised the 'full employment' level of unemployment. Some measures of this level depend on inflation, e.g. the Phillips curve, or the 'natural rate' or NAIRU. These we exclude here, leaving the issues they raise until the next section. But there are other measures which make use of data for unemployment and unfilled vacancies. Among them are the estimates of Brown (1985), who makes use of UV curves, plotting unemployment and unfilled vacancies against one another. His conclusion was that, between the mid-1950s and the 1980s, there had been little increase in labour market imperfection in Germany and Japan, whereas in the United States, France and the United Kingdom market imperfection could account for rises of the order of 2 per cent in the full employment level of unemployment. Much of the rise in unemployment between the mid-1950s and 1979, and nearly all of it between 1979 and the mid-1980s, was due to demand deficiency.[7] For Britain, and for many European countries, the story of the 1970s is one of lapses from the full employment which had lasted through the 1960s. This was not the case for the United States, but that story can be conveniently left for the next section.

Wage inflation

Why did wage inflation increase in most, if not all, industrial countries towards the end of the 1960s, and did that increase contribute to the rise in unemployment? When we speak of inflation without qualification, we usually have in mind the sustained increase in some general price index, such as a consumer price index, or a deflator of GDP or GNP. Such inflation can arise when there is an increase in total expenditure not matched by a corresponding increase in real output. The increase in total expenditure can be a spontaneous rise of the market sector, or it can be induced by monetary policy (e.g. an increase in the money supply) or by fiscal policy, whether by tax cuts or increases in public expenditure. Inflation can also arise from a spontaneous increase on the side of costs, whether wage or non-wage costs, notably import prices. Whether an inflationary impulse, originating in demand or costs, will continue depends on many things, including the elasticity of the monetary system, whether expressed in changes in the velocity of circulation or in the willingness of the monetary authorities to 'accommodate' the higher levels of prices and total expenditure. It will also depend importantly on two real factors: the initial degree of capacity utilization, and the growth of productivity. The categories of demand and cost inflation are commonly defined in relation to an initial position of stable prices, but the fact is that in most countries prices have risen in almost every year in the past half-century. This has two implications. As regards theory, we might introduce a third category of 'spiral' inflation to represent the fact that a first round of price increases brought about by demand-pull or cost-push may give rise to further 'rounds' of inflation, which may either converge on a finite total or diverge. In countries where nominal wages respond more quickly, or more completely, to price increases, inflation is likely to be higher than in countries where nominal wages are less sensitive to prices. Faster productivity growth will, in general, damp the spiral, though there are models of a 'wage–wage' spiral in which, if wages in following sectors maintain relativities, faster productivity growth in a leading sector could generate faster overall inflation. Second, when prices have been rising for many years, the *level* of prices is replaced in ordinary discourse by *inflation*, which is the time rate of change of the price level. When we say that inflation has fallen this year, we do not mean that goods and services are cheaper, but that the rate at which they have been getting dearer is less than it was.

When inflation has been going on for many years, the question of what is 'causing' the inflation resembles the grin of the Cheshire cat. But this was the position already reached in the 1960s. From 1870 to 1913, the annual average change in consumer prices in sixteen industrial countries was a rise of 0.4 per cent, and from 1920 to 1938 it was a *fall* of 0.7 per cent. The peace-time norm was price stability. The United States and the United Kingdom had falling prices in both periods. But, from 1950 to 1973, the average annual change for the sixteen countries was a rise of 4.1 per cent, a rate which was more than doubled in 1973–9.[8] Thus post-war inflation is in strong contrast with previous peace-time experience. Unfortunately, however, it was not steady, but showed considerable year-to-year variation. This makes it difficult to discern 'trends' and changes in trend, and even more difficult to pin down the causes of such changes. However, it is possible to point to the proximate factors making for changes, and a valuable analysis of inflationary and disinflationary impulses has been provided for the period 1951–79 by Brown (1985: ch. 4). He concerns himself with changes in the time rates of change of prices (or wages), and similarly for output to changes in its rate of growth. He distinguishes four kinds of inflationary impulse: M, money injection; E, expenditure-pull;

W, wage-push; and I, non-wage-push, predominantly import-price-push. He classified 308 cases of changes in annual inflation rates in eleven industrial countries, and also provided data for changes in the rate of growth of real GDP. He concluded that there is evidence of the counter-inflationary incidence of (negative) money-injection, and a pro-inflationary incidence of both wage-push and import-price-push, but the strongest statistical association was between expenditure-pull and accelerating output growth, much stronger than its association with rising inflation.

Brown's analysis does not throw up any single explanation of the acceleration of wage inflation experienced in most industrial countries in the late 1960s and the first half of the 1970s. A thorough study of the thesis concerning wage inflation would require detailed case studies of many countries. Here, however, we shall concentrate on two countries only, the United Kingdom and the United States.

In the British case, average inflation of hourly earnings in manufacturing from 1955 to 1959 was 5.9 per cent per annum. Average inflation for the first five years of the 1960s was also 5.9 per cent per annum. Although no acceleration was present official concern that perhaps wage inflation might do harm was growing to such an extent that a Council on Prices, Productivity and Incomes was appointed in 1957, to study the facts and report to the public. This was followed in the 1960s by various kinds of action: 'pauses', i.e. postponing pay increases in the public sector; a 'freeze' for six months on all increases; and the creation of a Prices and Incomes Board. The effect of all these measures of 'incomes policy' on holding back nominal wages is disputed, though I find it hard to believe that it was zero, and if there was a positive effect it would leave room for a 'rebound' as policy was relaxed at the end of the decade. The extra 0.5 per cent or so of unemployment generated in 1966 might conceivably have had a damping effect: on the other hand, the rise in import prices after the devaluation at the end of 1967 could have added to the net effect of the previous two factors in making for higher wage inflation. A different kind of explanation, of a longer term nature, was that offered by Henry Phelps Brown who observed the Hinge, an upward discontinuity in the curves of wage inflation in nine industrial countries in Europe. This, he thought, was the outcome of a continuous drift in the attitude of wage earners. Older workers had memories of the Great Depression of the 1930s and tended to rate job security above militancy, but younger workers had experienced only the high employment of the post-war years, with its rising living standards; they had higher expectations and believed they knew how to fulfil them. As time passed, the balance of power within trade unions gradually shifted from the older to the younger generation.[9] The 'events of May 1968' in France exercised a demonstration effect. The view that there was intensified wage-push about this time receives some corroboration from Brown's table of inflationary impulses (1985: 94–5, Table 4.1), which shows Ws for France in 1968, the United Kingdom in 1970 and Italy in 1969 and 1970. By 1970, our measure of wage inflation reached 13.9 per cent in the United Kingdom, double the average rate of the previous five years. At the same time, unemployment was drifting upwards.

The course of wage inflation in the United States during the 1960s stands out in contrast with the United Kingdom and many other European countries. Wage inflation (of hourly earnings in manufacturing) in 1960 was a mere 3 per cent and falling. In 1964, it set out upon a long and comparatively steady climb to a peak in 1975, whereupon it held steady around 9 per cent before tumbling sharply in the 1980s. There was no discontinuous Hinge at the end of the 1960s. The rise in wage inflation through the 1960s roughly mirrors the fall in unemployment from nearly 7 per cent in 1961 to under 3.5 per cent in 1969. In fact, at the end of 1961, the United States had embarked on a period of over a hundred months of uninterrupted expansion which was to carry it to the end of the decade. Before 1961, the longest expansion in the previous century had been one of eighty months across the Second World War, and, before that, the fifty months of expansion after the Great Depression (Pechman 1983: 424). The expansion relied heavily on fiscal policy, in particular the very large tax cuts of 1964 and 1965. Monetary policy was accommodatory.[10] It was only towards the end of the 1960s that the United States experienced the 'high pressure' which European countries had already been experiencing for many years. The United States did have 'non-accelerating wages' until the mid-1960s, but by the time high pressure was reached wages had begun to accelerate, albeit fairly slowly. Thus the United States does not fit the pattern implied in the question in the title of this paper. Nevertheless, it had an important impact on those countries which did. The dollar was the key currency of the Bretton Woods system. When the Korean War was over, the US consumer price level settled down to an annual average rate of increase of the order of 1.5 per cent. But, by the end of the 1960s, the annual rate exceeded 5 per cent. Given the weight of the US economy in the world economy and the size of its trade, such an increase was bound to be carried across, in various ways, to other members of the Bretton Woods system.

We have identified two factors making for higher rates of inflation and of wage inflation going into the 1970s than the steady, albeit quite widely varying, rates inherited from the 1950s. We have to consider whether it was these increases which brought to an end the era of high pressure, and, if so, whether avoidable mistakes had been made during the 1960s themselves. Before tackling these questions, however, we need to look briefly at the changing attitudes to inflation.

Attitudes to inflation

We saw earlier that the peace-time norm for industrial countries before 1938 had been stable, or even falling, prices. The average increase for sixteen industrial countries from 1950 to 1973 was 4.1 per cent. In many cases, there appeared to be no acceleration, and people became accustomed to rising prices. Quite a number of European countries which pursued policies of high pressure also established incomes policies, while in the United States after the Korean War low wage inflation was not tested, during the 1950s, by high pressure. By the end of the 1960s there had been, as we have seen, acceleration of wage inflation in most countries, and there is no doubt that 'concern' about rising prices grew stronger, leading some countries, such as Britain, to launch new incomes policy initiatives. But, though wage inflation at the end of the 1960s was higher than it had been at the beginning, there was as yet no sign of backing down from the full employment objective. In Britain the doubling of wage inflation did not inhibit the launching of a conventional expansion after 1972 (the Heath–Barber boom). The United States, whose commitment to full employment was weaker, allowed unemployment to rise sharply in 1970 and 1971, and wage inflation duly responded a little later. It is interesting to speculate whether, had the differing accelerations of wage inflation of the 1960s not been followed in 1973–4 by even bigger increases, the system might not have settled down with a steady 5 or 6 per cent superseding the 4 per cent which had hitherto prevailed. After all, what economists say about *steady* inflation is right, and it is not necessarily the case that higher average inflation entails higher variability. Brown (1985) has pointed out that in the British case the standard deviation of inflation rates between 1953 and 1970, when the mean annual increase was 4.25 per cent, was not greater than between 1929 and 1938, when the mean annual change was – 0.2 per cent. However, this has to remain a hypothetical question, since, in most instances, the accelerations of the 1960s were followed by even more dramatic developments in the 1970s.

The first shock came in 1973, in the form of a steep rise in commodity prices: the NIESR index of the export prices of primary products rose nearly 50 per cent between 1972 and 1973. This could, of course, be traced back to the exceptional degree of synchronization of boom conditions in industrial countries, and it could be expected that when demand was restrained primary product prices would fall back, which they duly did, though not as fast as they had risen. Nevertheless, from the point of view of the individual industrial country, the primary product price increase presented itself as an exogenous rise in import prices. Nine out of eleven countries in Brown's table of inflationary impulses registered an I, the only exceptions being Australia and the United States. In the following year, all eleven registered Is. This time the impulse was genuinely spontaneous, the quadrupling of the oil price by OPEC. Import price impulses work first of all into producer prices and then into consumer prices. The critical question then is the response of nominal wages. The extremes are illustrated in Figure 2.2. In the British case, wage inflation jumped from 11.1 per cent in 1973, when it had been falling, to 27.6 per cent in 1975. In the United States, wage inflation did little more than continue the gently upward path it was already on, rising from 7.1 per cent in 1973 to a peak of 9.1 per cent in 1975. The responses of other countries fall between the extremes of the United Kingdom and the United States. A similar, albeit smaller, divergence of wage inflation response is to be seen after the second oil shock in 1979 – a year in which ten of the eleven countries registered Is in the Brown inflationary impulse table.[11]

It was the combination of speed and scale of price and wage increases in the mid-1970s, reinforced by the further cost impulse of the second oil shock, which made the majority of countries abandon full employment and put the reduction of inflation at the top of their priority list of objectives. And if demand management is assigned to reducing inflation, it is no longer available to sustain output and employment. This was the main cause of the growth of unemployment in the 1970s. It was reinforced, in the case of the first oil shock, by the inability of oil-producing countries to expand imports in line with the transfer of purchasing power from the oil-consuming

DAVID WORSWICK

countries, thus deflating real demand for the world economy to an extent commonly reckoned to have been of the order of 2 per cent.

To the extent that countries were able, during the 1960s, to combine high pressure with non-accelerating wages, their success may be attributed to two main factors, one positive and one negative. The positive factor was that many governments had learned how to use the instruments of macroeconomic policy, monetary policy, fiscal policy and in some cases incomes policy to maintain effective demand and to offset quickly any recessionary tendencies which might appear from time to time. The negative factor was that the shocks (notably the first shock), which made the pursuit of non-inflationary full employment with these instruments no longer feasible, did not appear until the 1970s.

Were mistakes made in the 1960s?

On this reading of events the avoidance of policy mistakes made during the 1960s would have made little difference to the outcome in the next decade, notably the switch of policy objectives from output maintenance to reducing inflation. But one might ask a more limited hypothetical question. We did discern signs of acceleration of wage inflation in a number of cases during the 1960s, particularly towards the end of the decade. Suppose that the OPEC shocks were not to occur in the 1970s. Would the acceleration already observed have forced the switch of policy objectives in any case, or were policy mistakes made during the 1960s whose avoidance would have allowed the continuance of high pressure with non-accelerating wages? The question is not without interest, because one or two countries, notably Sweden, did contrive to carry on without complete abandonment of the employment objective.

I will mention two types of mistake whose avoidance was feasible and might have made a difference. One example comes from the United Kingdom and the other from the United States. As we saw earlier, throughout the 1960s the British government was attempting to set up some sort of incomes policy. This involved continuous discussions with trade union leaders. In 1969, the government appeared to give up on pay, and instead switched the focus of interest to strikes, putting forward a famous White Paper entitled *In Place of Strife*. This worsened relations between the trade unions and the Labour Government of the day, a worsening intensified under the succeeding Conservative Government, which made the achievement of a viable

62

and sensible way of keeping the inflation of money wages within reasonable bounds far more difficult. It would have been better to have kept the eye firmly on the ball of pay policy, notwithstanding all the difficulties. The other error was committed by the US authorities in allowing their own inflation rate to climb throughout the period from the mid-1960s to the mid-1970s. An increase in price inflation of 3 or 4 percentage points over ten years would not have upset the system if it had occurred in a small or medium-sized country such as Sweden or the United Kingdom. But the dollar was the effective key currency of the international payments system. If US prices had continued to rise at only 1.5 per cent per annum, it is conceivable that the US government might have striven harder than they did to maintain the Bretton Woods system, which seems, in retrospect, to have been a factor favourable to the maintenance of non-accelerating wages combined with high pressure.

The avoidance of the UK and US mistakes might have left economies better placed to continue with high pressure and non-acceleration in a normal world. But the shocks of the 1970s would still have upset the balance, and policies would still have been switched from sustaining output and employment to reducing inflation.

AMPLIFICATION

In explaining his use of the available data Mr Worswick started from the British case, using unemployment as a measure of pressure and wages and salaries per unit of output as the one index of wages covering the whole post-war period. Unemployment had remained very low from the 1940s until the 1970s, fluctuating between about 1.5 and 2.5 per cent; and while there had been oscillations in the rate of wage increase, there was no distinct upward trend before the late 1960s (Figure 2.1). In most other countries (Table 2.1) the 1960s had been a period of exceptionally high pressure. In the case of the United States, unemployment in 1961 was the second highest since the war, and pressure was increasing over the decade, in contrast with the fall in pressure in the United Kingdom. In America this was accompanied by a clear but gentle acceleration in wage increases between the beginning and end of the decade although fluctuations tended to be smaller than elsewhere. In the United Kingdom, France and Germany wage inflation showed no acceleration until 1968–9, with steeper rises at the time of the first oil shock in the United Kingdom and France but, exceptionally, a peak in the rate of wage inflation in Germany as early as 1970.

Mr Worswick then turned to an analysis of the forces producing high pressure in the 1960s and the subsequent ending of full employment in the 1970s, drawing attention to Brown's estimate that labour market imperfections might account for a 2 per cent rise in unemployment between the mid-1950s and the 1980s in Britain, France and the United States, while demand deficiency was likely to account for most of the rest (Brown, 1985). As to the acceleration in wage increases in 1968–9, he pointed to two factors at work: first, the relaxation of incomes policy, and second, the repercussions of devaluation on import prices and the cost of living.

In addition, Phelps Brown (1983) had detected in many European countries a discontinuity in wage movements at the end of the 1960s which he called the Hinge and attributed to a third, sociological, factor. Memories of the pre-war depression had caused the generation of workers after the war to practise systematic wage moderation and this could be illustrated from the willingness of the trade unions to hold back after the devaluation of 1949. But as the younger generation took over – with experience only of high employment and social security, entertaining rising expectations and conscious of their bargaining power – wage demands increased. The decline of centralized wage bargaining and the rise of the shop steward and factory bargaining told in the same direction. In the British case the change was typified by the Jack Jones approach where he acted simply as the representative of the militants making the demands. Whether there was a similarly explosive situation in other countries was for discussion. Some evidence for such a view would be found in Brown's treatment of wage-push in a number of countries.

Mr Worswick asked whether it was conceivable that, in the absence of the exceptional events of the 1970s, there might have been a steady, if somewhat higher, rate of wage and price inflation. There had been a period of a hundred years in which the price level in most countries had remained stable or even, in the case of the United Kingdom and the United States, fallen a little. By the 1960s the norm in most countries had become an annual rise of between 3 and 5 per cent. In Britain the norm was 4 per cent for prices and 6 per cent for wages; these rates might cause concern but were not deeply upsetting. If there had been no further shocks to come, would the outlined changes in the 1960s have simply pushed up the rate of 'tolerable' inflation from 4 per cent to 6 per cent? The question had to remain hypothetical, for there were much more dramatic impulses in store in the 1970s, due to commodity prices and the oil shock. In the 1970s, inflation had originated on the side of cost in the form of either the oil shock or the doubling of international commodity prices. No doubt the latter arose out of world demand pressures; but from the point of view of individual countries the rise in import prices was a cost-push. It was striking that in one of Brown's tables import price impulses figured as the dominant source of inflation in all countries in 1974 and in nearly all countries in 1980. These cost impulses, and the rise in wages that followed as wage earners tried to catch up with the rise in prices, carried things beyond the level of tolerance: so much so that the attitude to inflation was fundamentally changed. It did not happen all at once or in each country in the same way. But by the 1980s all countries were agreed that the priority in economic policy was the reduction of inflation.

Demand management, Mr Worswick argued, had been a major factor in prolonging the Golden Age. The policy, much criticized at the time on account of stop–go, was very much superior to what went before. But a policy addressed to maintaining employment cannot, without an incomes policy, be addressed simultaneously to combating inflation. It cannot combine expansion and contraction. By the end of the 1970s the authorities in all the major countries were addressing their policies mainly against inflation and had virtually given up on the maintenance of employment. That highly important change in attitude explains the disappearance of pressure and the persistence of unemployment: there is no need to look for more complex causes.

Summing up, Mr Worswick said that the acceleration in wages had many causes. In Europe, but not the United States, there had been an extra wage-push towards the end of the 1960s in several countries. That might have been absorbed, but the next push in the 1970s associated with the rise in import prices and the oil shock pushed inflation beyond the level of tolerance and changed the attitudes and priorities of national authorities. A similar change took place in international institutions.

On mistakes of policy, with which he had been asked to deal, he had time to mention only two. One was the shift in the United Kingdom from trying to secure the agreement of the trade unions to some kind of incomes policy to trying to deal with strikes (*In Place of Strife*, Cmnd 3888). A second was the acquiescence of the United States in an increase in price inflation in the 1960s from 1.5 per cent to 5 per cent. A key currency could not afford to tolerate prolonged excess demand; the consequence had been to give an inflationary push to prices not just in America but in all other countries linked to the dollar.

COMMENTS BY DAVID VINES

INTRODUCTION

I am very sympathetic to David Worswick's paper, and the question which he set himself set me a real challenge. His question is such a fundamental one that anyone trained in macroeconomics ought to be able to answer it straightforwardly using his or her most basic equipment. And yet I did not find his question straightforward to answer at all.

Thus my comment is set out as follows. First I review Worswick's argument. Then I set myself a simple question. What answer to Worswick's question – I asked myself – could I give to my undergraduate students, using only the simplest textbook tools to hand? In answering this question I split the textbook-driven explanation into three components. Then in a final section I argue that, as we step away from the textbooks, it makes sense to keep the same three components of the argument, but that each of them needs radical amendment compared with what the simple textbook story suggests. The role of history seems to become vitally important compared with a rather mechanical textbook view.

WORSWICK'S VIEW

Worswick argues first of all that what the question implies is what happened: by and large demand pressure was high across the OECD and wage inflation did not accelerate. He then concentrates upon answering his question for the United Kingdom alone.

His answer has two parts. First, the end of the Second World War saw governments committed to preserving high levels of activity.[12] This led to increases in the ratio of investment to output which in turn helped to keep output high. As the capital to output ratio rose in the 1960s, Worswick argues that there may have been some need for fiscal policy to take over a stimulatory role from investment if the boom was to be sustained. But, had inflation not accelerated in the 1970s, Worswick sees no reason why this process could not have continued, with either investment-led or fiscally supported growth.

Second, inflation took off largely for cost-push reasons. These included both the wage-push of the late 1960s and also the OPEC shock of the mid-1970s. But, although Worswick does not make so much of this, he also cites the extended demand pressure of the later 1960s, associated with the Vietnam War, which was transmitted to Europe.

His conclusion immediately follows. The reason that what was possible in the 1960s was no longer possible later was the cost impulses in wages and oil of the late 1960s and early 1970s and their effect in changing the priorities of government policies towards the deflationary policies necessary to contain inflation.

A TEXTBOOK VIEW

My simple textbook story has three components.

1 *The growth stimulus*: From the simplest Swan–Solow neoclassical growth model one could argue as follows. The possibility of techno-logical 'catch up' with the United States after the Second World War meant that the marginal product of capital was high, buoying up investment demand.[13] Even with exogenous growth in the labour force the rate of growth was transiently high as the economy converged to a new steady state with a higher capital to labour ratio and an increase in output per man hour.[14]

2 *Demand management and inflation*: Next one might argue that the British government wisely chose to utilize Keynesian demand management so as to keep this buoyant investment demand from causing sustained overheating during the period.[15] Furthermore, in particular, taxes remained high enough that national savings (public and private savings) matched the high level of investment[16] without interest rates, either real or nominal, having to be high.

3 *A low non-accelerating-inflation-rate level of unemployment (NAIRU)*: The level of unemployment at which overheating could be avoided was very low. This was because – one would say – the labour market was such that the NAIRU was itself very low. In the light of the work by Layard and Nickell (1987) one would argue that this was due not just to happenstance but to rising real incomes which satis-fied wage bargainers' aspirations.[17] This in turn was explained by three factors:

(a) technical progress and increasing capital intensity of pro-duction (for reasons connected with the high growth rate, explained in 1 above);

(b) improving terms of trade as a result of falling prices of primary commodities;

(c) relatively low levels of government expenditure (which meant that the tax rates necessary to manage demand in the way described above were not as high as they later had to become).

I have spelled out the three components of my argument because I think that they are logically separable, and that all three components are needed for a discussion of the 1960s. Abandon the first component, but keep the second and third, and you would have an explanation for full employment and low inflation but not for a high growth rate. I do not think that Worswick quite makes this distinction between the first and second components, but it seems to me to be important. The first component is at the centre of Kindleberger's analysis.

Notice that, in discussing the third component, I have not made use of any idea that there was *money illusion in wage demands* during the 1960s which allowed the economy to be run at a lower level of unemployment than the NAIRU. The idea that during this period there was wage moderation partly because wage bargainers continued to be fooled by the level of inflation which emerged seems to me to be inherently implausible. But my point 3 is not at all inconsistent with the Phelps Brown 'Hinge' idea, interpreted as a (probably unobservable) *moderation of real wage demands* during the 1950s and 1960s, which broke down in the late 1960s for reasons which both Worswick and Kindleberger describe.

IMPROVING ON THE TEXTBOOKS: THE ROLE OF HISTORY

I think that we must do better than the simple textbook story for each of the three components of my discussion above. Let me take them in turn.

(i) The new growth theory of Romer (1986) and Lucas (1988) enables one to produce a sustained permanently higher growth rate if investment prospects improve. The key idea concerns research and development, but it could be extended to include resources devoted to technology transfer. In such models the growth rate is proximately determined by resource devoted to a knowledge-creating activity (research and development or learning by doing in technology transfer); spillovers from the innovating activity to the rest of the economy play a crucial role in making higher long-run growth sustainable in the face of fixed factor supplies when the productivity of the knowledge-creating activity increases. Krugman (1990) has produced a Schumpeterian model with different underpinnings but with the same sort of outcome. Innovation (or technology transfer again) gives rise to transient monopoly rents; the bigger the return to the innovative activity the greater the amount which will be undertaken and the greater the steady state growth rate even for a fixed supply of primary factors. These stories – they are no more than that yet for they are not tested – are I think persuasive. And they gel nicely with the Singh *et al.* positive feedback mechanism from profits to investment to rising productivity to profits – which Kindleberger cites approvingly. Growth creates an environment in which growth can thrive. That is a bootstraps kind of argument. But the bootstraps feature seems important. This is the sense in which the historical explanation seems vital.

(ii) We have to do better on demand management than the simple textbook story. The reason that the British government prevented overheating during this period was fundamentally due to the balance-of-payments problem under the Bretton Woods fixed exchange rate system, not to its intrinsic fear of inflation. In the early 1970s Matthews and Ball, amongst others, joined what Kindleberger calls the 'damn the torpedoes school' in supporting the Heath–Barber boom: now that at last we have got rid of the balance-of-payments constraint we can press on and grow our way out of difficulty. Similar pressures, and the inflationary consequences, would have come stronger and earlier in the absence of the fixed exchange rate constraint. Mrs Thatcher and Nigel Lawson provided a further example of the same phenomenon: in the absence of a fixed exchange rate commitment, domestic anti-inflation resolve may not be adequate. The Barro and Gordon (1983) argument suggests that even if the tendency to *inflation acceleration* is avoided in such circumstances, the equilibrium *level of inflation* will be higher, because the temptation to inflate in the search of transient output gains cannot be resisted at low inflation rates. Again we have a bootstraps kind of argument, this time about the policy regime. The policy regime prevented inflation running away. But the policy regime could only be maintained because inflation had not run away already. In the face of such apparent circularity one needs historical specificity in arguing why the policy regime did in fact disintegrate in the late 1960s.

(iii) It is on the NAIRU that the problems are most severe. The work of Layard and Nickell referred to earlier, and also recent work by Rowlatt (1988), has dissected the changes in NAIRU over the past two decades. But one is left with a suspicion that something is missing in the account of why the NAIRU was so much lower in the 1950s and 1960s. Is it partly that disaggregated labour markets acted in a more fix-price manner than they did with the more competitive wage and salary bidding of the 1970s and 1980s? Or is Kindleberger right, even for the United Kingdom, that it was the demographics of labour reserves that really mattered? Or is it simply hysteresis: that unemployment could remain low because it already was low, whereas subsequently any attempt to remove high unemployment has run into supply-side constraints? Again one is up against a real circularity, and particular historical discussion seems inevitable.

After this brief review, I must confess that I remain somewhat in the dark about the answer to Worswick's question. A simple textbook explanation seems possible. But the true one seems likely to be richer, problematic and inevitably historical.

DISCUSSION

Lord Jenkins raised two points. First of all, he expressed doubts about David Worswick's proposition that, had inflation not been given a particularly strong external boost by the first oil shock, we might have moved to a slightly higher rate of inflation with which we could have jogged along almost indefinitely. If it was possible to live with 4 per cent, as we did, couldn't we have lived – unwelcome though it might be – with 6 per cent? But if that were to be posed as a genuine option, one had first to abstract the international factors at work in the early and mid-1970s and then, second, explain why if inflation could be held at 6 per cent it could not be held at 4 per cent. He could see no great difference between the two.

His second point related to the policy errors of British and American governments in the late 1960s. The British example should provide great solace to Lord Callaghan since it implied that he was right and the Government wrong about *In Place of Strife*. There had been a deliberate policy decision by the Government – though not one that was effectively implemented – to go for the one thing (*In Place of Strife*) rather than the other (incomes policy) and indeed in the spring of 1969 there was a direct trade-off between the two. The Government agreed to go ahead quickly that year with the necessary legislation (but never did) and announce that the stringency of the wage-freeze would be somewhat relaxed in the autumn. David Worswick had therefore been correct in pinpointing this trade-off; and the decision probably did have some adverse effect on wage movements over the next few years. But he had then implied that the whole issue of dealing with trade union power was a diversion. Could one really envisage – as he personally could not – that it would have been possible to go on through the 1970s and 1980s without any curbing of trade union power? Yet such an assumption was necessarily involved in regarding the whole business as a diversion. He doubted whether Lord Callaghan would regard it in that light (and Lord Callaghan indicated agreement).

As for the American example of a policy error, it was on a rather different footing. The British government had taken a specific decision: the American government had taken no decision but had financed the Vietnam War in an inflationary way. To avoid that mistake it would either have had to terminate the war or raise much heavier taxation.

Sir Donald MacDougall said that he agreed with David Worswick that it had been a great mistake to give up incomes policy towards the end of the 1960s. He well remembered being summoned, along with Lord Croham, by the Chancellor (Lord Jenkins) to be told that it was not possible to have an incomes policy and engage in trade union reform. Asked what he had said on that occasion, Sir Donald replied 'I listened with respect . . . but was rather dismayed'. It had also been argued then that prices and incomes policy was breaking down and could not be continued although he was not altogether convinced.

He was in agreement, too, with David Worswick that incomes policy had had a positive effect, if only a small one, in keeping down wage inflation in the 1960s. It was not something he could prove statistically but from 1965 until 1969 wages and salaries per unit of output (in the whole economy) rose by just over 3 per cent per annum while unemployment averaged less than half a million, which was not bad going. More than incomes policy had been involved, however. There had been a tripartite consensus among employers, trade unionists and governments of both colours to the effect that it was not possible to sustain full employment and a high rate of economic growth if pay increases were excessive. The private discussions between the three parties in the early days of the National Economic Developmental Council (NEDC) had been taken very seriously indeed and had been helpful in establishing a consensus. Nowadays meetings of 'Neddy' are held for half a day at intervals of three months. But early in 1963 in the course of just over two months there had been six full day meetings, including two consecutive days (a Sunday and a Monday) when the Council went through the *Green* and *Orange Books* paragraph by paragraph and finally agreed them for publication. Later the Council had gone through a long period of mutual education on the subject of inflation. After one meeting at which there had been some letting off of steam it was possible to discuss pay, prices, profits and productivity calmly and objectively.

In a series of papers which Sir Donald had written for the Council month after month in collaboration with Fred Jones, a former assistant to George Woodcock of the TUC, the discussions had been carried forward step by step on such matters as the different characteristics of profits and wages; the determination of prices; possible forms of control of pay, prices, profits and dividends; what the criteria might be; even the machinery that might be used for administering the necessary policies. In Sir Donald's view, it had been the mutual understanding resulting from these discussions that enabled George Brown to secure agreement so quickly with the TUC and what became the Confederation of British Industry (CBI), and why it was possible to maintain and toughen the policies in the years that followed.

Professor Artis began by expressing sympathy with David Vines in his effort to invoke the NAIRU to explain how low unemployment could be combined with low wage inflation. It was easy to engage in the circular argument that the natural rate of unemployment 'must have been' very low if wage inflation was so low. David Vines had sought to give substance to this argument by pointing to a number of real factors at work, such as the contribution to real wages of improvements in the terms of trade, low rates of tax etc. Reference had also been made to labour supply as an influence on wages, both by Vines and Kindleberger, citing the Lewis model. Labour supply could have been important in the form of immigration, especially as the immigrants went as a rule to the bottlenecks in the labour market. At the time there had been much discussion of optimal Phillips curves and the directing of immigrants to the areas with the most acute shortages.

David Vines had also referred to the folk-memory of inflation. In

Barro–Gordon language one might suppose that people would lose their aversion to inflation over a period of time, partly under the influence of economists perhaps: the Barro–Gordon indifference curves would then steepen in slope and the 'reputational equilibrium level of inflation' might rise. This would provide quite a respectable and straightforward explanation without dragging in money illusion.

A final point related to the hysteresis line of argument: that as the actual rate of unemployment rises it drags the natural rate up with it because people become less employable and more habituated to unemployment. This argument was symmetrical and hence implied that we had a low NAIRU in the Golden Age because we had had a low NAIRU for a long time.

Alan Budd had a comment to offer on the labour market in the 1960s and the Phelps Brown 'Hinge' theory. A more extreme version of the theory had been put forward by Glyn and Sutcliffe (1972) in the late 1960s. They had referred not only to the trade unions' memories of the horrors of unemployment in the depression of the 1930s but also to the general strike of 1926, which was seen as a crushing defeat of the labour movement. The conclusion they drew was that this explained the docility of the trade unions when, as in the war, they did not attempt to exercise their enormous power and long afterwards when they continued to be led by right-wing leaders. The theory went on to suggest that in the 1950s and 1960s the workers came to realize their power and proceeded to exercise it, encouraged by the commitment to full employment. The share of GNP going in wages rose steadily and had the trend continued profits would eventually have disappeared. It had been Alan's first job in the Treasury to explain the phenomenon and this was what caused him to read Glyn and Sutcliffe.

Several writers, including Brian Reddaway (1965), explained the rising inflation of the 1960s by the conflict between labour and capital for a share of income. It could also be argued that the process of accelerating inflation helped labour to gain share – a view never expressed before the war – because of the practice of historic cost accounting which concealed the loss of share from firms pricing on that basis. Prices and incomes policy also tended to operate more strongly on prices so that profits were squeezed and the share of wages expanded.

All this might be dismissed as Marxist claptrap. But if one accepted that it was happening there were various possible responses. Two responses after 1970 were of interest. One, the Heath–Barber response, was to attempt to buy labour out of its demands and hope that the faster you grew the more readily you could satisfy wage claims or reduce the pressure for nominal wage increases. This would be so if, the faster real wages grew, the lower was the nominal increase demanded the following year – a theory developed in Cambridge. Unfortunately this response ended in the miners' strike in 1974.

A second attempt was made in 1980–1 under another Conservative administration – the Thatcher–Howe administration – and could be described as bringing about an old-fashioned crisis of capitalism, generating a massive slump and recreating a reserve army of labour. This had two consequences: it brought down inflation and at the same time restored profits to their previous level. The incredible rise in profits was an aspect of events that should not be overlooked. Perhaps there was something in Glyn and Sutcliffe after all! Quite how John Major and Norman Willis fitted into the story he could not say, not being a Marxist historian.

Christopher Dow wanted to address the very large question that had formed the first half of David Worswick's problem: why had inflation been so low for so long in spite of undoubted high demand? He had a possible answer not so far mentioned: a rather simple explanation appropriate to such a large-scale, long-continuing phenomenon. All inflations contained a cost–price element. Once started, inflation generated repercussions which perpetuated it through a cost–price spiral. But what determined the speed of the spiral? On that, economics had little to say. He suggested that experience of living with inflation tended to accelerate the process. What people were trying to do in a spiral was to protect their real incomes against erosion by previous inflation. The question was how quickly did they react? How far did they go? Reactions had speeded up. In the early post-war period wage rounds had not been universally annual but by the 1960s they were accepted as an annual occurrence. There was no reason why they should not become six-monthly, three-monthly or even weekly. The same applied to profits. The interval between a rise in costs and an adjustment of prices was not fixed. The delay had often been extensive in earlier years but firms had learned to price on replacement cost instead of historic cost and the adjustment had speeded up.

This speeding up had happened and was surely bound to happen. In his view it had been a major factor: it was only to be expected that inflation would accelerate over the period. Indeed, it was surprising that inflation had not accelerated more. Perhaps that could only be explained by a fundamental sluggishness in human nature. People had other things to attend to and could not spend all their time protecting themselves against inflation.

A second reflection was that if inflation could be slowed down, presumably by changing expectations, the benefits would grow the longer the process could be continued. Over a decade, if it could be sustained, the benefits could be very considerable.

Lord Callaghan went back to the discussion of *In Place of Strife*. At the time he had been opposed to the proposals but now wanted to recant, although not wholly. He had been brought up in the tradition of Ernest Bevin that if you entered into an agreement you stuck to it until it was due to expire. This was not the doctrine of some trade unionists in the 1960s and 1970s. He had taken the view, no doubt idealistically, that the trade unions ought to reform themselves and given Bevin-type leadership they could have done so. This was preferable to a Labour government reforming them by the law, which was so inherently opposed from 1904 onwards to everything in which the trade union movement believed. The behaviour of the trade unions in the 1970s had made him change his views and he had reluctantly accepted the need to turn to the law in spite of his preference for self-discipline whenever possible. The rot had set in and things had gone too far.

He had been interested, as the least economically educated person present, in the non-economic factors cited by David Worswick, believing that economic theory could not explain how the situation arose. Jack Jones's encouragement of the shop steward movement, quoted by David Worswick, illustrated the significance of sociological factors. Another example was television, which had brought into the lives of his constituents familiarity with a way of life previously unknown to them and the thought that they, too, might enjoy that way of life. Christopher Dow had mentioned the institution of the annual wage-round, but there had been no trace of this in the 1930s when he was engaged in wage negotiations and prices had tended to fall, not increase. If the wage-round became annual in the 1950s or early 1960s it had preceded the acceleration in wages and so, too, had television.

But the main change had come in 1968, the year of revolution when de Gaulle retreated from Paris, American students burned down their dormitories, and Charing Cross Road was closed while people with iron bars 20 feet across rushed down the road shouting 'Ho-Chi-Minh' at everybody. He himself had been taken aback at

75

that time to find a revival of Trotskyite views in Labour circles. The Trotskyites had never carried the great mass of the workers with them but it was they who set the pace on a great many of the issues. They worked themselves in by great stamina, out-staying everybody at shop stewards' meetings, putting up more resolutions than anyone else could think of and winning support for wage claims that trade union discipline then forced on the mass of workers. What had the universities been teaching? Were they perhaps responsible for what happened?

Professor Kloten reminded the group of the establishment in Germany in 1967 of 'concerted action' as part of the law on stability and growth. He had attended the sessions between 1969 and 1976. 'Concerted action' was intended to make wage movements compatible with overall economic data as interpreted by the government and the Council of Economic Experts. It provided a platform for the exchange of opinions, although there was hardly any thorough discussion of the opinions advanced. Nevertheless 'concerted action' proved useful. It helped to restore confidence after the recession in 1967, for example, and to limit the increase in money wages. But the wage contracts, applying for longer periods than usual, turned out not to be in line with the dynamics of the following upswing. In 1969 there had been a super-boom in which real wages lagged far behind the rise in labour productivity. The workers felt betrayed and reacted with wild cat strikes. The unions were startled and tried to get the situation under control. In the second half of 1969 they saw their opportunity and what followed was the strong rise in nominal wages (and of the price level) referred to by David Worswick.

A second strong rise took place in 1974 after the first oil shock. The trade unions tried to anticipate the rise in consumer prices and secure an even higher increase in wages. The result was a rise in wages (e.g. in the public sector) by about 16 per cent. Monetary and fiscal policy did not keep step so that there was a clash between the movement in wage costs and the data set by monetary policy. It was this clash that mainly accounted for the downturn in 1975. A second consequence was that the Bundesbank, on the recommendation of Helmut Schmidt and the Council of Economic Experts, became willing to publish annual monetary targets to give the public and the labour unions a lead. This had functioned fairly well, particularly from the end of the 1970s onwards.

In conclusion, Professor Kloten argued that the rate of increase in wages in Germany was determined, first, by the economic situation which governed the amount of leeway available; second, by monetary and financial policy; and third, by incomes policy. But in his view incomes policy, as carried out in 'concerted action', was a weak instrument that did not help much and that risked being based on wrong forecasts. There might, however, be special situations calling for discussion between government, employers and trade unions, as, for example, in the case of East Germany where wages had ceased to bear any relation to labour productivity.

Mr Brittan said he would confine himself to a question. Why had the academics abandoned the idea of money illusion so quickly? Was it just a matter of fashion? It seemed to him that money illusion took many years to fade: it was a very long time before people learned to think in real or indexed terms. Sociological factors such as pre-war memories and a less aggressive trade union style no doubt entered into it: all these influences related to a kind of subconscious, pre-war anchor to the price level. If prices rose in a particular year, it was thought of as a disturbance. None of this was clearly articulated; but it took some time before behaviour was adjusted completely to a world in which money lost a few per cent every year.

NOTES

1 There are no continuous series for unemployment totals and rates for the United Kingdom in the post-war period. There have been adjustments, from time to time, in the numerator (the numbers unemployed) and in the denominator (whether it be total employees or the labour force, including the armed services). The adjustments in the 1980s were sufficient to take between 2 and 3 percentage points off the 'unemployment rate'. But we are only concerned with the overall picture: so, for 1950–64, I have taken the figure reproduced in the National Institute *Economic Review*, and since 1965 I have used the official estimates given in the 1990 edition of the Annual Supplement to *Economic Trends*.

2 There are series for weekly and hourly wage rates from 1950, and also for hourly earnings in all industries: but they were discontinued in 1974. There are series of weekly earnings and of hourly earnings in manufacturing, from 1955 to date. The figures of weekly wage rates and of weekly earnings have broadly similar shapes to that of wage and salary costs over the relevant periods. Weekly wage rates fluctuate rather less than either weekly earnings or wage and salary costs. All three series show no trend, or even a faintly downward one (according to whether you start in 1950 or 1952) until 1967. All show jumps after 1967, and a big leap from 1973 until 1975. A second leap occurred after 1977, although the 1980 peak of around 20 per cent was only two-thirds that of 1975.

3 A decade runs from 0 to 9, except that the 1930s decade is 1930–8. For the inter-war decades and the 1950s, 1960s and 1970s, I have drawn on

Maddison (1982). For the 1980s, I use OECD Standardized Unemployment Rates, which are broadly consistent with Maddison. The OECD
table for the 1980s is littered with asterisks, denoting 'provisional', and
vertical lines, denoting breaks in the series. I have ignored them all.

4 The UK figures were taken from the National Institute *Economic Review*
(NIER): Statistical Appendix. All the other figures come from the ILO
Yearbook of Labour Statistics. The *Historical Statistics* supplements of the
OECD *Economic Outlook* carry tables labelled 'hourly earnings in manufacturing' and 'hourly wage rates in manufacturing', which are easily
accessible, but only go back as far as 1966. Nevertheless, they suggested
themselves as a check on the NIER and ILO figures. I found, however,
that in six of the seven countries the figures given for year-to-year percentage changes in 'earnings' and in 'wage rates' were identical. Only for
Germany do they differ in the kinds of ways one would expect. Apparently, the practice is that when there are national data for only one of
'earnings' or 'wage rates', they are used as a proxy for the other, which
has, of course, the effect of making both series useless for someone who
has access only to the *Economic Outlook* supplements. Fortunately, OECD
Main Economic Indicators (MEI), from which I imagine the *Outlook* figures
are drawn, does specify whether the figures refer to 'earnings' or 'wage
rates'. With the aid of MEI, I was able to check on NIER and ILO
figures and found that in most cases the discrepancies were not large.
There was one exception, namely the year-to-year percentage changes in
wage rates in France between 1972 and 1975. ILO makes French wage
rate increases peak in 1973, a year earlier than in any other country, most
of whose earnings figures peak in 1974, with one or two in 1975. OECD
makes French wage rates have a slightly lower, but more clearly defined,
peak in 1974 than the ILO peak in 1973. On not very strong grounds, I
am inclined to prefer the OECD story for these few years from 1972 to
1975, switching back to the ILO series in 1976.

5 In the *Origins of Trade Union Power* (1983) Henry Phelps Brown observed
an increase in the rate of rise in money wages in nine Western countries
around 1969, which he called the Hinge. He did not include Canada but,
besides the other six which we have charted, he included the Netherlands,
Belgium and Italy. He, too, noted that the United States, Germany and
Japan did not fit into this picture.

6 It is true that the British cost-of-living index was substantially fiddled. But
there was no inflationary outburst such as had occurred in the First World
War, when prices doubled, nor, again, after the war.

7 For a discussion of these and other measures of structural unemployment
in the United Kingdom, see Worswick (1991: ch. 5).

8 All these figures are taken from Maddison (1982).

9 In the British case the move had already begun away from industry-wide
pay bargains between employers' organizations and trade unions and
towards plant bargaining, a move which was favourable to militancy.

10 Brown's inflationary impulse table shows Es for 1962 and 1965, and Ms
for 1961, 1963 and 1967.

11 Some countries appear to have learned the lessons of the 1973–4 shocks
more quickly than others, and weathered the 1979 shock with less

disturbance. One might mention Germany, Sweden and Norway, all countries with 'incomes policy' arrangements.

12 Robin Matthews argued in 1968 that investment demand was high because of the post-war commitment of policy to maintain a high level of activity. The important fact was, he argued, the commitment, and not the actual carrying out of stimulatory Keynesian policies.

13 Strictly one needs a vintage model, so that this is only true for new investments, not for all of the existing capital stock.

14 Sato once demonstrated that convergence to a steady state in the neoclassical growth model may take as long as 100 years following a disturbance to a parameter or to initial conditions. This would be plenty long enough for adjustment to a higher marginal product of capital to have sustained the growth rate throughout the 'Golden Age', even though it did not lead to a permanent increase in the growth rate.

15 Notice that this appears to argue the opposite from the view attributed to Matthews in note 12. But the points of view are not in conflict. The maintenance of a *regime* in which high demand was assured could have so stimulated investment that *individual actions of demand management policy* had to be contractionary. This is in accord with the observation of Matthews that the *ex post* budget deficits did not give evidence of expansionary policy.

16 Or nearly did so: I abstract from the gap between national savings and national investment represented by the balance-of-payments deficit, which in the light of later experience was always small, as work by Feldstein and Horioka (1980) and Baiyumi (1990) has shown.

17 And shifted out the labour supply schedule at any level of the workforce.

BIBLIOGRAPHY

Baiyumi, T. (1990) 'Saving and investment correlations: immobile capital, government policy or endogenous behaviour?', *IMF Staff Papers* 37 (June).

Barro, R.J. and Gordon, D.B. (1983) 'A positive theory of monetary policy in a natural rate model', *Journal of Political Economy* 91: 589–610.

Brown, A.J. (1985) *World Inflation since 1950*, Cambridge: Cambridge University Press.

Clark, C. (1937) *National Income and Outlay*, London: Macmillan.

Feldstein, M. and Horioka, C. (1980) 'Domestic saving and international capital flows', *Economic Journal* 90 (June): 314–29.

Glyn, A. and Sutcliffe, R. (1972) *British Capitalism, Workers and the Profit Squeeze*, Harmondsworth: Penguin.

Department of Employment (1969) *In Place of Strife: A Policy for Industrial Relations*, London: HMSO, Cmnd 3888.

Krugman, P. (1990) *Rethinking International Trade*, Cambridge, MA: MIT Press.

Layard, R. and Nickell, S. (1987) 'The labour market', in R. Dornbusch and R. Layard (eds) *The Performance of the British Economy*, pp. 131–79, Oxford: Clarendon Press.

Lucas, R.E. (1988) 'On the mechanics of economic development', *Journal of Monetary Economics* 22: 3–42.

Maddison, A. (1982) *Phases of Capitalist Development*, Oxford: Oxford University Press.

Pechman, J. (ed.) (1983) *Economics for Policymaking*, Selected Essays of Arthur M. Okun, Cambridge, MA: MIT Press.

Phelps Brown, E.H. (1983) *Origins of Trade Union Power*, Oxford: Clarendon Press.

Reddaway, W.B. (1965) *Reasons for Rising Prices*, University of Cambridge, Department of Applied Economics, Reprint Series 230, Cambridge: Cambridge University Press.

Romer, P.M. (1986) 'Increasing returns and long run growth', *Journal of Political Economy* 94: 1002–37.

Rowlatt, P.A. (1988) 'Analysis of the recent path of UK price inflation', *Oxford Bulletin of Economics and Statistics* 50.

Solow, R.M. (1956) 'A contribution to the theory of economic growth', *Quarterly Journal of Economics* 70: 65–94.

Swan, T.W. (1956) 'Economic growth and capital accumulation', *Economic Record* 32: 334–61.

Worswick, G.D.N. (1991) *Unemployment: A Problem of Policy*, Cambridge: Cambridge University Press.

3

WERE THE INSTRUMENTS OF CONTROL FOR DOMESTIC ECONOMIC POLICY ADEQUATE?

Lord Croham

Why was it not until the 1960s that the adoption of a full employment objective began to produce serious inflation in Britain? Were there instruments available in the 1950s for controlling the domestic economy which had been lost by the 1960s or were there some other developments which required entirely different instruments?

Economic management in the late 1940s and 1950s had made full use of the various economic instruments, as was made clear in the description of how it was done which was published in the *Economic Survey* for 1947.

Looking back after two periods of very high inflation this early post-war period seems to have been remarkably successful in producing a combination of very low unemployment, an average annual price increase of about 3 per cent per annum and an average growth rate for the economy of 2–2.5 per cent. Unemployment was lower than in the pre-war period, the growth rate was higher and the rate of inflation, though higher, was considered by many to have almost as many advantages as disadvantages. But of course there was one big and not unexpected snag. The balance of payments kept giving trouble.

Were the direct controls in any way responsible for such economic management 'success' as occurred in the early post-war period when unemployment was so low? As regards the low level of internally generated inflation it is more probable that the main explanation for it was the adherence to the fixed exchange rate between 1949 and 1967 and the resultant stop–go policies. The familiar cycle was of expanding demand, rising employment, increased domestic expenditure, wage and price rises, the current balance of payments going into deficit, deflationary measures, public expenditure slowed, unemployment rising, the balance of payments improving and then, for political reasons, a fresh expansion of demand to start the cycle going again. Lags in both the reaction of the economy to fiscal change and the recognition of what was happening resulted in government interventions in the economy nearly always being seriously mistimed so that stability was never achieved. But would the stop–go sequence itself have been avoided if the objectives set for the economy had been more realistic?

As the controls were progressively removed, ways of managing the economy had to change, putting more emphasis on general macroeconomic instruments, though the cycle continued. At the same time new priorities were emerging. It was realized as the 1960s approached that although the British economy was growing at a faster rate than pre-war it was growing much less rapidly than the economies of most of our European competitors, especially France and Germany. Moreover, trade competition was increasing.

When the government decided to go for faster growth in 1961–2, Britain had already substantially reduced government intervention in the economy and therefore economic management had to rely more heavily on indirect methods and on exhortation. Private sector investment in the home economy had been freed and there was no pent-up demand. Central government could still control a large investment programme in the public sector. On the balance-of-payments front, quantitative import controls and most of public purchase had gone; tariffs were being progressively reduced through GATT negotiations; a contingency plan for reintroducing import quotas was kept in reserve. Imports of manufactured goods were on a steeply rising trend. Exchange controls were still in force. Internal financial controls had been relaxed though recourse was still made from time to time to credit restriction by tightening hire-purchase restrictions and by requests to the banks about their lending policies. Interest rate policy had become more flexible and bank rate was being raised quite sharply when the balance of payments was under threat. In short, the direct influences on the economy were limited in scope and uneven in application.

The balance of payments was still the main weakness, especially as the foreign exchange reserves had become subject to fluctuations of greater amplitude than previously, partly because UK deficits tended to coincide with 'rest of the sterling area' deficits. It was also becoming necessary to pay more attention to wage claims and settlements. An advisory body, the Council for Prices, Productivity and

Incomes (the Three Wise Men), had been set up in 1957 and lasted until 1961, but its advice could not be made effective.

The general philosophy for creating the new regime of growth was that the government should commit itself to a specified higher rate of growth and attempt to establish confidence in both sides of industry that growth would be sustained, so that productive investment would be expanded to match that rate of growth and restrictive labour practices might be dropped. There would as a result, after an unspecified interval, be higher productivity, higher exports and the establishment of a virtuous cycle. It was claimed that it had been demonstrated that higher growth produced higher productivity, rather than the other way round.

The way to bring all this together would be an economic plan, or programme for action, drawn up under the aegis of a National Economic Development Council (NEDC), composed of representatives of the government and of the two sides of industry, plus independent members. It was given a staff who were entrusted with the production of the programme for growth, including the identification of specific weaknesses in the economy which might otherwise cause overheating or balance-of-payments problems. It was hoped that the existence of the Council would make it possible to deal with some of these weaknesses. The two problems which called for most attention were the risk of increasing cost pressures and balance-of-payments deficits as the economy expanded. There were other issues, however, like regional imbalance and shortage of industrial capacity in some sectors. It was largely in connection with this new approach to growth that it began to be argued more vigorously that more policy instruments, or at least more imaginative applications of existing instruments, would be needed. Some form of national incomes policy and a temporary control of imports were both being widely urged. And as people began to manipulate figures, many of those concentrating on the balance-of-payments problem began to speculate in private on the need to devalue sterling.

Because exchange controls existed, the long-term capital account of the balance of payments was not seen as a serious problem, though speculative short-term capital movements, for which no effective controls have ever been devised, were to frustrate many of the ambitious plans.

What was insufficiently recognized in much of the discussion of planning in the early 1960s was that the major defect of the British economy was not that it was short of manufacturing capacity but that its capacity was high cost and its middle management relatively ineffective. This weakness would take a long time to put right and would require a more fundamental treatment than a few investment incentives, wage and price policies or successive devaluations. (The subsequent setting up of the 'little neddies' was a partial recognition of the problem of inefficiency, as was the creation of the Industrial Reorganization Corporation, though one may doubt whether the solutions proposed were the right ones.)

The main impetus to growth after 1961 was given by expansionary fiscal policy in successive budgets. By 1964 there was no doubt that the economy was expanding but it began to look increasingly doubtful whether it could be sustained until the hoped for longer-term benefits were realized, because the balance-of-payments outlook was beginning to deteriorate very sharply. What was subsequently to become more worrying was that wage and price movements claims were beginning to increase in size, though they were still modest compared with later experience. There was an attempt to develop agreement about pay settlements in the NEDC but the trade unions were reluctant to do any deals with a Conservative Government with a General Election impending. The Government created some new machinery to examine wage claims in the National Incomes Commission. Most of the unions refused to co-operate with this body. The most important case with which the Commission had to deal in its short life was the examination of a pay claim in the engineering industry, in the course of which it fell to Alec Cairncross to put the Government's case for moderation. Nor was anything done at this time to quell the rise in imports, though Kahn had been subjecting both the Prime Minister and the press to a barrage of advocacy for import controls, quoting Keynes as regarding import controls as an essential measure of economic control: 'If higher earnings lead us to import more than we can afford, this cannot be remedied by the Treasury chastising itself with a high rate of interest.'

Although things had not got out of hand by the General Election of October 1964, the incoming Labour Government was immediately faced with both a gloomy forecast of the balance of payments and a worrying account of prospective public expenditure. Some of its advisers recommended an immediate devaluation of the pound. The pound was not devalued. Reliance was placed on a reduction in public expenditure programmes and on a temporary surcharge to make imports more expensive and to add to revenue. The import charge attracted vigorous international criticism, especially from European Free Trade Association (EFTA) countries. But it was not until the first budget in November, which was believed to be insufficiently deflationary to match the situation described in the Government's White Paper, that external confidence fell away sharply and required repetitive action to protect the reserves. At the same time, the Labour Government which initially had been disposed to stand back from wage issues was coming to the view that it would have to have a comprehensive prices and incomes policy. Such a policy, in various forms, became a key feature of economic management from 1965 to 1970 and again from 1972 to 1974. It was first introduced on a basis agreed with trade unions and employers' organizations and was therefore largely voluntary. Subsequently, guidelines were tightened more than once and enforced by statutory powers. One of the reasons for a step change to a tougher policy after 1965 was to persuade international opinion that this was an adequate substitute for a more restrictive fiscal policy, which would otherwise have been a pre-condition of US support for an approach to the IMF.

The Labour Government's programme for growth, which was set out in the National Plan of late 1965, indicated the need for both an incomes policy and some means of restraining imports. But this does not prove that these instruments would have been indispensable for any growth objective. The growth objective chosen was not modest. Not only was the planned rate of growth, at 4 per cent per annum, a substantial jump over previously sustained rates of expansion (believed to be 1.5–2.5 per cent), but the public expenditure programme which had more chance of being achieved was set at 4.25 per cent per annum.

I think that it is quite clear that the advocates of faster growth objectives in the 1960s believed that the traditional instruments of fiscal and monetary policy would not be sufficient. For most of them this went beyond the feeling that some form of incomes and prices policy and of import control was necessary. Attention was paid to new ideas within the fiscal field which might promote higher investment or reduce regional imbalances. Ingenious new taxes and grants were dreamed up, and old ones modified, in the hope that they would meet these needs without infringing international agreements about quotas and subsidies. Most of these were of a discriminatory nature, such as the Selective Employment Tax, and contained various regional incentives. Most had comparatively short lives, not so much because they were shown to have failed as because the government changed in 1970 and 1974.

Were there deficiencies in the traditional instruments of economic policy which required (and may still require) devices like these? Did the problem lie in the impracticability of the growth and public expenditure objectives combined with the incompetence of much government intervention when it tries to be selective? Or were there reasons why Britain could not achieve the objectives it had set itself within the confines of a fixed exchange rate so that it needed to be able to float sterling? The very low rate of unemployment in the 1950s (less than 2 per cent in contrast with Beveridge's target of 3 per cent) created a conviction that any higher level of unemployment was politically disastrous, regardless of circumstances, and this pre-disposed governments to try to run with a pressure of demand which was too high. Nor was the situation helped by the adoption in the 1960s of over-optimistic growth targets purely on the grounds that the target figure had to look large, regardless of our ignorance about what caused steady growth.

It is convenient that the problems of the British economy in the mid-1960s were comprehensively reviewed by the Brookings Institution in 1968, and that their report was in turn discussed at a Ditchley Conference chaired by Alec Cairncross in 1970.

The Brookings Report (Cairncross, 1970) highlighted a number of features of the UK situation. It noted that in the period 1950–62 Britain's economic growth had been slower than that of the United States and Europe and had still been punctuated by recurrent crises. Changes in fiscal policy had had to be geared to the payments situation. The household sector in much of this period had been a net saver but government expenditures appeared to have led an inde-pendent life. Governments had been slow to take fiscal action to impose a general restraint on private consumption in the face of rising public expenditures. Monetary policy had been relied upon to restrict specific sectors of private expenditure such as consumer durables. The Brookings Report suggested that monetary policy should have been targeted to regulate the balance of payments and that the main instru-ment for the attainment of domestic objectives should be fiscal policy. It was not thought that incomes policy could guarantee a reconcilia-tion of full employment with price stability or a manageable balance of payments. It was believed that the recurrent payments problem was the result of an attempt to maintain too many policy commitments –

domestic growth, full employment, a foreign and military presence and an international central banking role – in the face of insufficiently favourable circumstances both at home and in the world economy. Given the time at which the Brookings Report was written, it was optimistic about the results of the 1967 devaluation.

The Brookings Report concluded that it was not an insufficiency of policy instruments that was responsible for the disappointing British economic performance but the existence of too many objectives to be consistent with the reality of Britain's position in the world. The key judgement was that growth should be encouraged by increasing economic efficiency rather than by encouraging investment or aggregate demand.

Those assembled at Ditchley in 1970 to review the Brookings Report did not accept all the arguments. There was a fairly broad agreement, however, with the proposition that Britain had had too many policy objectives and had erred in believing that full employment, steady growth, stable prices and an absence of balance-of-payments troubles were compatible with each other. Some participants implied that the objectives should be different. Robin Matthews believed that the objectives had not been absolute but could have been characterized as the achievement of as high a level of activity as was compatible with the state of the balance of payments. In the post-war period it was impossible to achieve both a satisfactory level of demand and a satisfactory balance of payments, especially when the level of demand regarded as satisfactory was a very high one. David Worswick argued that correct fiscal and monetary policies were necessary to achieve various economic objectives but they were not sufficient. Additional instruments were required, such as a permanent incomes policy. Roy Harrod wanted a more vigorous import restriction.

Robert Hall pointed to an alternation of objectives and stressed the significance of the desire of governments to win elections. Stimulus after a deflationary phase was always overdone because governments could choose the date for a general election during the upswing but before prices had been much affected. He pointed out that from mid-1967 to 1970 some spare capacity had always been maintained in the economy.

The question whether there was a close relationship between the level of aggregate demand and the price level exercised both the Brookings team and the Ditchley discussion, as did the proposition that the maintenance of a high level of demand would lead to a high level of productivity. The conclusion was that there appeared to be some relationship between the pressure of demand and prices but it was not a fixed one. The rate of growth in productivity appeared to be unaffected by the pressure of demand.

Richard Caves, representing the Brookings Institution, argued at the Ditchley Conference that maintaining equilibrium in both aggregate demand and the balance of payments required separate policy instruments of adequate strength and flexibility, and that more instruments were needed if separate aspects of aggregate activity (prices, growth rate) were to be controlled. His main conclusion about the United Kingdom was that the need to adopt fiscal and monetary policy to cope with recurrent crises of the balance of payments rendered them relatively ineffective as stabilizers of the fluctuations of domestic policy targets. Either sufficient policy instruments were not at hand or they were not used with sufficient force or analytical insight. As regards incomes policy, Caves pointed to the danger that incomes policy might have perverse effects – the maximum norm for wages could easily become a minimum as well.

At this time in the late 1960s there were several different views within the official Treasury. From 1964 onwards there were nearly always four senior economists advising the Chancellor who were not always in agreement with each other. As regards the senior non-professional Treasury officials (if I may speak for them), we believed that the economy was overloaded and that the main need was to reduce the load of public expenditure. We were particularly concerned about the levels of defence expenditure and of government expenditure overseas. There were also some very worrying forecasts being made of increased social expenditure, especially pensions, which would add to the overload problem. Given that most attempts to bring about substantial reductions in public expenditure failed, we were somewhat reluctant to lose any policy instruments that were to hand which might reduce aggregate spending or assist the balance of payments. Most of us did not have great confidence in prices and incomes policies except as short-term measures. But we were afraid of the effect on external confidence of abandoning the incomes policies once they had been introduced. This was especially so after 1965, when a tougher incomes policy had been publicly presented as a substitute for a tighter fiscal policy. But few officials had any doubts about the concept that governments could and should manage the economy by a combination of fiscal and monetary measures (supported to an unquantifiable extent by residual controls of which exchange control was the most significant).

By the end of the 1960s, however, there was less optimism about economic management than there had been earlier. This was not because we felt short of instruments but because the development of the British economy was consistently disappointing. We were no longer so sure about what ought to be done. Alec Cairncross, no longer in government by the end of the decade, summed up the new attitude in his concluding reflections on the Ditchley discussion with a sentence which gained in truth in the years that followed: 'We do not know for sure how the economy works and it certainly does not work in the same way for long.'

AMPLIFICATION

Lord Croham said that he would confine himself to UK policy largely because he knew more about it after 'dabbling in it' between 1947 and 1977. On incomes policy he had had responsibility for the detailed work between 1965 and 1970 and again in 1973–4.

The question with which he was asked to deal could be put another way: did policy-makers think that they were short of macroeconomic instruments to secure the policy objectives set for them? The short answer is that the available instruments were clearly not adequate for the actual tasks which had been set. But was that the fault of the instruments or of the tasks to be carried out? What did the policy-makers most want to have? In his view they were in the position of the alchemists of old, wanting the impossible, in search of a philosophers' stone that would control wages, incomes and prices.

He apologized for the absence of statistics, charts and equations in the paper he had circulated. He had been tempted to refer to the events and attitudes which affected the development of thinking in government in the 1950s and 1960s, and which helped to explain how the situation in the 1960s arose and how things actually turned out. There had been great enthusiasm for economic planning in Britain in both these decades, and governments published documents describing how it would operate. But the thoughts about how it would work were totally different in the 1960s from what they had been earlier. What was common was the existence of multiple objectives; and very often in both periods there was a feeling that too much was being attempted.

In the first period there were many highly detailed controls over the economy surviving from war-time; and, as was explained in the *Economic Survey for 1947*, these were to be manipulated so as to control industrial output, investment, private consumption, imports etc. Much more confidence was shown in the survey in the ability of the government to succeed in these efforts than was felt at the time in Whitehall.

By the 1960s, opinion about how the economy could be run had totally changed. Most of the controls had gone. Was this the reason for both the change in opinion and the policy failure? Lord Croham thought not. In the early post-war years the shortage of resources was far more a source of concern than any shortage of instruments of control. There was always a lurking fear in people's minds that full employment would be bound to lead to inflation. But in 1945–7 it was the early collapse of the economy through a shortage of foreign exchange that was the real danger. The balance-of-payments problem continued to be a dominating thought during the 1950s and 1960s and played an important part in the experience of that period. There was less fear of a total collapse after the years of Marshall Aid but there was a continuing problem and it called increasingly for new economic instruments. These were usually of two types. The level of unemployment was politically very sensitive, partly because it had been possible to keep it very low and partly because it was confidently assumed that it could continue to be kept low. This meant that if for any reason unemployment increased, even if only to a level that has long now been unachievably low, there was intense pressure to bring it down again. But any expansion of demand for that purpose soon affected the balance of payments. The tendency for wages to rise was, at that time, of much less concern than the failure of exports to increase fast enough and the tendency for imports to grow too quickly. It is surprising, therefore, in the light of the figures now produced about the level of inflation in the 1950s and 1960s, that the most constant demand for an additional instrument was for something affecting incomes and prices. What gave rise to this was not so much a fear of wage inflation as a fear that if wages rose too much it would upset the balance of the economy, reduce industrial investment when it was inadequate and stimulate consumption.

Although from a long-term point of view there was need of much more industrial investment, and there were regional imbalances, somehow there was less pressure for new instruments to deal with those problems than with prices and incomes, and it was believed that some ingenious use of existing instruments would make it possible to cope with them. Indeed, in the 1960s some highly ingenious new forms of taxation were developed and tried out. There was also, from time to time, pressure for some instrument to deter imports, especially after import controls had been relaxed. Roy Harrod, for example, bombarded the Prime Minister at the end of the 1950s with letters about the need to control imports of manufactures. At that time I was the custodian of a contingency plan to restore import controls in case of need; but by the early 1960s it had become more and more impracticable to reintroduce them because of the lack of an adequate basis on which to allocate import licences. (What basis there was relied on pre-war share of trade figures and was therefore hopelessly out of date.) There was also an obvious danger of retaliation against our exports. It was at this stage that pressure increased for a floating exchange rate; and although that may seem entirely a matter of external economic policy, the main reason for it was as a way of coping with the tendency of British industry to be uncompetitive in foreign markets.

The phasing out of most controls in the 1950s had gone reasonably smoothly, with few demands for reinstatement apart from import controls. There had been little experience of incomes policy; and this helped to make it seem attractive as a relatively new instrument. Nothing much was done until the idea spread in the early 1960s that the UK economy was not performing as well as had been thought and that other countries were doing very much better in the growth stakes. People looking across the Channel were impressed by the success of France. The thinking of both our political parties was then imbued with the concept of 'going for growth', finding an instrument for that purpose and getting agreement on a growth target.

Donald MacDougall had earlier in the day referred to the NEDC and to early success in spreading understanding of economic affairs. When Maudling followed Selwyn Lloyd and was tempted to go for demand expansion, he relaxed fiscal policy so as to encourage growth but badly wanted to secure an agreement in the NEDC on an incomes policy. The approach of a General Election prevented the trade unions from collaborating.

Growth rates, Lord Croham argued, were something politicians were extremely naive about. Whatever the achieved growth rate, they wanted a target significantly bigger and that was liable to mean bigger by more than 1 per cent. Alec Cairncross had recently described in a broadcast how difficult it had been to persuade Selwyn

91

Lloyd to accept a target of 4 rather than 5 per cent; and 4 per cent itself was substantially higher than the rate experienced in the 1950s.

A further reflection was this. Anyone trying to recount the history of a period in which he was active, relying on memory and the material available at the time, would be totally astonished to find that most of the figures for the same period produced by other people twenty or thirty years later were quite unrecognizable. The most important instrument lacking was a position-finder to tell us exactly where we were at any given moment. Nearly all statistics, and especially those made on the basis of trends, are subsequently changed and yield quite a different picture with the passage of time. It might well be, therefore, that many of the things that happened in the 1960s took place because of inadequate guidance and information.

When the Conservatives failed in 1964 to secure agreement on an incomes policy, it was left to George Brown to take over most of the work and staff of the NEDC (including Donald MacDougall) and demand the production of a National Plan in which a comprehensive prices and incomes policy was to be a key feature. (An import deterrent in the form of a temporary import surcharge was also introduced about that time.) In the light of later experience, the rapidity of the development of prices and incomes policy in the 1960s was remarkable. In the first phase extensive negotiations with employers and unions were directed towards winning acceptance of a broad voluntary policy. The application of the policy was delegated to a Prices and Incomes Board. The job of the Government was to establish guidelines, to refer cases for study to the Board which appeared to infringe the guidelines and, if the Board reported that the increase was not justified, to take over and try to persuade the parties to delay the increase.

This procedure had the great merit of keeping the Government at arm's length from price and wage fixing. But it was not likely to be successful once inflation had taken hold and gained momentum. At an early stage it became clear that voluntary co-operation was not always to be relied on. The first case on the prices side related to the price of soap, which was largely made in the United Kingdom by two firms, one British and one American. The British chairman, called in by George Brown and asked to hold the price, agreed at once. The American chairman, when appealed to, was prepared to defer the price increase only if the Government could point to legislative powers. In such a situation only a statutory policy will work.

In fact, within a few months, because of balance-of-payments problems, the incomes policy was being made more rigorous as a substitute for a stiffer fiscal policy. The Government, in need of support from the IMF and the United States, was under pressure to tighten control of the economy. Support would be conditional on a firmer budgetary policy or a tighter incomes policy. Lord Croham personally had had to develop the necessary framework for tougher control of incomes and prices and then go and sell the proposals to the US government.

Were incomes policies of this kind really macroeconomic instruments? They certainly could not be expected to operate with any quantitative precision. In the 1960s the incomes and prices policy was moderately successful in damping wage and price movements: this was probably the most successful phase of this kind of policy in the whole post-war period. But any effect on external confidence was very short-lived, although one of the main reasons for the more rigorous policy had been to boost external confidence. Moreover, a heavy backlog of pressure built up on the wage front so that, as soon as the Government felt obliged to easy up on the policy, it broke through.

Thus there had been no experience of maintaining prices and incomes policy for any length of time; nor was there ever likely to be such experience unless the starting point was a level of inflation close to zero. In the light of later experience of prices and incomes policy in the 1970s Lord Croham doubted whether anyone who had been close to this kind of policy could have any confidence in its use as a macroeconomic policy instrument. There had been a period when there was only a prices policy: but all it did was to destroy the financial integrity of the nationalized industries by denying them the power to adjust prices when wages were increased.

In conclusion he referred to the Ditchley Conference of 1970 at which many round the table had been present when the Brookings Report of 1968 had been reconsidered. Although he had disagreed at the time with the Brookings team, he came to the conclusion that the argument of the report was convincing. This was to the effect, first, that the United Kingdom had an inefficient economy and was trying to grapple with it by ineffective means, and second, that it had far too many objectives to be dealt with successfully by any combination of economic instruments. His considered belief was that it was not necessary to have a great many instruments provided that there was a sensible set of objectives and the economy was not overloaded – in particular not overloaded by public expenditure.

93

COMMENTS BY MICHAEL ARTIS

The question set for discussion asks whether the instruments of control for domestic economic policy were adequate. Like Lord Croham I take British economic policy to be the referent here. There is a well-known and natural temptation, if you do not like the outcome of your efforts very much, to say that of course you did not have the right tools for the job. But we should beware the adage 'It's a poor workman who blames his tools'. It might not be right to jump to the obvious conclusion too quickly. First, you need to ask whether the toolbox was not perhaps half-empty, and check whether the tools were in good condition. Then we have to ask whether they were the right tools for the job. Finally we must enquire whether the economic policy journeymen of the time were competent – did they handle the tools properly, use the right ones at the right time and so on.

To answer the first question, I would say that the toolbox was certainly quite large – indeed impressively comprehensive in some ways. Some old tools had been discarded, as Lord Croham reminds us. During the 1940s and 1950s a set of direct controls was available to the economic planner which were gradually eliminated from the toolbox. But these tools had been useful in rationing scarce resources in detail and the name of the policy game changed as the constraints on the British economy were eased; the elimination of these policy tools can hardly be accounted a loss, therefore. In any case, quite a number of controls survived which could be used to address the problems of the 1960s – exchange controls, Industrial Development Certificates, hire purchase controls and so on – and by the standards of today, certainly, the range of policy instruments available was very large. Correspondingly, there were major policy initiatives in areas untouched by policy today: there was a highly active regional policy, an incomes policy, the National Plan and an attempt at indicative planning.

Nevertheless, some tools were better (more effective) than others. Some of the tools were themselves 'under construction'; or they were rather frail – this was so for planning and for incomes policy, for example. They were not necessarily very reliable – even the description of them as tools or instruments might be challenged as suggesting too strongly that we can think of them on the same level as, say, rates of taxation (Frank Blackaby makes such a point in the introductory chapter to his (edited) volume on British economic policy in the 1960s (Blackaby 1978)). The best tools were surely the standard instruments of demand management policy, especially variation in tax rates and monetary policy instruments. The use of these was not even confined by the annual budgetary timetable. There was the 'regulator'. The financial system was highly constrained by today's standards, so there was really no doubt that tax rate variation would work.

My argument so far, then, is that the toolbox appeared quite comprehensive but some tools were of a better quality for the job than others.

What about the tasks set for the users of these tools? Here it seems clear to me that there was a degree of unrealism about the way in which it was supposed that some of these tools could be used. I refer specifically to the fact that by the middle of the decade the chief problem for policy had been supposed to be that of deficient growth, with indicative planning as part of the solution. In fact, not only was it unclear that the solution proposed matched the problem, but the chief problems for policy turned out to be more mundane and closer to home – first the recurrent balance-of-payments problem and then, near the end of the decade, the beginnings of the inflation problem that was to dominate the 1970s. Did the policy-makers also attack these problems with a misconceived view of what was possible – subsequently blaming their tools instead of their misconceptions? To a degree, the answer to this question also must be 'yes'. Policy-makers had in view that the Phillips curve offered an exploitable trade-off and that incomes policy could shift the trade-off in a favourable direction. Among the intellectual foundations for the devastating monetarist counter-revolution of the late 1970s were denials of propositions like these (of course, these denials themselves represented misleading half-truths . . .). Still, the policy-makers themselves (according to Lord Croham's account) heavily discounted the effectiveness of incomes policy and there were certainly many 'unbelievers' in the Phillips curve among the British economic establishment. What of the balance of payments? Here, interestingly, intervening fashion provides some support for those who were sceptical of the effectiveness of devaluation – though equally it seems clear in retrospect that a real depreciation was required and that this, in the circumstances of the time, would have involved a discrete devaluation of the nominal peg.

What seemed to work very well, though, was demand management, in the sense that control of demand was feasible, the instruments of policy were flexible and demand management could 'solve' each of the main problems – inflation, unemployment and balance-of-payments disequilibrium (but not growth) – at least temporarily. The criticism that demand management tools were harnessed to the creation of a political business cycle is after all a disguised endorsement of their flexibility and effectiveness. Nevertheless, the basic problem was that, in the absence of additional tools, the demand management 'dose' required to 'solve' the balance-of-payments problem at any time was liable to be too big to permit employment to be maintained at a desirable level, and might not be at the right level to control inflation. The result was a 'fire-fighting' approach to economic policy in which these problems were perforce tackled sequentially – and repeatedly.

Sceptical policy-makers probably knew and discounted the weaknesses of some of their policy instruments (or at least acted with instinctive conservatism amounting to the same thing); they knew that they were condemned to a fire-fighting manipulation of the instruments of demand management policy. They sought some medium-run room for manoeuvre by campaigning for more discipline over government spending (or, again, were led by innately conservative instincts to adopt this posture). This was appropriate in so far as government spending lay – in principle at least – in their own sphere of control. But this did not do anything for the rest of the economy. When Richard Caves summed up for the Brookings side at the Ditchley Conference (Caves 1971), he drew attention to the sheer inefficiency of the British economy and the Americans' scepticism that demand management could have great effect one way or the other on that problem. This was a perceptive comment. Demand management tools were effective and flexible. But the *best* they could do would be to iron out the fluctuations in output around its trend – and in fact they did not even do this because they were enlisted in the fire-fighting approach.

The supply-side deficiencies of the British economy are, it is well known, of long standing. There is every presumption that they are deep-rooted. Solving the problem probably therefore takes *long-run* commitment to a suitable range of policies and institutions – if indeed there is any solution.

DISCUSSION

Opening the discussion, *Lord Callaghan* agreed with Lord Croham about the naivety of politicians in relation to growth rates, but added

96

that he was not at all sure that only politicians should don the dunce's cap. He clearly recalled that it was not only the Labour party that had endorsed 4 per cent. The Tory party, in its manifesto, said it intended to aim for a 4 per cent growth rate. Indeed, the Tory Government had begun to try to do that, and growth had reached 6 per cent under the chancellorship of Reginald Maudling (1962–4). All the press including 'brilliant young commentators like Nigel Lawson' complained about how ineffectual Mr Selwyn Lloyd had been (Chancellor, 1960–2) and demanded that 'Maudling stop dawdling'. But as authoritative as anyone was the OECD. Lord Callaghan recalled that the OECD had set a target of 50 per cent growth over the decade, which would imply growth close to 4 per cent per annum, and that Robert Shone, the Director General of the NEDC, also persuaded the NEDC to adopt a target of 4 per cent.

Christopher Dow pointed out that that target had been for the whole OECD area; that it had been explicitly recognized that the rate of growth of countries would vary, and that Britain would have a slower-than-average growth rate. The rate predicted for Britain had been around 3 per cent, which was not unrealistic. Lord Callaghan replied that no politician, fighting an election, could have been expected to exclude Britain from the whole OECD area. He had no doubt that it was very hard to alter the long-term trend of growth. He remembered how, when the Department of Economic Affairs had come to discuss the National Plan with Sir William Armstrong (permanent secretary to the Treasury, 1962–8), Sir William had convinced him that it would be absolutely impossible to achieve 4 per cent because of balance-of-payments constraints. The government had therefore aimed at 3.8 per cent. The whole thinking of the time had been in favour of higher growth targets, and politicians had responded to such social pressures.

The Government had set splendid objectives, but failed to carry them out. It had intended to make structural changes in the economy, redeploy labour and keep wages in line with productivity. The aims had been fine, but the tools simply could not achieve them.

Lord Callaghan made what he described as 'one other confession': he had been very much against devaluation in the 1960s. His reasons were partly moral, which might now seem ridiculous. But he had also thought, and still believed, that with new young ministers coming into government after thirteen years in opposition, determined to put their policies through in the first twelve months, devaluation would merely have added to the problems. With hindsight, he wished that the Labour Government had devalued after winning the General Election of 1966. Before that, devaluation would have been impossible: the Tories would have said, 'Return a Labour Government, and that is what you get'.

Terence Higgins put the question of the session, about the adequacy of economic controls, into the broader context of the legacy of the 1960s. The Conservative Government of 1970, in which he had served as a Treasury minister, had inherited that legacy. What did the Government inherit, he asked, and was the inheritance frittered away or improved?

The Conservative Government, coming into office in 1970, inherited the aftermath of what was undoubtedly the most rigorous incomes policy ever introduced. He recalled, night after night in the House of Commons, an hour and a half at a time, with a vote at the end on a three-line whip, debating whether a particular wage settlement was in excess of the policy or not. On one occasion, the question had been whether two particular individuals in the public sector had had a 20p a week increase more than the policy allowed. That was debated for an hour and a half. He had handled most of the debates, against Roy Hattersley, occasionally assisted by another shadow Treasury spokesman called Margaret Thatcher.

The Tory Government, having opposed the policy in opposition, abandoned it on coming to power. Lord Croham had referred, in his paper, to the incomes policies he had been involved in from 1968 to 1970, and then from 1972 to 1974. He left out 1970–2, the period of the so-called '$n-1$' policy, which had been very much the best incomes policy Britain had had. It had been run by a very small group of ministers – just three people – who took the view that, if the level of public-sector settlements could be reduced, the level of private-sector settlements would follow. For two years, the team had ground down every spending minister, week after week, to reduce the level of settlements. The general rule taken by the team, on which Mr Higgins had served, had been that the true level of settlements was generally roughly double whatever the spending minister said his wage settlements were. David Worswick's data in his paper had been rather misleading, because they related wage settlements to output. In fact, the government had halved the rate of settlements between 1970 and 1972. The policy came unstuck with the first miners' strike. Ministers had made very clear to Derek Ezra (then chairman of the National Coal Board) what was the most he should offer.

Unfortunately, Mr Higgins recalled, Derek Ezra rushed off one evening to the miners' headquarters. The Treasury team actually sent someone to chase him down the Euston Road to try to stop him. He offered the miners' leadership more than anything the Government had in mind. The Government was then stuck with the offer, and the whole incomes policy was destroyed. Mr Higgins still believed that the policy had worked well, and might be useful today, even though the public sector was smaller now than it had been in the early 1970s.

The Tory Government had also become worried by the rise in unemployment. It hoped to raise the rate of demand until it came in line with productive potential, and then to keep the two together. It was true that the level of spare capacity the Government envisaged was much less than was really needed to keep a grip on inflation. But there had been no intention of allowing demand to expand indefinitely. Unfortunately, one weekend Edward Heath made a speech which the Treasury team failed to catch, in which he gave the impression that growth would go on forever. In this lay the foundation of the Barber boom.

The Conservative Government had taken the view that the exchange rate should not be a barrier to its expansionary policy. Tony Barber said, on a number of occasions, that, if need be, the Government would allow the rate to float. As a result of the miners' strike and the collapse of incomes policy, that eventually became necessary. Mr Higgins recalled a meeting, at 9 a.m. one morning, which he attended with Tony Barber, Douglas Allen and Frank Figgures. They had agreed that it might be necessary to float, depending on what happened on the foreign exchanges by midday. Leslie O'Brien had not been at the meeting because he had been at a meeting in Switzerland. And they had discussed whether bringing him back would make floating inevitable, because of the risk that he would be detected on the way home. They even wondered whether he could be suitably disguised. (Lord O'Brien, much amused, interjected that he had actually been in the south of France, on holiday.)

By midday the loss on the exchanges had become so great that floating was inevitable. The Nixon tapes recorded how the news reached the American President. An assistant had rushed in to announce that the British were floating. 'Gee,' said the President, 'that's devaluation.'

In summation, concluded Mr Higgins, the inheritance of the 1970 Tory Government had not been an easy one. The Government had probably been right to abandon the statutory prices and incomes policy, although it had been forced to revert to it in 1972. The voluntary policy might have been retrieved: most of the expansion in the money supply that worried Margaret Thatcher and Keith Joseph was absorbed in the housing market. But in the end, the Government had been forced to call an election: the Tory party was determined to go, and in those circumstances Mr Heath had no other option.

To one who had not been involved at the time, said *Andrew Crockett*, it was interesting to compare the situation of policy-makers then and now. Today's policy-makers frequently regretted the shortcomings of what was dubbed 'one-club golfing'. Changing Michael Artis's tool-kit analogy he reflected on the very large variety of clubs available in the 1960s: not just putters, but drivers and mashies and niblicks. He was interested to hear how much people at the time realized that those were relatively weak instruments that could not be relied on. Some of the commentary on the period suggested a good deal of confidence: if the government had five objectives, and had five instruments, then everyone knew from Tinbergen that it was home and dry.

Several problems were obviously realized at the time. First, a number of these instruments operated with lags that were larger and more variable than their most enthusiastic proponents assumed. As a result, when their effects came through, the underlying situation had changed. That meant, as Lord Croham had noted, knowledge of what the underlying situation was at any given time was deficient.

Second, as had increasingly been realized, some instruments of demand management had potential adverse effects on the efficiency of the economy. Some involved attempting to influence prices, whether the exchange rate, interest rates or incomes, to fend off influences coming from the market. You should not assume that because a price developed in a market it was the most efficient price. But you ought at least to ask whether, when you intervened to alter market prices, you were correcting a distortion or adding to it. It had often been argued, for instance, that the 'dash for growth' – high demand, maintained for a long period – would lead to Kaldor-type productivity increases. That view would now be greeted with scepticism.

Mr Crockett also felt that the importance of structural policies had not been sufficiently appreciated. The effective functioning of the economy called for a range of measures which might either directly affect the way the economy worked at a micro level, or, more importantly, create the conditions for markets to work more effectively. That might include, for instance, measures to promote flexibility in the process of wage determination, or education. Growth could not

be promoted simply by using the instruments of demand management and indicative planning. It was also essential to address
structural weaknesses in the economy.

This seemed to *Samuel Brittan* a perfect occasion to make a conditional defence of what he had thought in 1963, 1964 and 1965. He
had been involved in drafting the first chapter of the National Plan,
the only chapter, as he put it, that was in prose, rather than numbers.
The chapter contained a defence of the market economy. Indeed,
Thomas Balogh had complained about it, and said that it leant too far
towards being fair to Reginald Maudling. Samuel Brittan had not
been at all interested in specific targets for the steel industry, the coal
industry or the iron filings industry; nor in ringing up manufacturers
to tell them not to put up the price of something. As a spoof, he had
once drafted a letter to his laundry drawing their attention, in the
most bureaucratic language he could muster, to various documents
on prices and incomes policy and asking them under what head they
justified their latest price increase, and whether they had first
exhausted all productivity improvements. He was glad that he had
not sent the letter, because a few months later the laundry industry
was referred to the Prices and Incomes Board, and these very bureaucratic questions had been put to people who could not even send him
the correct shirt.

Mr Brittan had never believed in physical intervention of this sort.
But, for a time, he had believed in the bootstraps effect of going for
rapid demand growth and leaving the exchange rate to take care of
itself. He accepted that the policy he had advocated had probably
been wrong, but he felt that he had no apologies to make to the
Establishment. He had continued in his belief because the case
against it had been argued appallingly badly by the English advocates
of sound money. Hardly anyone – whether in the Bank of England,
the Treasury or the academic world – had said to him, 'you won't get
growth if you boost demand – or at least, not for very long'. Instead,
people had used the argument that Lord Callaghan had referred to:
that abandoning the exchange rate was immoral, because it would
harm the holders of sterling balances. Samuel Brittan's view had
been, and still was, that people held such balances at their own risk. A
price was a price, and that applied to the sterling exchange rate as to
anything else.

Samuel Brittan had changed his view when he read the more
fundamental arguments of those he called 'radical reactionaries' –
those such as Milton Friedman and Friedrich von Hayek – who did

not talk about the sterling area but who simply explained that the stimulating effects of relying on a bit of inflation worked only so long as people did not realize what was happening. Eventually the effects wore off, leaving in their wake higher or accelerating inflation and nothing much to show for it. The British sound-money people had never deployed these arguments.

Mr Brittan's greatest regret was that Operation Robot was not carried through in the early 1950s. This combined a sort of Erhard operation, to free the economy of controls, with a floating rate. If Britain had adopted that policy, the country would have discovered then, instead of twenty years later, the limits of pursuing faster growth by letting the exchange rate go. This was quite consistent with refixing the rate at a later date, as for instance on the establishment of the European Exchange Rate Mechanism.

Sir Donald MacDougall refused to be provoked into replying to Mr Brittan about Operation Robot. He had done so already, and so had Sir Alec Cairncross, and they were in agreement.

He had been closely associated with both the NEDC plan and the National Plan. The NEDC plan, published in 1963, had to a considerable extent been inspired and influenced by the French four-year plans. He recalled in 1960 going to France in a party of businessmen, trade unionists, academics, politicians and civil servants. The chief planner, Mr Massé, had been convinced that tripartite planning had increased the rate of growth in France. One idea behind the setting up of the NEDC was what Sir Donald called 'the confidence trick': you thought of a number for growth over a given period ahead which was rather greater than had been achieved in the past; worked out what it involved for industry and government; everyone would then work on the assumption that faster growth was going to happen and, lo and behold, it would happen. This might or might not have worked in France, but it certainly did not happen in the United Kingdom.

But the 'confidence trick' argument was not by any means the only element in the National Plan. The *Orange Book* (*Conditions Favourable to Faster Growth*), contained proposals for action, many of them on the supply side, which were quite independent of the growth target of 4 per cent. Indeed, the first chapter of the *Orange Book* was on education in all its forms, including training and business management. It was interesting that, thirty years later, this subject was still high on the programmes of the main political parties. Britain clearly had not done nearly enough in the intervening years.

The target in the NEDC plan of 4 per cent growth a year between

1961 and 1966 was the lowest that could have been picked in the circumstances. Productivity had accelerated from 1.5 per cent a year before the Second World War to an underlying rate of about 2 per cent in the 1950s, and about 2.5 per cent from 1955 to 1961. The members of Neddy honestly believed that it was nearer 3 per cent in 1963, when the National Plan was published. If you added the predicted growth of the labour force of roughly 0.75 per cent, which proved accurate, it came to 3.75 per cent. So 4 per cent was the lowest round number that could possibly have been chosen, given the need to play the confidence trick. Many people had wanted a higher figure, such as 5 per cent.

In fact, the country achieved 3.2 per cent. Sir Donald thought it would have been possible to do slightly better but for two big policy mistakes, though they probably had more effect on the National Plan, whose terminal date was 1970, than on the NEDC Plan, which ran to 1966.

The first mistake was what Sir Donald dubbed 'the Keeler public-spending boom'. When John Profumo resigned in 1963 over the Christine Keeler affair, he effectively postponed the General Election for about a year. Sir Donald recalled watching from the NEDC, with amazement and then horror, as the Government under Sir Alec Douglas Home made one announcement after another of increased public spending plans. These were well above what the NEDC thought could be afforded even with 4 per cent economic growth. So Labour, in 1964, inherited a big Conservative public-spending pro-gramme. This caused endless trouble, but could not really be blamed on the 4 per cent target.

The second big policy mistake had been not to devalue in 1964, or at least after the General Election of spring 1966, when the Labour Government had won a majority of nearly a hundred. This failure dis-torted economic policy and dominated it for at least four years, from 1964 to 1967, when we did devalue, and in 1968, when Britain suffered the nightmare of the J-curve after having borrowed up to the hilt.

Turning to the National Plan, produced by the Department of Economic Affairs in 1965, Sir Donald said he personally had been reluctant to have a plan at all. He was sick of visitors from centrally planned economies asking him how the plan was going to be imple-mented for individual industries when the government did not have the instruments for such an approach. He had become disenchanted with the confidence trick approach, which did not seem to be working, and he saw little future for growth if Britain did not devalue.

103

But George Brown had insisted; so Sir Donald had tried to get as low a figure as possible. The best he had able to do was 25 per cent over the six years from 1964 to 1970. That worked out at 3.8 per cent a year. In fact, 25 per cent was marginally less than had been achieved during the previous six years from 1958 to 1964. George Brown had wanted a higher figure than 3.8 per cent so that he could have a higher pay norm. But Sir Donald had dissuaded him by arguing that 1958 had been a below-trend year.

Robin Matthews found that one advantage of retrospect was that it was easier to see which problems were peculiar to Britain and which were common elsewhere. Quite a number were shared abroad.

The papers by Lord Croham and Professor Artis had set out a list of aims for some of which it was appropriate to look to government, such as avoiding inflation and avoiding slumps; with others, such as raising the growth rate, the role of government was more doubtful.

The low growth rate was a peculiarly British feature, not found in other European countries. However, the rise in unemployment was a general European phenomenon as, with the exception of some countries, was the rise in inflation. So it might be true that Britain had used economic tools inappropriately to try to achieve growth, but it was hard to see how that could be blamed for inflation and unemployment, since those occurred in countries which had not tried to raise growth in the way that Britain had done.

David Worswick wondered whether the target of 3.8 per cent or 4 per cent in the National Plan was reasonable, in the light of Lord Croham's observation that output was growing at 1.5–2.5 per cent. He had looked up the numbers being reported at the time by Christopher Dow and others from the National Institute and found that there had not been much change in the output estimates of GDP. There had, though, been enormous changes in the balance-of-payments figures; the great crisis of 1964 had almost disappeared. He was inclined to share Sir Donald's view of the actual state of the economy: the growth rate between 1955 and 1964 was around 3 per cent, and the rate between 1959 and 1964, from peak to peak, was about 3.6 per cent. So it would not have been possible to set a target of much less than 4 per cent if the whole exercise was to have any point. If a growth target had to be set, 4 per cent was not unreasonable in the light of what was known at the time. He had never thought that central government had the capacity to raise the growth rate; but that was a different matter.

Lord Callaghan interjected that, from his position in the Treasury, the target had been all right but the other figures had not added up. It had been other factors, such as the apparent balance-of-payments position of the time, that had made the target improbable.

Sir Alec Cairncross pointed out that, at the time, the French were thought to have achieved a high rate of growth through planning. In fact, this was not so. The French had maintained the rate of growth they had hit after the war. If anything, it was falling off by the 1960s. Britain was trying to raise the rate of growth by planning. That was an entirely different task. He thought it very unlikely that government, unless it approached the question indirectly and took a very long view, could have much effect on the rate of growth.

He also felt that Britain had set about planning without really understanding how growth took place – growth in productivity, rather than growth in output. There was little theory about what determined the rate of growth that was worth a hoot – though what there was was in the *Orange Book*. Indeed, that was the only attempt to set down what could usefully be done to affect the rate of growth.

Beyond that, Britain was trying to raise the rate of growth at a time when the exchange rate was uncertain. It was impossible to say 'devaluation will take place in year X'. Government was therefore trying to plan as if it knew what was going to happen when it did not know. There was a contradiction right at the heart of the plan, which made it very unlikely that it would work successfully.

Although the conference had been focusing on the growth of GDP, the real problem had been the growth of public expenditure. That had been set at 4.25 per cent. He had not known when that decision had been taken, and had been unaware of it for some time. When he had learned of it, he had thought it a frightful mistake. Government was treating the one thing it could control as certain, while assuming that the things it could not control would come about. In reply to a question from the chairman, Sir Alec recalled that the civil servant in charge of public spending at the time had been Sir Richard Clarke.

Christopher Dow wanted to distinguish between the concerns that were rightly felt at the time, and the concerns that the conference should concentrate on in deciding what relevance the experience of the 1960s had for the present day. He shared the view of Michael Artis and of Robin Matthews. A book he had written, published in 1964, *The Management of the British Economy 1945–60*, had helped to form present views of the 1960s. But its conclusion had been taken to be that the effects of demand management had been perverse; that that was inevitably so and that therefore all attempts at demand management should be abandoned. In fact, Mr Dow's argument had been, not that demand management should be abandoned, but that it should be improved. Subsequent research seems to have confirmed the conclusion that demand management exacerbated economic cycles in the United Kingdom during the period, but showed that in other countries demand management had diminished the violence of economic fluctuations. That suggested that Britain could have done better.

Such consensus of policy at the time now seemed minor: what had gone wrong since the 1960s had been much worse than any of the policy failures of that decade. After all, Britain had recovered rather quickly, and without any serious consequences, from the minor recessions of the 1960s. Looked at from that point of view, Mr Dow did not think one could say that the policy instruments were inadequate. Whether they were adequate to deal with the economic problems after 1973 was an altogether different question. Clearly we did not have adequate policy instruments to steer the economy without fluctuations or serious inflation in the face of the kind of external shocks the economy had suffered since 1973, but the question was whether any instruments could ever have done that; and the experience of the 1960s did not throw much light on that point. Mr Dow therefore saw no reason to blame policy instruments for events since then.

Professor Malinvaud wanted first to take up the point made by Sir Alec Cairncross in an earlier session, that it had been difficult at the end of the 1960s to forecast that an exceptional period had come to an end. He recalled that, from 1962, he and Professor Matthews had been involved in a project to try to understand post-war growth in their respective countries, under the leadership of Moses Abramowitz. He had been faster than Robin Matthews, and had published his results in 1972. In a final little section, probably written in 1970 and called 'What next?', he had argued that the recent rapid rate of growth could probably continue for some time.

Robin Matthews had been saved from such a mistake by taking longer to publish. When Professor Malinvaud had begun his study, in 1962, his preferred hypothesis had been that the 1950s and early 1960s were exceptional years, because the industrial countries were catching up with the growth in their underlying potential. He had expected this catching up to be exhausted by the mid-1960s. As the years passed, and growth accelerated instead of slowing down, he abandoned his original hypothesis.

The book had contained a chapter, that he would still stand by, on the role of French planning. He had presented planning as a pedagogical device appropriate for a country where economic education was deficient; where public opinion was divided; where there was a large public sector that had to be run in a rational way; and where the 1930s and the military defeat in 1940 had left a gloomy view of economic potential. Planning was one way of raising expectations of what might be achieved.

· Since then, French planning had been progressively abandoned, mainly because it was overused as an instrument. He felt there was still room for planning in a market economy, where the market gave some, but not all, of the relevant information.

Lord O'Brien recalled that he had entered the Bank of England in 1927 when Britain had been back on the gold standard for two years. In 1931 Britain left the standard again. The Bank of England, for the first time in its history, devised a foreign-exchange section to deal in foreign exchange, bringing in a man from the Kredit Anstalt in Austria to explain how to deal in foreign exchange. (Professor Solow promptly volunteered American advice with British building societies.) The Bank had seen itself as the inheritor of sterling as a great international currency.

After the Second World War, huge amounts of sterling debt had been given to countries for war supplies which could not have been paid for in any other way. It was not surprising, said Lord O'Brien, that the Bank had been a bit obsessed with dealing with this burden. Some of his colleagues had felt that sterling could be returned to the level it had occupied in the nineteenth century. Lord O'Brien admitted that he had had the distinction of being associated with all the devaluations of sterling since the war. At the time of the 1949 devaluation, he had merely been 'the boy who handed the letter to Camille Gutt [managing director of the IMF] saying we'd done it'. But he had always believed that sterling should have been devalued sooner after the war, and that the American loan should not have been dissipated in paying off sterling balances at the old rate of exchange.

But sterling had been a problem the Bank had to live with. The sterling area, which had been huge, had held all its foreign-exchange reserves in London, pooling them with Britain's reserves and drawing on them whenever they were needed. Australia, for instance, had to be able to meet its foreign-exchange requirements from the common pot in London. In 1968, he had gone to Australia to persuade the country

107

to continue to hold sterling because Britain could not have afforded to meet its claims. He recalled making the journey under the name of 'Mr Reed', to avoid detection by the markets.

Lord O'Brien still stood by his opposition to devaluation in 1966. It had not been to do with any moral sentiments about sterling. It was because he believed that devaluation would not do any good, and that it certainly would do no good with a government that was not prepared to scale down the economy and leave a margin of spare resources that could be exported. That was essential, if devaluation was to work even for a short time. Even once devaluation took place, as Lord O'Brien reminded Lord Jenkins, it had taken him some time, after he replaced Lord Callaghan as Chancellor, to decide what had to be done to make it work. Even after that decision had been taken, it had taken so long to start to have an effect that Lord O'Brien had reached a point where he thought the only option might be to float.

Sir Fred Atkinson argued that the statistics the conference had been looking at made it appear that the 1960s had been a period of success. That was not how it had felt at the time. There had seemed to be a series of sterling crises, almost every year. The fundamental trouble had been that the growth aims had been over-ambitious, and translated into absurd programmes of public expenditure. Reginald Maudling had started it: his boom had provoked one balance-of-payments crisis. The Labour Government had thus inherited an economic mess in 1964, but had been very unwilling to rein the economy back or curtail foreign expenditure. Instead, the public mood had been for outbidding even the Conservative growth targets.

After devaluation in 1967, the Chancellor had had a great deal of authority, and had been able to cut back spending, especially overseas spending, and to put up taxes to an unprecedented extent in 1968. There had been a more anxious year after that before the economy began to come right, but balance had been restored by 1970.

The Chancellor of the Exchequer's job, thought Sir Fred, was an incredibly hard one. In other countries it was distributed among several ministers. In Britain, all the blame fell on the Chancellor if the economy was mismanaged. He remembered Chancellors being tremendously respected in the Treasury which, being a small department, was greatly receptive to influence from the top. The whole department could be galvanized in half an hour. He was glad that the two ex-Chancellors at the conference could look back on the 1960s and feel that their record had not been a bad one.

Lord Callaghan wound up the session by arguing that the main lesson he drew from the period was that the best weapon a Chancellor could have to handle the economy wisely was the absence of an election manifesto. If the Labour party had not been committed in its manifesto to fulfilling so many pent-up ambitions at once, it could have taken more time to fulfil its objectives.

BIBLIOGRAPHY

Artus, J.R. (1975) 'The 1967 devaluation of the pound sterling', *IMF Staff Papers* November: 595–640.

Blackaby, F.T. (ed.) (1978) *British Economic Policy*, Cambridge: Cambridge University Press.

Cairncross, A. (ed.) (1971) *Britain's Economic Prospects Reconsidered*, London: Allen & Unwin.

—— (1985) *Years of Recovery*, London: Methuen.

Cairncross, A. and Eichengreen, B. (1983) *Sterling in Decline: The Devaluations of 1931, 1949 and 1967*, ch. 5, Oxford: Basil Blackwell.

Carré, J.J., Dubois, P. and Caves, R.E. (ed.) (1968) *Britain's Economic Prospects*, Washington, DC: Brookings Institution.

—— (1971) 'Second thoughts on Britain's economic prospects', in A. Cairncross (ed.) *Britain's Economic Prospects Reconsidered*, London: Allen & Unwin.

Department of Economic Affairs (1965) *The National Plan*, London: HMSO, Cmnd 2764.

Donovan Report (1968) *Report of the Royal Commission on Trade Unions and Employers' Associations 1965–68*, London: HMSO, Cmnd 3623.

Dow, J.C.R. (1964) *The Management of the British Economy 1945–60*, Cambridge: Cambridge University Press.

Fishbein, W.A. (1987) *Wage Restraint by Consensus: Britain's Search for an Incomes Policy Agreement 1965–79*, Boston, MA: Routledge.

Malinvaud, E. (1972) *La Croissance Française*, Paris: Editions du Seuil.

4

COULD INTERNATIONAL POLICY CO-ORDINATION HAVE BEEN MORE EFFECTIVE?

John Williamson

The 1960s have sometimes been idolized as the Golden Age of international policy co-ordination. In the first section of this paper I describe the two mechanisms that produced some sort of co-ordination of macro policies of the major industrial countries at that time. In the second section I note that the policy regime increasingly failed to deliver the desired results, and ultimately collapsed. Alternative possible explanations for these failures are then discussed.

THE MECHANISMS OF CO-ORDINATION

International policy co-ordination has been modelled in the literature of the 1980s as periodic encounters between the policy-makers of different countries designed to establish whether they can agree on any modifications of their planned policies that will lead to mutually beneficial results. They search for policy changes that would lead to a Pareto-preferred outcome.

The 1960s did have a mechanism that approximated this 'active' form of policy co-ordination. It was pursued through the OECD, following its pupation from the OEEC in the early 1960s. The Economic Policy Committee met three times a year at ministerial level, while its powerful subcommittee, Working Party 3, met at the level of senior home-based civil servants every six or eight weeks, rather on the model of how Keynes had hoped the IMF Executive Board would function. Between them these two committees monitored the development of the major economies, discussed the mutual consistency of their policy objectives, critiqued one another's policy stances and concerned themselves with trying to preserve the Bretton Woods system, whose health deteriorated as the decade progressed.

The OECD had the advantage of a degree of consensus on the intellectual paradigm guiding its efforts that has been absent since. The model was essentially a Keynesian explanation of the generation of demand supplemented by a Phillips curve to explain inflation and an exogenous natural (supply-side) rate of growth. The OECD had already tracked nine of the ten variables that the Tokyo summit designated as 'indicators' when the effort at policy co-ordination was resumed in 1986. (The included variables were output, growth, unemployment, inflation, trade balance, current-account balance, interest rates, budget deficit and reserves; the missing indicator was the money supply.)

The logic of OECD co-ordination as articulated in Cooper's classic study (1968) was that demand spillovers from one country to another create externalities that need to be internalized if policy is to be efficient. Specifically, demand growth needs to take account of the situation abroad as well as at home; for the stronger the demand is abroad, the easier it is to expand at home, but the more desirable it is that demand be restrained to avoid overheating the world economy. Hence the OECD was assigned the task of checking countries' forecasts of demand growth, adding them up, and comparing the result with estimated capacity expansion. Marris (1986) does not give the impression that this process had a great deal of impact on policy during the 1960s, though he cites periods just before (1959) and after (1971) when he claims it did.

A second function of co-ordination was to ensure that targets were internationally consistent. There was much concern in the 1960s about competitive balance-of-payments policies, either that countries were seeking a bigger reserve build-up than was collectively available, or that the OECD countries sought a larger collective current-account surplus than the sum of the deficits that the rest of the world would be able to finance. The first concern motivated creation of the Special Drawing Right (SDR), while the second led to discussion of 'Kessler matrices' in the OECD. These laid out a set of mutually consistent current-account targets (my recollection is that these were a 1 per cent of GNP surplus for each industrial country). Since countries had no policy instrument that they were prepared to use routinely to manage the balance of payments, the exercise struck me as academic in the pejorative sense of the term.

In addition to active policy co-ordination in which policy-makers agree to mutual adjustment of their policies when mutual gain is possible, policies may be co-ordinated passively, through the pursuit of a set of rules that are accepted by all participants and that induce a measure of mutual consistency in the policies of different countries. I have elsewhere (Williamson 1985) interpreted the Bretton Woods system as providing such a 'rule-based regime' (Cooper 1985). Let me review the rules of the Bretton Woods system and explain how they helped to secure policy consistency.

Exchange rates were normally to remain stable within narrow margins, but could, and by implication should, be changed when there was a 'fundamental disequilibrium'. Although never formally defined, there was never much doubt what this concept meant: a situation in which a country could not expect to achieve basic balance over the cycle as a whole without deflating output from full capacity or restricting trade or payments for balance-of-payments reasons. Thus the basic principle embraced was that exchange rates should be directed toward medium-run balance-of-payments needs rather than short-run anticyclical policy. The motivation was explicitly that of outlawing the beggar-my-neighbour use of exchange rate policy that had occurred in the 1930s.

It was universally assumed at the time of the Bretton Woods system, though not formally spelled out, that fiscal and monetary policy would be directed at the maintenance of full employment (or 'internal balance'). Reserves were to be used to avoid the need for continuous external balance. The absence of alternative provisions to deal with modest non-self-reversing imbalances suggests that the architects of the Bretton Woods system accepted that it would be necessary to shade fiscal–monetary policy with a view to the balance-of-payments position. This was explicitly endorsed by the OECD Report on the Adjustment Process (OECD 1966). (This report also endorsed another proposal for dealing with such imbalances that was not, so far as I am aware, conceived of by the architects of the Bretton Woods system: namely, Mundell's (1962) proposal to vary the fiscal–monetary mix. But, as I have argued elsewhere (Williamson 1971), the mix should be regarded as a way of financing a deficit rather than of adjusting it.)

Although Keynes did not get the negative interest rates on creditor bancor positions that he sought, the Bretton Woods reserve regime did imply something about the assignment of adjustment responsibilities. Countries were expected to restrict their deficits to the sums that could be financed from their available reserves supplemented by IMF drawing rights. Reserve currency countries had some additional latitude to finance payments deficits by issuing their own currencies, but it was assumed that this possibility would be limited by the need to maintain confidence in convertibility. Britain invested much energy during the pre-Bretton Woods negotiations in gaining an assurance that the United States would participate in the adjustment process, and secured the scarce currency clause to that end (although it was never invoked). This well-attested historical fact surely establishes that the Bretton Woods system was not intended to be a dollar standard.

I thus interpret the Bretton Woods system as far more than just a commitment to pegged exchange rates. It embodied, rather, a comprehensive set of rules for assigning macroeconomic policies: exchange rates to medium-run external balance, fiscal–monetary policy to short-run internal balance, and reserves to provide a buffer stock (as distinct from a monetary base) that would allow short-run departures from external balance. This is the intellectual position that Keynes had developed in the inter-war years (Williamson 1983). Keynes is usually thought of as having lost out to White in the design of the Bretton Woods system because of the absence of bancor and the other gimmicks (like negative interest rates) that he dreamed up during the war, but in a far deeper sense he was the victor. No other economist has ever seen the assignment rules that he developed over twenty years embodied in a policy regime that was intended to bind his successors.

How did the spontaneous pursuit of national self-interest, subject to continued observance of the rules of the Bretton Woods system, ensure a broad consistency between national and world interests?

There is now a significant literature (see Canzoneri and Gray 1983; Oudiz and Sachs 1984) showing formally that choice of monetary and fiscal policies with a view to short-run stabilization objectives (maximization of a utility function specified in terms of the activity level and inflation and/or the balance of payments on current account), taking other countries' policies as given and with exchange rates flexible, leads to an outcome (the Nash equilibrium) inferior to that available with policy co-ordination (the co-operative solution). A fixed-exchange-rate rule is a way of ruling out manipulation of the monetary–fiscal mix with a view to gaining short-run benefits at the expense of other countries. The first of the Bretton Woods rules introduced precisely this constraint, but in a form that did not preclude an exchange-rate change needed to facilitate payments adjustment.

The second of the Bretton Woods rules, as interpreted above,

assigned monetary–fiscal policy to short-run internal balance, subject
to the need to maintain the exchange-rate peg. As long as the basic
presupposition of Keynesian demand management, that price levels
are constant (or at least predetermined), remained approximately
valid, this worked rather well: with hindsight, fine-tuning surely has
to be rated a greater success than it was at the time. And, as long as
exchange rates remained properly aligned, the stop–go policies
imposed on demand management by the Bretton Woods constraints
served a social function that few appreciated at the time (but see
Triffin 1960: 82–3). With a correctly aligned exchange rate, an
external deficit provides an early warning that deflation is needed,
while the automatic stabilizer provided by the deflection of excess
demand into an external deficit constitutes a safety valve that helped
prevent the development of inflationary inertia.

The third of the Bretton Woods rules required countries to respect
a (reasonably symmetrical) reserve constraint, while using reserves as
a buffer stock to reconcile continual pursuit of internal balance with
only medium-run pursuit of external balance. The major benefit that
arose from this rule, in conjunction with the first two, is that it helped
to avoid a synchronized world business cycle. Robert Lawrence
(1978) found that there was practically no synchronization during the
period 1959–67 when the Bretton Woods system was functioning
properly, with adequate but not excessive liquidity. There was
synchronization in an earlier period, 1950–8, which he explained by
a liquidity shortage that forced other countries into following the
United States, especially during and after the Korean War. The
recession of 1958 was the one case of a synchronized (but nonetheless
relatively mild) world recession during the Bretton Woods period.
Thereafter, until 1969, recessions were essentially national, induced
primarily by a need to curb payments deficits: France in 1959; the
United States in 1960; Britain and Canada in 1962; Italy in 1963–4;
Japan in 1964; and Germany in 1966. Under the Bretton Woods
rules, other countries tended to offset those recessions by expanding
demand so as to preserve internal balance when exports fell, while
one country's deficit (that pushed it toward restraint) was another's
surplus (which nudged it toward monetary expansion). Thus the
world as a whole did not deviate significantly from full employment
because of payments imbalances. The mechanism that was supposed
to secure this result under the gold standard (though it is doubtful
whether it did; see Eichengreen 1984) seems actually to have
functioned during the Golden Age of Bretton Woods.

JUDGING THE SUCCESS OF CO-ORDINATION

The objectives sought by macroeconomic policy were growth, full employment, low inflation and balance-of-payments equilibrium. For a decade or so, the Bretton Woods system worked like a charm in achieving all four. Not only did gross world product (GWP) grow faster during the 1960s than in any decade before or since, but employment was high and inflation was low. (The average inflation of 4.1 per cent in 1990 was higher than in any year in the 1960s prior to 1968, when the Bretton Woods system was already beginning to disintegrate.) Perhaps it needed the OECD to create peer-group consensus among the major members as to how they should be interpreting the rules,[1] but the system worked on any reasonable test of performance.

The system broke down when the assumptions on which it was based – capital immobility and an absence of inflationary expectations – ceased to be a reasonable approximation to the facts. Macroeconomic performance began to deteriorate in the late 1960s, and then worsened conspicuously in the early 1970s. The Golden Age of policy co-ordination ended with an inflationary explosion that was controlled, at great cost, only a decade later. Not only did the 1970s open with an evident failure to achieve the goals that policy co-ordination was intended to further, but the mechanism that was supposed to promote implicit co-ordination, the Bretton Woods system, itself collapsed.

What explains the failure of the policy regime, first to deliver the macro goods, and then even to sustain its own existence?

At the time I placed major emphasis on the inadequacy of the economic instruments deployed by the authorities to secure the objectives that they set themselves. Specifically, I believed that simultaneous achievement of low inflation and full employment required an incomes policy, and that simultaneous achievement of internal and external balance required an element of exchange-rate flexibility. (I favoured a crawling peg rather than floating rates in order to reconcile enough exchange-rate flexibility to achieve external balance in the medium term with preservation of the advantages of the Bretton Woods system as analysed above.)

I would not today expect as much from those policy innovations as I did then. Incomes policy has proved a less useful instrument than many of us hoped in the 1960s (though I still find myself unable to join the chorus that declares categorically that incomes policies are, always and everywhere, at best useless). Exchange-rate changes can still facilitate adjustment to real shocks and can reconcile differential rates of inflation, which may be useful when inflationary inertia differs between countries. But the accelerationist theory of inflation implies that the freedom to choose an independent national inflation rate, on which so much seemed to hang, is of no long-term value at all. Indeed, the drive for European Monetary Union (EMU) reflects a new-found conviction that ready accommodation of differential inflation can be an error because it invites the development of differential inflationary inertia.

In retrospect I would attach more significance to the charge that the intellectual framework underlying the policy regime was deficient, at least in the one key respect just alluded to. The theory of inflation embodied in the official view of the world was clearly inadequate. Until some date in the first half of the 1970s, policy was based on what we now refer to as the naive Phillips curve, without an expectations-augmenting (accelerationist) term.[2] This led to far too much tolerance of accelerating inflation and the devastatingly damaging co-ordinated push to reflate in 1971.

Is it possible to argue that better co-ordination could have avoided the failure of the policy regime? The only instance that strikes me as a failure of active co-ordination is the OECD support for concerted reflation, in 1971, in the face of growing stagflationary pressures. But I have never believed that the active co-ordination provided in the 1960s by the OECD (and nowadays by the G7) is as important as having a sensible set of rules to provide implicit (rule-based) co-ordination. (I failed lamentably in persuading my colleagues of this during my spell in the Treasury in 1968–70, doubtless due to my inability to articulate what was at that stage more a gut feeling than a coherent intellectual position.) And the Bretton Woods rules were progressively subverted as the decade went on.

The basic problem was that the expedients adopted to deflect countries from buying gold from the United States transformed the system gradually into a dollar standard, which meant that the centre country set the pace of monetary expansion and escaped discipline, including any external discipline over its inflation rate. The system collapsed as other countries found the need to import inflation imposed by a fixed exchange rate intolerable.

How could that development have been reversed? I still think the only chance was to reform the exchange-rate system adopted at Bretton Woods in order to make devaluation a feasible policy option for the centre country in the new environment of capital mobility. A crawling peg with a gold–SDR pivot would have given the United States the option of devaluing without wrecking the system, which would in turn have allowed other countries to put pressure on the centre country. The failure to make timely repairs and renovations to the Bretton Woods system (beyond introduction of the SDR) was a major failure of the 1960s.

The Bretton Woods system worked as well as it did for a little over a decade because of a series of fortunate accidents: liquidity was about right despite the absence of any mechanism to secure that result, exchange rates were reasonably aligned despite the attempt to suppress realignments, inflation was low and the reserve centre still acted as though the suspension of gold convertibility would be a disaster.[3] The basic inadequacy of the system was the absence of mechanisms capable of maintaining such a satisfactory conjunction of circumstances. The SDR agreement was intended to provide that flexibility with regard to the quantity of reserves, but it was not complemented by those additional reforms (limited exchange-rate flexibility, asset settlement) that were needed to allow the system to survive. The neglected virtues of the Bretton Woods system were sufficiently real to make that failure a matter of regret. (On the other hand, you could argue that capital mobility would in any event have eroded the system's utility within another decade.)

CONCLUSIONS

The 1960s opened with the best international monetary system the world has ever had finally starting to operate as had originally been intended, supplemented by a newly created mechanism for policing the Bretton Woods rules and allowing active policy co-ordination when necessary. A decade later the international monetary system collapsed and the policy co-ordination mechanism was allowed to atrophy as a punishment for having been abused in intensifying the inflationary explosion of the early 1970s. It is a rather sad story. I cannot see how the policy-makers of the 1960s can avoid responsibility for having allowed it to happen.

The moral that I would draw for the 1990s is that there are virtues in a rule-based regime, if the right rules are found and they are updated to keep the system in good working order. Those rules would need to be interpreted, which would provide a role for the G7. Of course, the rules could not be those of Bretton Woods; they would have to make appropriate allowance for the pervasive phenomena of capital mobility and inflationary expectations.[4]

In fact, when the world tired of macroeconomic *laissez-faire* in 1985, it reverted not to a rule-based regime but to active policy co-ordination by the G7. That is better than nothing, but no more than second best.

AMPLIFICATION

Introducing his paper, John Williamson said that he had been told of an occasion when the Chairman had said at the conclusion of a meeting that he never thought that he would enjoy a discussion of international liquidity. As his paper was on that subject he hoped that this would not prevent the Chairman and others from enjoying it.

In his paper he argued that there were two forms of policy co-ordination. One was the rule-based system embodied in the Bretton Woods arrangements. The essence of this was a set of assignment rules, as they would now be called, i.e. a set of principles as to what policies should be directed to what objectives. The particular set of assignment rules built into the Bretton Woods system was very much the set that Keynes had developed during the inter-war period. This might explain why he commended the Bretton Woods system to Parliament with such energy, in spite of the rejection of all the institutional arrangements that he personally had suggested in the Keynes Plan and the acceptance instead of the White Plan as the basis of the system. However, it had been the assignment rules rather than the institutional details (e.g. the price of gold) that had formed the central part of the system.

The three assignment rules included were as follows.

1 Exchange rates should be directed to the medium-term needs of the balance of payments rather than to the short-run needs of demand management. This derived from the experience of competitive devaluation in the inter-war period and the belief that the use of exchange rate policy in that way could be damaging to other countries. This idea has now been modelled in much of the literature of the 1980s on policy co-ordination, on the argument that an exchange-rate rule can prevent countries from playing games at one another's expense.

2 Reserves should be used as a buffer stock to permit short-term deviations from external balance. Continuous external balance,

unlike continuous internal balance, was not a target to be met in every period. There was no loss of welfare if a loss of reserves one year was offset by a gain next year, whereas it was not possible to set two jobs next year against no job at all this year. A second function of reserves was to produce desynchronization of the business cycle internationally. If there was a reasonably symmetrical reserve constraint and each country sought internal balance, the loss of reserves by one country would be balanced by a gain by another, with contraction in the one offset by expansion in the other. A series of national recessions under the Bretton Woods system did not produce a world recession, the nearest approach being in 1958. There were two asymmetries in the system: one between surplus and deficit countries because of the greater compulsion to adjust in the case of deficit countries; and a second between reserve currency countries and others, the former having an extra latitude in running a deficit. These two asymmetries tended to cancel out in the 1960s, the leading deficit countries being also reserve currency countries.

3 Monetary–fiscal policy should be used to maintain internal balance – a quintessentially Keynesian rule not written into any agreement but tacitly accepted. In the 1960s, as the OECD Report on the Adjustment Process explained, there was agreement that, with relatively mild disequilibria, the internal balance target could be shaded in order to preserve external balance. It was also agreed that the policy mix could be varied in order to reconcile external and internal balances. This proposal by Robert Mundell was accepted in the 1960s with rather too much enthusiasm since it left the current-account adjustment hanging without an adequate mechanism to address it.

One of the social functions of these rules was that they tended to lead to stop–go policies. There was more sense in these than was conceded at the time because, with a balance-of-payments obligation, if the exchange rate was about right, excess demand would find a safety valve in the balance of payments which would also provide an early warning of inflation.

John Williamson had argued that these added up to a helpful set of rules for the operation of the international economy in the 1960s. He had made no reference to the price of gold although that was an important element in the system. It was part of what lay behind the reserve constraint of the United States, which distinguished the Bretton Woods system from the dollar standard into which it evolved towards the end of the 1960s.

A dollar standard was something over which John Williamson had been in disagreement with Professor Kindleberger ever since they first met in 1967. If the centre country behaved responsibly, he agreed that the system would be difficult to abandon, but he preferred a more symmetrical arrangement and believed that it had some technical advantages such as the desynchronization benefits of the Bretton Woods system.

A second form of policy co-ordination was that described at the beginning of his paper involving bargaining on modification of existing policies. There had been a meeting answering to this description on interest rate disarmament in 1967 under Lord Callaghan – perhaps the clearest example in the 1960s.

Most people thought of the OECD as the place where meetings of this kind usually occurred, either in the Economic Policy Committee or Working Party 3. It was difficult to decide how much the bargaining process amounted to or what co-ordination of growth policy was achieved, but the OECD had undoubtedly served as a complement to the rule-based system by providing a kind of peer review of how each country was applying the rules. In this way it helped to make the Bretton Woods system work more smoothly and effectively.

There had thus been two complementary forms of co-ordination, one passive and consisting of rules, and the other active and involving meetings. Judging by results, all this activity was not as successful as one might have hoped. There was a deterioration, with accelerating inflation and rising unemployment, beginning in the mid-1960s and becoming very clear by the early 1970s. Why was policy co-ordination a failure? At the time, John Williamson put it down to instrument inadequacy: incomes policy, for example, was regarded as indispensable to low inflation combined with full employment; and in order to reconcile internal and external stability, exchange-rate flexibility was needed. He had argued for the use of a crawling peg rather than floating exchange rates, since the former was an institutional development of the Bretton Woods system and could allow it to survive longer. It would have given the United States a mechanism with which to improve its balance-of-payments position without bringing down the whole system; at the same time it would have enabled other countries to bring pressure on the United States.

In retrospect neither incomes policy nor exchange-rate flexibility had been sufficient. Inadequacy of instruments had not in fact been the main problem. The intellectual framework underlying the system in the 1960s had been inadequate in at least one critical respect: there had been no accelerationist theory of inflation such as was introduced by Friedman and Phelps in the late 1960s. Allowing inflation to build up was a fatal mistake. The Germans had been right in their determination to prevent it and had been spared a lot of unemployment as a result.

A third line of explanation had been that a set of coincidences had allowed the system to operate reasonably satisfactorily in the 1960s. It was not any in-built mechanism that kept the system in balance then but a fortunate accident. Liquidity was about right without any mechanism to secure that result. A mechanism – the SDR – was created in the 1960s and came into operation on 1 January 1970, and might have been important had it been complemented in other ways. But in fact it had not amounted to much. Exchange rates, too, had been reasonably aligned in the 1960s, although there was an attempt to suppress realignments. But there had been no mechanism of the European Monetary System (EMS) variety to prevent exchange rates from getting out of line. Inflation was low in the 1960s, but there was not sufficient determination to keep it low, and differences in inflation rates were on the increase. Another coincidence had been that the United States was still acting as if the suspension of gold convertibility would be a disaster: it had not yet learned benign neglect.

So the Bretton Woods system worked well because of these coincidences, without any guarantee that the same constellation of factors would continue into the 1970s. The system might have been prolonged by something like the SDR, an adjustment mechanism such as the crawling peg and something on the lines of asset settlement. But with rising capital mobility, would that have been enough? Perhaps all that was lost was five to ten years of useful life for the Bretton Woods system.

Mr Williamson concluded by citing the final paragraphs of his paper. He expanded his reference to the errors of the OECD in 1971 in using the co-ordination mechanism to give a reduction in unemployment precedence over checking the acceleration of inflation. On the other hand, the story he had told did not account for the major problems of the 1970s and 1980s. The system, to judge from the evidence of recent history, was far more resilient than had been thought in the 1960s. If there was no boost to demand in the budget it would be provided later in one way or another, through lower interest rates, for example, or a growth in exports. The system, unless badly abused, was fundamentally quite resilient. Something might be lost through inadequate policy co-ordination but not nearly as much as had been imagined in the 1960s. Supply-side activities were more important, and it was in activities of this kind – meetings of fishery experts and proposals for protection of the environment – that the OECD was most useful.

COMMENTS BY ANDREW CROCKETT

It is an honour and a pleasure to be invited to participate in this conference to mark Alec Cairncross's 80th birthday. I have admired and been influenced by his work since I was a first-year under-graduate. I first met him in person at an event in the UK Treasury that was known to the British side as 'the IMF seminar'. It was an occasion on which an IMF team led by Jacques Polak sought to explain to a sceptical British audience the Fund's version of the monetary approach to the balance of payments. The British side, on the other hand, sought to tell an equally sceptical IMF that trying to apply the Western hemisphere model to an advanced industrial country with a developed capital market was a failure to understand economic theory or monetary statistics or both. (At any rate, it displayed woeful ignorance of the conclusions of the Radcliffe Report!)

I do not fully recollect the intellectual outcome of the seminar. What I do remember quite clearly from the occasion were two things. The first was Alec Cairncross's exceptionally skilful and patient chairmanship. The second was a series of titanic clashes between Jacques Polak and Nicky Kaldor about the role of money in the economy. Neither persuaded the other but I gave the verdict to Kaldor on points, if only because he spoke longer and with even greater conviction than did Polak.

I mention all this, not simply because it is customary to begin remarks at a conference like this with a personal reminiscence (and I'm afraid 1968 is as far back as I can go), but because it symbolizes an important point about international policy co-ordination. Co-ordination can only work provided there is broad agreement about, first, the fundamental objectives of economic policy; and second, the basic model underlying economic processes. Failure to agree on a model, or the use of the shared model to achieve inconsistent ends, will produce friction at best and conflict at worst. Moreover, the model must be more or less right. Co-ordination on the wrong model can also produce disastrous results.

Williamson's paper is, as usual, excellent – full of common sense and useful insights. My main comment is that he does not quite do justice to the complex of factors that led to the demise of the Bretton Woods system. In his oral remarks, he suggested that, with appropriate 'repairs and renovations', the rules of Bretton Woods could have survived, at least for a significant period. This leads him to underestimate the difficulties of returning to a rule-based system, and perhaps does not do full justice to the more informal co-ordination now being pursued by the G7.

The main thesis of the Williamson paper is as follows. The Bretton Woods system involved a comprehensive, if implicit, economic model in which there was a fairly clear assignment of instruments to targets, and a mechanism (fixed exchange rates) for avoiding the *negative* externalities of self-interested policies. Grafted onto this was an instrument for active co-ordination (the Working Party 3 consultative machinery) which tried to go further and reap some of the advantages of *positive* externalities.

The chief deficiency in this policy model, according to Williamson, was the absence of a satisfactory intellectual explanation of the inflationary process and, more important, of any mechanism to harmonize divergent inflation rates or at least offset their consequences for balance-of-payments equilibrium. The misunderstanding of the inflation generation process led to excessive tolerance of policies leading to acceleration of inflation. And the lack of an effective means of dealing with differential rates of price increase led to the collapse of the system.

The conclusion is that, if only we could find a technique for rectifying this crucial weakness in the functioning of the Bretton Woods system, we would have a valid basis for a return to rule-based arrangements. These could perhaps deliver co-ordination that would be as effective in the 1990s as it appears to have been in the early 1960s.

If achievable, this would certainly be a prize worth having. Williamson's preferred solution, I take it from his other writings, is to return to an exchange-rate rule but to apply it with more flexibility than under Bretton Woods (through using wider bands and a greater willingness to adjust them). This would then accommodate differential trend inflation, without permitting the competitive policies the Bretton Woods system was designed to avoid.

I agree with Williamson that the inability to prevent inflation divergence was a crucial flaw of the Bretton Woods system. But I do not believe the adaptation of rules would have sufficed to save the system, nor that the reintroduction of exchange-rate-related rules would be successful today. I have several reasons for this scepticism.

First, the Bretton Woods system had been made more brittle by the relaxation of capital controls and the growth of international financial markets. This not only introduced the possibility of speculative capital flows overwhelming central banks' powers to resist through intervention, but it also made the whole concept of an equilibrium exchange rate much harder to grasp.

Second, the consensus on the underlying objectives of economic policy was beginning to break down. During the early part of the post-war period, high employment and low inflation went fairly well together, and fears of disorder if exchange rates were allowed to float convinced most policy-makers that it was worth paying a price to preserve the fixed-exchange-rate system. In the 1960s, US administrations gave growing emphasis to promoting employment and growth and less emphasis, in relative terms, to price stability. Conversely some European countries were giving increasing attention to price stability. It is possible that greater co-ordination would have preserved fixed exchange rates for a little longer, but not, I submit, by very much.

Third, no rule-based system can easily adapt to, rather than control, inflation. I would be quite doubtful about the ability of the greater use of adjustments to fixed rates to offset inflation divergences satisfactorily. Most experience suggests that devaluation is a temporary expedient that can only work if the breathing space it provides is used to secure a better balance between demand and supply. If used deliberately to offset differences in inflation aversion, then inflationary differences are likely to grow.

Fourth, the consensus on the underlying Keynesian model was eroding chances of saving the Bretton Woods system because the underlying economic model of the economy on which it was based was losing favour. The Keynesian consensus was losing its persuasive power, in part because of its perceived policy shortcomings, and also because of the seductive simplicity of the monetarist paradigm that was offered as an alternative.

Could international policy co-ordination have been more effective? This is different from asking whether the Bretton Woods system could have been saved. I believe co-ordination could have been better, but it would have involved designing better rules for the functioning of flexible rates rather than additional rules to enable fixed rates to survive. The trouble with the flexible rates system is that its active proponents believed it could be an essentially self-regulating system, so long as a few simple rules, such as no intervention in exchange markets, were followed. This is a simplification. What was needed was a thorough exploration of the spillover effects of domestic economic policies on trading partners, and a continuous assessment of which policies could be regarded as beneficial or legitimate and which should be discouraged.

What are the lessons of all this for the present day? Disillusion with flexible exchange rates and unco-ordinated policies is quite widespread. Could we therefore return to more formal exchange-rate rules, buttressed perhaps by the kind of policy assignment guidelines Williamson has described in a number of his published papers? In favour of this is the fact that most members of the European Community have now opted for membership of the Exchange Rate Mechanism, and have apparently been increasingly successful in reconciling lower inflation with adequate growth. Does this suggest that the world economy at large may soon be ready for a more rule-based regime?

I do not believe this is likely for the simple reason that the successful operation of a fixed rate system (*even* if periodic realignments are allowed) requires the acceptance, *de facto*, of a single monetary authority. This acceptance may be emerging in Europe, but it is not present at the world level. Monetary convergence in Europe has been achieved in recent years because of the overwhelming importance attached to bringing inflation down and keeping it down. The credibility anchor of the Deutschmark and the Bundesbank has plainly been crucial in that regard. (It is interesting to note that Britain did well outside the Exchange Rate Mechanism (ERM) for the first half of the 1980s, but was unable to sustain its performance in the absence of a credible anchor.)

Europe is able to accept the notion of the monetary hegemony of the Bundesbank because it is looking forward to eventual monetary union, and because markets in Europe (labour, capital, goods and services) are becoming increasingly integrated. Moreover, economic structures are converging and steps are being taken towards convergence in conjunctural performance.

The situation is quite different when you consider the world level, and the potential differences in economic objectives and performance between the three main economic 'poles' of Japan, the United States and Europe. It is inconceivable to me that any one of the 'poles' would accept the monetary hegemony of another. So it is not possible to replicate a situation akin to the US leadership in the world economy in the 1950s and early 1960s, or like Germany's leadership in Europe in the 1980s. Nor do I think it is possible to have, formally, shared monetary management such as McKinnon (1984) suggests in his proposal for a jointly determined G3 monetary growth.

There are several reasons for my pessimism in this regard, but it is enough to note two here. First, there are still important differences in economic objectives that are likely to emerge in time. When a government that is determined to change the emphasis it gives to either growth or price stability arrives in power, it will not be possible to deflect it easily by considerations related to the functioning of the international monetary system. Second, we are unlikely to recreate the degree of consensus about the functioning of economies that we experienced in the 1960s. Think of the doubts that mainstream economists had about Reaganomics or the Thatcher–Howe policy mix. Such changes in political and economic fashion are bound to recur, and we need to devise co-ordination mechanisms that are resilient in the face of these.

So where does this leave us? I do not see any realistic alternative to a process of continuous policy co-ordination, informed by an attempt to develop a coherent economic model that reflects the highest common factor of agreement among the countries concerned. This is indeed what the G7 has attempted to do in the post-1985 period.

The basic model was described in successive issues of the IMF *World Economic Outlook* from 1986 to 1988. It involves a greater recognition of the complexities of international capital flows than is sometimes reflected in the work of those who treat the capital account as largely exogenous. Starting from the insight that movements in the balance of payments reflect shifts in saving–investment balances, this approach involves an attempt to identify the factors that underlie differential rates of savings and investment across countries. These factors may be appropriate and sustainable (such as differential rates of return on capital), or unsustainable and distorting (such as consumption-related budget deficits, or artificial inducements to save). The task of policy is to remove distortions to the efficient mobilization of saving and allocation of investment. Exchange rates, in this approach, are an important potential indicator of a policy problem. But the objective is not to establish constraints for policy (say in the form of exchange-rate objectives), but to provide a framework which enables inconsistent or unsustainable policies to be identified and corrected in a timely fashion.

DISCUSSION

Christopher Dow, opening the discussion, agreed very much with John Williamson's support for Bretton Woods, which had been a highly satisfactory system. It was not automatic but was backed by a 'policeman' in the shape of the IMF to make sure that it worked. OECD's role was supplementary to that of the IMF and was to create a kind of intellectual consensus by a rather informal discussion among a peer group drawn from the major powers. Without consent from the major powers any international organization had no power of its own. But discussion, of itself, would lead nowhere without agreed rules of behaviour to provide a basis for it. The best way of ensuring the successful operation of a system relying on such rules was to write them down and make them public so that nobody could be in doubt what the rules were. Thus a rule-bound system and a process of informal discussion were not distinct but complementary parts of the same arrangement.

The Bretton Woods system, while it operated, was well balanced and the fruit of much thought before its creation. In his view it would be wise to aim at restoring a system as close to it as possible. This might be old-fashioned but there was good hope that the system could be recreated. There were arguments against it, such as Andrew Crockett had given, but for each of these there were counter arguments.

Professor Kindleberger doubted whether rule-based systems in monetary affairs were ever symmetrical. The gold standard had been a sterling system. The Bretton Woods system was a dollar system which broke down in 1970–1 because the United States persisted in reducing interest rates when Germany was tightening policy quite rapidly. In the 1960s the United States had an average deficit of about $2–4 billion a year. This was not an accident: the United States was feeding dollars into the system at the rate people wanted them in order to add to their liquidity. John Williamson had made no mention of the G10, the Basle Agreement or the lender of the last resort function when the system got into trouble – a function that had to be introduced from time to time under the gold standard and under the dollar standard. The dollar standard had broken down because it was not perceived to be a symmetrical system. It was no doubt unattractive and undemocratic but it seemed to function better than a system in which everybody had a say. Special Drawing Rights (SDRs) had been created to provide more liquidity for the United States, but in a democratic system they had to be spread around every other country and this killed the idea because it no longer served the function of providing base money for the banker to the system. Rules were all very well but money evolved in a Darwinian way and evolution did not conform to strict rules. Peel, in the Bank Charter Act of 1844, had declared that if some contingency had not been covered there would be men of responsibility who would do what was needed. An asymmetrical system was needed. There was talk of one run by Germany or Japan but it would evolve, not be created by constitution-making (to which the United States was addicted). Money should have an unwritten constitution.

Lord O'Brien queried whether the United States had been providing dollars that other countries wanted. Had they not been thrusting them in enormous quantities on countries that tried to convert into gold because they did not want or trust them? The United States, instead of parting with gold, provided gold certificates that only the Germans were prepared to take. It had then become necessary to create SDRs, in place of dollars, that other countries *would* take. Unfortunately, the SDR never really got off the ground and the system broke up.

Professor Kindleberger rejoined that the United States was in current-account surplus until about 1966 and other countries were borrowing more than they needed to meet the cost of goods and services. They were deliberately adding to their liquidity and using the United States as a bank. Earlier there had been no international capital market in the United States so that borrowing was not possible, but latterly it had become too easy to sell bonds and raise dollar loans. John Williamson had not mentioned the lack of monetary co-ordination that made the deficit of $4 billion in 1970 rise to about $20 billion in 1971 and $30 billion in 1972, so bringing down the system.

Lord Callaghan recalled a Lancaster House meeting of the G10 in the 1960s at which Joe Fowler, the US Secretary to the Treasury, who had been strongly opposed to SDRs, suddenly reproached him as Chairman of the G10 for not pushing through a decision more quickly in face of French opposition. Was the United States conscious of its liquidity-creating function then? To which Professor Kindleberger replied: 'Just the three of us: Despres, Kindleberger and Salant!' (Despres, Kindleberger and Salant 1966).

Professor Solow began by expressing surprise at John Williamson's contention that what led to the breakdown of the Bretton Woods system was not simply some inability to avoid divergent national inflation rates but an intellectual failure to understand accelerationist inflation theory. Had everybody understood, and had it been true, that a correct theory of inflation was one of acceleration with well-defined natural rates of unemployment for each country, that might conceivably have helped; but with ill-defined, unknown, variable natural rates that go, for a country like Germany, from 2 per cent in the 1960s to 8 per cent in the 1970s, accelerationist theory would have made little difference. It was also an error to think that the US administration, as a matter of deliberate policy, favoured high employment rather than low inflation in the late 1960s. It was trying to prosecute the war in Vietnam in a way that would not turn the great middle class against it and feared that a tax increase would do precisely that.

In citing fisheries as the only example of a good thing that the OECD did, John Williamson could have paid no attention to what the OECD actually did about fisheries. All the OECD did was talk about them. It could not even collect the data showing what each country took from the world's stock of fish. All the talk had done was to lead to the 200-mile limit and national over-fishing everywhere.

Andrea Boltho pointed out that there was no reference in the paper to the efforts that had been made to mend the Bretton Woods system before it broke down. A major attempt at international co-ordination had been made at the Smithsonian Conference but it came too late and was too little, probably for the reasons given by Andrew Crockett, such as the expansion of capital flows. The expansion in 1972–3 had been synchronous and its inflationary consequences should have been foreseen. At that time he had been in charge of forecasting in OECD and the forecasts of output had been very close to the mark in both years, but a major error had been made on inflation. Why? For three major reasons. First, and in corroboration of John Williamson's point, sufficient account had not been taken of acceleration: not because of inattention to some natural rate of unemployment, but simply because of neglect of the inflationary atmosphere created by the cost-push inflation of the late 1960s. Second, there was a conviction that there was much more slack in the economies than there turned out to be. Productive potential had been estimated for every country and checked with national authorities and account had been taken of existing unemployment, but the natural rate of unemployment, unbeknown to the forecasters, had risen everywhere. There were many bottlenecks in 1973 in spite of the existence of more overall slack than at the previous peak.

Third, the OECD did not foresee the commodity boom. In early

1972 Christopher Dow had brought Wynne Godley to see him, and Godley had put forward the 'preposterous' forecast of a massive deterioration in the terms of trade of Western countries with repercussions on real incomes and inflation. Relying on the experience of the past twenty years, OECD had dismissed this forecast, regarding a deterioration of 1 per cent or so as the utmost to be expected. Boltho had consulted all the in-house economists he could on the danger of a major upswing in commodity prices, and not one had thought it at all likely. So there had been an underestimation of inflationary expectations, of the degree of full employment already reached and of the likely swing in the terms of trade that would follow the failure of commodity supply to expand *pari passu* with output over the period of falling commodity prices in the 1950s and 1960s. In his forecast he had been very badly wrong. But did it matter? Had he forecast an unsustainable boom with two-digit inflation would governments have listened? They were all fighting elections and were determined to expand to improve their chances. Nor would the first oil shock have been much affected since it was not inflation and high demand pressures so much as the Yom Kippur War that had produced it. The intellectual mistake was probably of limited significance in the event.

Professor Kloten recalled how the influx of foreign currency in 1968–9 had undermined the German stabilization policy. This had led to the *de facto* revaluation of the Deutschmark in December 1968 by means of taxation measures. It had propelled the super-boom of 1969, gave a reason for the short period of floating rates in the middle of 1971 and also accounted for the restrictions on the foreign currency imports in 1972 and the subsequent resignation of Karl Schiller. His successor Helmut Schmidt continued to believe, until January 1973, that the danger was not of a breakdown in the Bretton Woods system but of a collapse of the German economy following a revaluation of the Deutschmark.

Professor Kloten favoured a rule-based system with rules to be updated if required, and implemented with adequate discretionary measures. In any new system, whatever the intellectual foundation, it was a necessary condition that the framework should be accepted and adopted by the politicians. As matters stood, he found himself in agreement with Andrew Crockett in his expectations for the 1990s.

Sir Ralf Dahrendorf asked what, if the arguments against a rule-based world system applied also to Europe, should be done in the event of a European Defence Community disaster in the monetary field within the next few years?

Andrew Crockett replied that that was an argument for extreme caution in moving forward from the existing rule-based EMS, with its escape hatches, to a monetary union from which there would be no escape hatch and which would have to be very carefully prepared both at the institutional level and in terms of structural convergence.

James Meade went back to his association with Keynes in his proposals for a clearing union. These had assumed control over capital movements and indeed Keynes had hankered after control of imports as well. The enormous volatility of capital funds, which Andrew Crockett had emphasized, presented a difficulty in John Williamson's argument since short-term capital movements could swamp the use of reserves in maintaining stability in the exchange rate while adjustments were made in the domestic economy. Keynes would have regarded both monetary policy and fiscal policy as available for the control of demand.

Professor Meade also wanted to raise a fundamental issue in the choice between a rule-based system and policy co-ordination. He was convinced that it was not possible to succeed if monetary policy was assigned to the control of inflation and fiscal policy to the control of demand. Both instruments have very substantial effects in both directions. He was a believer in rules rather than planned co-ordination, but not in making central banks independent of Treasuries, or *vice versa*, because it was always necessary to have a package of monetary and fiscal measures to suit the circumstances.

James Tobin said that there had been much discussion of appropriate policy mixes in Working Party 3 in the 1960s: for example, the United States was recommended to use fiscal policy in recovering from the 1960 recession so as to avoid lowering interest rates, which would be inappropriate to economic conditions in Europe.

In any international monetary system, whether with fixed or flexible rates, the world average level of interest rates is left loose, unless a single dominant country determines the rates or there is a co-ordinated decision by the leading countries. However the world level is determined, it should be possible for individual countries to deviate to some extent from the world level. A co-ordinated decision by the G7 countries would still allow appropriate deviations. The world as a whole might be homogeneous in the long run and neutral to monetary values, but this is compatible with differing speeds of adjustment, different initial conditions etc. He had suggested in the 1960s, and more recently, that each country should frame its own targets for macroeconomic policy. These would not then be imposed on it; but what would be imposed would be policies consistent with their own targets. This would lead logically to some determination of what movements and differences in interest rates should be permitted in different countries.

Lord Callaghan asked to be allowed to draw on his recollections of a situation in the late 1970s after the breakdown of the rule-based system of the 1960s. Three heads of state, who had all been finance ministers in the 1960s and experienced the system in operation then, had asked themselves whether something better was not possible in the G7. At the Bonn Summit each country was given a specific and separate target after a process of bargaining. The Americans undertook to raise the price of oil nearer to the world level; the British undertook to bring inflation down; the Japanese were persuaded to increase public expenditure; and the Germans agreed to increase the growth rate in the Federal Republic. This was a deliberate attempt to co-ordinate policy and get a greater degree of stability and confidence in the international scene: to achieve what might even be regarded as a primitive element of world government.

Professor Tobin interjected that Helmut Schmidt looked on this agreement as the source of the Iranian revolution and the rise of the Ayatollah, but Williamson claimed that he had changed his mind and now thought well of the Bonn Summit.

Lord Croham said that the Bretton Woods system had been excellent in many ways, and designed to avoid a repetition of the excesses of the 1930s. But it was asymmetrical in that the United States, which believed that it could always obey the rules, never expected to be subjected to the supervision of the IMF. Right from the outset, some of the rules to which Keynes attached importance were blocked, the scarce currency clause for example. Nor was there anything in the system to ensure that the base currency would provide just enough liquidity but not too much. In the early years, the United States behaviour fitted the system remarkably well: the only major problem initially was the dollar shortage. Later, the creation of too many dollars would have caused any other country to come before the IMF. As the system began to break down, consideration was given to all sorts of modifications that might make it work, such as SDRs and crawling pegs. But by that time excessive dollar creation meant that things were out of control when the external shocks occurred.

John Williamson, replying to the discussion, said that asymmetrical systems were no doubt the ones that evolved naturally. The Bretton Woods system had been intended to be symmetrical but it had evolved asymmetrically and thus had been easier to create. The world, however, was not in a position to accept an asymmetrical system now: any system would have to be symmetrical. His blueprint for policy co-ordination did provide an alternative to having a single monetary authority and this accorded with what Professor Tobin suggested. This would be to commit the average world rate of interest to a world growth target (a nominal income target). In deciding whether deficit or surplus countries should adjust, the criterion would be whether world income was expanding too fast or too slowly. Such a rule would give each country considerable freedom and still introduce a measure of consistency.

He disclaimed optimism that such a solution would ever be adopted. It was unlikely that the world would do anything so sensible. All one could do was to think out what was desirable and how it could be done, and it was in that spirit that he made his proposals.

Finally, it had always been his view that there was an element of financial intermediation in the US deficit in the 1960s, but there was also involuntary dollar accumulation and other countries had not been able to bring about adjustment since there was no proper adjustment mechanism and they couldn't bring pressure on the United States. The cost of all this was the explosion in dollar holdings in 1971–2 referred to by Professor Kindleberger, which was exactly what one would expect from a dollar standard and the reason for rejecting a return to a dollar standard.

AFTERTHOUGHTS BY SAM KATZ

John Williamson has given us a valuable overview of the analytical underpinnings of the Bretton Woods system, but I have misgivings about the special role in the breakdown of that system which he assigns to the dollar. I thought at the time that the dollar's role as reserve currency did not merit the attention given it during the reform debates of the 1960s and, in my view, it deserves even less attention today.

Was 'the only chance . . . to reform the . . . system' really 'to make devaluation a feasible policy option for the centre country'? I doubt it. After all, the dollar was eventually devalued in 1971. The procedure adopted then could have been exploited at any time during the 1960s: the United States had only to accept a higher gold price and the Europeans a general appreciation. One further point. The broad support among Europeans for a uniform rise in the price of gold as a fundamental systemic reform was a special, but significant, obstacle to dollar devaluation. The United States would have obtained no relief from an overvalued dollar had its higher gold price been followed by a worldwide increase.

To be sure, American policy-makers share responsibility for the system's breakdown. In particular, they failed to provide a stable domestic base for the international system. In addition, they were naive in convincing themselves that the dollar alone – as anchor of the system – could not, or should not, be devalued. But European officials shared responsibility in refusing to revalue and in pressing measures of demand restraint upon an American economy in which unemployment was already at levels they would have regarded as unacceptable.

In short, it was as critical for system stability that the European currencies be revalued as it was that the dollar be devalued. Much of the strain on the system might have been mitigated had the mid-1973 levels of European currencies been put in place by 1967. Let me add a further point. It was not alone 'the expedients adopted to deflect countries from buying gold from the United States' that 'transformed the system gradually into a dollar standard'. Policy-makers on both sides of the Atlantic agreed to discard the 'adjustable' elements of the Bretton Woods regime. They managed exchange rates so that changes in parity were to be made only as a last resort – that is, only after four other options had been tried and failed. This rigidity became entrenched, in part, because the political cost of *any* exchange-rate action proved to be unexpectedly high, as those who participated in the Wilson debate about sterling devaluation in 1964 can confirm.

Even a system with rigid rates might have survived had the major trading countries agreed upon alternative mechanisms of international adjustment. But balance-of-payments adjustment was regarded as an autonomous policy area – not subject to international surveillance – by two powerful groups of IMF members: deficit countries not requiring Fund financing, such as the United States, and chronic surplus countries, such as Germany and Japan. Fund officials never obtained – or sought – specific commitments for remedial action from these countries, regardless of the size or chronic nature of their imbalances. Under Fund practice, their adjustment responsibilities remained entirely voluntary.

I view the experience of the 1960s as evidence that the international character of exchange-rate actions cannot be maintained without a functioning system of international adjustment. To achieve such a functioning system had been a priority concern during the Bretton Woods negotiation. The earliest proposal – set out in Keynes's original memorandum on a world clearing union of September 1941 – stipulated that members with debit and with credit balances were to be treated with an even hand by the Managing Board. This formulation was drastically revised by British financial officials because it provided too little liquidity and too much adjustment. Their amended White Paper was rejected by the Americans because it provided too much liquidity and too little adjustment. The latter offered as a compromise the creation of a fund with limited quotas but with a scarce currency clause designed to ensure creditor (not reserve currency) co-operation in adjustment action. This clause was intended by American officials to serve as an incentive for IMF members to pursue 'good creditor' policies on a voluntary basis, not to be the basis for initiating IMF sanctions. This 'good creditor' attitude governed American leadership initiatives in restoring liberal trade and payments arrangements during the 1950s. It was an aspect of international finance almost entirely neglected in the prolonged reform negotiations of the 1960s.

The breakdown might have been avoided, or postponed, had adjustment imperatives been stressed in the formal negotiations of the 1960s. But the deliberations were preoccupied with world liquidity in general and the dollar's special role in particular. This perspective, and this emphasis, I have regarded as an anachronism from the Genoa Conference of 1923, when French representatives rejected the proposal to confer reserve status on the pound and non-reserve status on the franc. The formulation of the debate during the 1960s was based on the Triffin paradox: the conviction that international breakdown was inevitable unless the world economy could be freed from dependence upon the dollar for its reserve needs. As it turned out, the innovation of the decade – the introduction of the SDR – neither rescued the system nor became a substitute for the dollar. On the contrary, the international community maintained an extraordinary appetite for dollar assets throughout the oil crises of the 1970s and the absurd American deficits of the 1980s. Thus, the preoccupation with liquidity matters during the 1960s proved to be a detour from the main lines along which the international monetary system developed in the next two decades.

The exchange-rate and adjustment difficulties of the 1960s were momentarily resolved by the floating of the major currencies after 1969. A regime of floating rates imposes a symmetry in that surplus and deficit countries are brought directly into the stabilization process through fluctuations in currency values. The fall in the dollar means a reciprocal rise in the values of the European currencies. With floating rates, partner countries share the economic costs of adjustment; each avoids the domestic political costs of a formal exchange-rate decision; and neither is required to initiate domestic policy changes as a result of external constraints.

The world has found no other practical way to achieve even this degree of symmetry. To be sure, the Fund was intended to encourage prompt and balanced adjustment action by all its members; but the Bretton Woods arrangements proved to be unworkable over four decades, particularly for the key-currency countries.

It is altogether timely, therefore, for Williamson to suggest that we should initiate a search for orderly rules and more effective mechanisms for co-operation so that the international system will no longer have to rely upon a floating regime which has been governed by the market-driven forces of currency fluctuations. The currency alignments – or misalignments – of the 1980s have not been realistic measures of international price competitiveness nor have they helped much to restore tolerable balance to the structure of world payments. The adjustment experience during the period of 'hands off' floating in the first half of the 1980s was little short of disastrous.

Many of us can join Williamson in a preference for trying in the 1990s to establish common rules for timely balance-of-payments adjustment action by all Fund members, be they a reserve or non-reserve, deficit or surplus, less developed or industrial country. However, the international economy has probably already moved too far in the direction of regional fragmentation to get agreement among the major trading countries on global rules for a global system. As a result, the key-currency countries are likely to continue their drift towards larger groupings, with each currency floating widely against the others.

Our immediate alternative, therefore, is to strengthen the casual arrangements for international co-operation which the industrial countries have depended upon over the past two decades. These have provided more than occasions for the interchange of information and for policy discussion. For the industrial countries were able to utilize them to organize *ad hoc* international rescue intervention during moments of imminent crisis: the Mexican debt collapse of 1982; the dollar overvaluation of 1985; and the Wall Street declines of 1987 and 1989. This *ad hoc* approach to international co-operation is clearly a second-best arrangement and gives us a monetary order markedly inferior in structure to one based upon global rules. But even the strengthening of second-best arrangements could be a substantial advance if only it shielded the world economy in the 1990s from the misalignments of currencies and the massive surpluses and deficits of the 1980s.

NOTES

1 Christopher Dow made the interesting suggestion during the conference at Glasgow that that was the major role of the OECD, implying that active and passive forms of co-ordination are complements.
2 Several other attacks on the model of the 1960s, such as monetarism, the monetary approach to the balance of payments, the Lucas supply function, the policy ineffectiveness theorem, Ricardian equivalence, real business cycle theory and new classical economics, have in my view left it largely unscathed. The subsequent macroeconomic developments that do need adding are the Lucas critique, rational expectations and time inconsistency; but none of these seems to me to play a fundamental role in explaining the debacle of the 1960s.
3 This was crucial to the system operating with reasonable symmetry, which is how it was designed and how it operated for the brief ten years between the restoration of European convertibility in 1958 and the suspension of the gold pool in 1968. Once the gold pool was suspended, everyone assumed that the United States would react to a run on its gold stock by suspending convertibility, and the United States therefore began to assume that it could treat its balance of payments with what was euphemistically known as benign neglect. Worldwide inflation was the malign outcome.
4 My proposals for rules adequate to present circumstances are to be found in Williamson and Miller (1987).

BIBLIOGRAPHY

Canzoneri, M.B. and Gray, J.A. (1983) 'Monetary policy gains and the consequences of non-cooperative behavior', *International Finance Discussion Paper 219*, Federal Reserve Board.
Cooper, R.N. (1968) *The Economics of Interdependence*, London: McGraw-Hill.
—— (1985) 'Economic interdependence and coordination of economic policies', in *Handbook of International Economics*, vol. II, Amsterdam: Elsevier.
Despres, E., Kindleberger, C.P. and Salant, W.S. (1966) 'The dollar and world liquidity – a minority view', *The Economist* 218 (6389), Feb. pp. 526–9.
Eichengreen, B. (1984) *International Policy Coordination in Historical Perspective: A View from the Interwar Years*, London: CEPR.

Gilbert, M. (1980) *Quest for Monetary Order*, New York, Chichester: Wiley.

Lawrence, R.Z. (1978) 'The measurement and causes of the synchronization of the international business cycle', Doctoral Dissertation, Yale University.

McKinnon, R.I. (1984) 'An international standard for monetary stabilization', in *Policy Analysis*, vol. 8 (March), Washington DC: Institute for International Economics.

Marris, S.N. (1986) 'Managing the world economy: economics, institutions, and politics', Gaston Eyskens Lectures, University of Leuven.

Mundell, R.A. (1962) 'The appropriate use of monetary and fiscal policy under fixed exchange rates', *IMF Staff Papers*, March; reprinted in R.A. Mundell, *International Economics*, London: Macmillan.

OECD (1966) *The Balance of Payments Adjustment Process*, Paris: OECD.

Oudiz, G. and Sachs, J. (1984) 'Macroeconomic policy coordination among the industrial countries', *Brookings Papers on Economic Activity* 1.

Solomon, R. (1977) *The International Monetary System 1945–76: An Insider's View*, New York: Harper & Row.

Tew, B. (1985) *The Evolution of the International Monetary System 1945–85*, 3rd edn, London: Hutchinson.

Triffin, R. (1960) *Gold and the Dollar Crisis*, New Haven, CT: Yale University Press.

Williamson, J. (1971) 'On the normative theory of balance-of-payments adjustment', in G. Clayton, J.C. Gilbert and R. Sedgwick (eds) *Monetary Theory and Monetary Policy in the 1970s*, London: Oxford University Press.

—— (1983) 'Keynes and the international economic order', in D. Worswick and J. Trevithick (eds) *Keynes and the Modern World*, Cambridge: Cambridge University Press.

—— (1985) 'On the system in Bretton Woods', *American Economic Review*, May.

Williamson, J. and Miller, M. (1987) *Targets and Indicators: A Blueprint for the International Coordination of Economic Policy*, Washington, DC: Institute for International Economics.

5

DID THE SIXTIES SWING TOO FAR?

Ralf Dahrendorf

Much of this colloquium is about the rigorous analysis of economic policy with special reference to Britain. In my musings on the 'swinging sixties' I shall adopt a lighter tone, deal with softer subjects, and take you to another country. To me, the 1960s bring back memories of politics in Germany, first as a government adviser, then as an elected member of Parliament, and my subjects at the time were education, social policy and the general need for change. *Nach dem Ausbau der Umbau* – after expansion, reform – was the theme of political debate.

When Willy Brandt had formed his government in the autumn of 1969 – a coalition of Social Democrats and Liberals – he made a moving government statement in Parliament. Many people still remember its key sentence: 'We must venture more democracy!' No one quite knew what he meant even at the time, but it sounded right; it had the ring of the reforming climate of the time. Memories of the preceding year, 1968, were ubiquitous. 1968 had been a revolt without evident objective; when its protagonists were invited to television and radio programmes on the occasion of the twentieth anniversary in 1988, most of them looked unlikely revolutionaries – even 'Red Danny' Cohn-Bendit is now a councillor in the city government of Frankfurt – and no consensus emerged as to what it had all been about. Vietnam? Sexual freedom? Educational opportunities? 'We must venture more democracy' sums it up.

For some of us, the disappointment of Brandt's Government was its failure to initiate social reforms. The only serious project in the early weeks was a measure which had acquired a symbolic significance out of proportion with its apparent importance: a bill to force employers to continue paying wages and salaries during the first two days of sickness of employees. Already rules concerning sick pay were generous; but the first two days had remained what seemed to some an unacceptable gap in the safety net of the welfare state. The gap had to be filled, and so it was. The result turned out to be dramatic. Absenteeism rose, and the first two days turned out to be more costly than the next ten. Did the sixties swing too far? The example may well be worth examining more closely. It marks precisely the point at which legitimate social policy turns into unaffordable yet tempting nannying from the cradle to the grave.

There were other reasons why Willy Brandt's Government failed to fulfil its promise of reform. It was a coalition, and not all – indeed not many – Liberals actually wanted much change. Also, *Ostpolitik* soon moved to the centre of the stage. For the first three years, foreign policy dominated cabinet discussions and parliamentary debates to the point of exhaustion; there was simply no time and energy left for other matters. Above all, however, what needed to be done had largely happened already, partly by stealth – social trends rarely have a beginning and an end – and partly by a hundred flowers blooming in schools and churches, political parties and local communities, even businesses and the military, to say nothing of families and other small social units.

Let me highlight three sets of changes, of which only the first is strictly the result of deliberate action. It has to do with education. After 1958, the OECD began to take a consequential, though initially controversial, interest in education. A conference in Kungälv in Sweden assembled in 1961 the small band of social scientists who were then interested in education. The proceedings were published under the title *Ability and Educational Opportunity*. An unlikely title, one might think, for an organization dedicated to economic development! Three years later, in a paper called *Economic Aspects of Higher Education*, the OECD explained its interest. The argument was simple. By the late 1950s, economic reconstruction was complete and growth became a subject of concern. Growth, however, required not just capital investment but highly skilled people to deal with new technologies. Educational expansion had become – so the OECD Commission for Scientific and Technical Personnel (as it then was) argued – a necessary condition of economic growth.

The argument caught on, especially when, in the mid-1960s, a number of countries experienced recessions and sought new ways back to the growth path, 'Keynes plus' policies as it were. In Germany, a dramatic plea by the Protestant theologian and educator Georg Picht, entitled *The German Educational Catastrophe*, correlated economic growth and the proportion of university entrants, observed a growing gap, and predicted ruin. I argued against this thesis at the time (in a pamphlet called *Education is a Civil Right*) and am still convinced that the economic case for the expansion of secondary and tertiary education is weak once a country has reached a certain level of educational participation. There may be a case for more and better vocational training, but it does not follow that universities must grow in size. Organizational and political reasons, such as the need for the OECD to make a case for its interest in education, or the readiness of politicians to listen to 'economic' arguments, however phoney, led to the prevalence of a mistaken and misleading theory which in turn led to useless and costly manpower planning. However, this is another matter, though perhaps one of some relevance to the British debate in the early 1990s.

In the 1960s the deeper question was never relevant because all roads led to Rome, or rather, to educational expansion. After all, I had only given different reasons for the policies advocated by Picht, and all of us followed the lead of the OECD. In Britain, the Robbins Committee (which had sat from 1961 to 1963) made a similar case. And expansion happened, at the secondary and tertiary level at any rate. The 'scholarship boy' (R. Hoggart) came from being the exception to being the rule, with consequences for schools as well as for the structure of social classes (a subject to which I shall return). New universities were founded everywhere; the teaching profession, both secondary and tertiary, grew rapidly. In the 1960s, the groundwork for an unprecedented expansion was laid. The German example is not untypical at least for the continent of Europe. With population stable (indeed the relevant population declining in the 1960s), the number of students in tertiary education gradually doubled from 120,000 to about 250,000 between 1950 and 1965. Within the next eight years it doubled again, and then, between 1973 and 1988, it rose from just over 500,000 to three times that number, 1.5 million. One side effect of this process is not often mentioned, though it has significant social and political ramifications. The number of voters who work full-time in educational institutions as teachers or students has risen from under 5 per cent in 1960 to more than 10 per cent, and in some countries nearly 15 per cent, by 1990. There is today an educational class whose rootlessness makes it a breeding ground for all kinds of political ideas.

Did expansion swing too far? The British case is nowhere near as dramatic as that of Germany and others, and has other special features which is why I shall return to it at the end of my remarks. Leaving Britain on one side, there are those who would argue that the educational expansion begun in the 1960s has destroyed continental universities. (In Germany, this is personalized by some who claim that Picht – and Dahrendorf – should be held responsible.) Admittedly, if I was asked today to name the top twenty universities of the world, they would not include a single one in Continental Europe; and even outstanding departments or specialist centres are more sparse than expenditure on tertiary education would suggest. Masses of students pass through barely structured courses and, if they do not drop out, they eventually attain devalued if not worthless degrees. There are reasons why so many of the best apply for a place in a British or American university.

The reasons have to do with a subject of general relevance. The weakness of educational expansion in continental countries was that it took place without corresponding changes in academic structure. Existing institutions were simply blown up in size. Today, universities which have the number of students which, say, Oxford has (14,000), are regarded as failures and candidates for merger or closure. Teaching has suffered by unmanageable numbers, and research by sprawling bureaucratic requirements. Thus universities fail their students and their teachers alike.

These are large generalizations, and they must be taken with more than a grain of salt. Of course one can point to the *grandes écoles* in France, to private universities like Bocconi in Milan, to the Federal technical universities in Switzerland. Still, the 1960s reforms suggest one serious lesson. The alternative to mindless expansion would have been structural reform. For example, a well-organized undergraduate-type degree course would have made sense. It was proposed by some, but foundered on the rock of vested interests. As one of those who experienced such failure, I have come to a melancholy conclusion. (It is one shared by others; Lionel Robbins made a similar point in his late reflections on the Robbins Report and its consequences.) Expansion, at least in education, requires accompanying measures of differentiation in order to achieve its purpose. But differentiation is almost impossible to bring about by deliberate action. Difference grows, it cannot be made. At the same time, differentiation and structure can be destroyed, and the risk is great that even the most well-meaning expansion will destroy the structures which it is intended to offer to more people.

I have no answer to this dilemma. It is the dilemma of universities and polytechnics in a growing tertiary system. Expansion is a leveller, and this is certainly one of the themes which one must associate with the 1960s. I do not mean this in any simple sense of the defence of advantage against levelling-down. The abolition of privilege was a necessary and a desirable process. I mean it rather in the sense that structures were dismantled which had held people and given their aspirations and actions meaning. A Czechoslovakian writer was recently quoted with the observation: 'In the old days, nothing was allowed and everything mattered. Now everything is allowed and nothing matters any more.' No one would wish the old regime back, least of all in the post-communist democracies of East Central Europe. But a milder version of this experience has swept the free world since the 1960s, as we went from constraints and prohibitions to a climate in which anything goes.

'We must venture more democracy.' *Democracy*, democratization was the second main theme of the decade with which we are concerned. The meaning is rarely very clear, though the tangible effects of the trend are. Their name is, in a word, co-determination. The German system of industrial co-determination is of course much older; it stems back to 1950–1, and in part to 1919 – though it is relevant to note that the Brandt government extended co-determination to enterprises with fewer than a hundred employees which had previously been exempt. In higher education, legislation or statute changes have taken place all over Europe which give junior staff a say – in some cases, a majority – in decision-making bodies. More unlikely institutions followed suit, such as churches, including even the Catholic Church. The Second Vatican Council can be seen as an instrument of democratization, all the way to the introduction of the vernacular at mass and a new church architecture which puts the altar in the centre of the community and at the same level. Conscript armies have adopted the principle of the 'citizen in uniform' which makes them much like other fields of employment, and incidentally allows a growing number to opt out. It might be amusing to pursue this argument all the way to the phenomenon of the democratization of family life and, more generally, the new role of children.

Did democracy swing too far? Again, it is well to beware of knee-jerk reactions. Much needed to be done to encourage participation and accountability. The fact that some changes overshot the mark is perhaps neither here nor there. One of the more catching slogans of German students in 1968 is hard to translate: *Unter den Talaren der Muff von tausend Jahren* ('Underneath the gowns the musty smell of a thousand years'). One would have thought that the right response should have been to give the gowns a good airing; instead they were abolished altogether. But there are more serious consequences.

One is bureaucratization. Universities provide a good example, though by no means the only one. I hesitate to postulate a general law to the effect that democracy means bureaucracy, but it certainly appears that democratization has, as its inevitable consequence, more formal procedures, more paper, more committees and more administration. The choice is odd and worrying. It seems to be one between personal and unaccountable power and the bureaucratic dissipation of decision-making. At any rate, these are the Scylla and the Charybdis between which a course has to be found. Most European countries did not find it. If one is looking for explanations of what Mancur Olson called the 'social rigidities' of the 1970s, it may make more sense to look at the causes and consequences of bureaucratization than at the 'logic of collective action' in his terms.

The other consequence of democratization is an immense suspicion of power, indeed of authority of any kind. This takes us to more intangible trends. Few would deny that since the 1960s there has been much doubt in the right of those in positions of power to do anything, and in many institutions a consequent paralysis of authority. The family may well be the most extreme example, though there are others, all the way to the political process. The growth of civic, often local, initiatives is on the one hand a desirable expression of democratic participation; but on the other hand it is a result of deep distrust in governments and established political parties; and incidentally, given the essentially negative preoccupations of such initiatives – as a rule, they want to prevent rather than promote decisions – it is another cause of the retardation of change in many countries.

In many, not in all: once again it will be evident to most that the statements made here about trends originating in the 1960s are less true for Britain than for the rest of Europe, and need considerable qualifications for the United States and other parts even of the OECD world. Britain, in particular, has kept its peculiar combination of traditional structures of authority and privilege with modern features of democracy and participation. Only recently, and from a surprising political corner, have these structures been attacked and partly dismantled, first in the name of a radical individualism of market accountability and now, it appears, in that of a classless society conservative-style.

Before I take up this important point once more, let me at least mention a third trend commonly associated with the 1960s which is moral, or perhaps immoral, even 'demoral' (as one might be tempted to say). I have never found it easy to make confident statements about social values. If values are real, they must be reflected in more tangible structures, and if this is not the case, there is little to say about them. Yet a vast literature has emerged around the subject of values since the 1960s. Daniel Bell (1973) was the first to speak of a 'post-industrial society'. Ronald Inglehart (1977) has tried to establish the prevalence of 'post-material values' on the basis of survey research. More recently, a veritable torrent of articles and books have been produced about 'post-modern society'. More to the point perhaps, the 'permissive society' is associated by many with the 1960s. It is still praised by some as a liberation from the claustrophobia of censorship in the widest sense of the term. At the same time, no subject has raised the question of whether the 1960s did indeed swing too far more insistently than that of a world in which apparently anything goes.

The theme can be described in a few simple statements. Since the 1960s most developed societies (and some others too) have seen a strong trend from social control to anomy, from overregulated to underregulated lives. In sexual behaviour, fashion, literature and art, spoken language and personal appearance, in short, in public and private mores, powerful codes have been replaced by near-total choice. This was, and is, a process of liberation. Few want to return to the stifling prescriptions and hypocritical realities of an older morality which is still at times described as Victorian. At the same time, more and more people wish that there was something to hold on to, some core of values which commands general acceptance. Connections are seen between the destructuring of social mores and the problems of law and order, including drug addiction and other forms of disorientation, especially in young people. There are good reasons to introduce the word anomy in this connection. It was first used by Emile Durkheim in his explanation of suicide, and applied in particular to those who had lost the firm railings of moral certainty; city-dwellers, protestants, members of incomplete families.

I have tried to give such observations some substance in my Hamlyn Lectures on *Law and Order* (1985). There, I have also argued that, while it is not very difficult to dismantle structures which for many have lost their meaning, building new institutions is all but impossible and certainly a long process. (The discussion about 'civil

society' in the destructured countries of East Central Europe high-
lights the problem.) Thus the risk is great that in the place of institutions we get mere façades of order, more policemen instead of a
greater acceptance of the law. The point is relevant for a final
comment which is about Britain. If these musings have a common
theme, it is that the 1960s gave a strong push to increase people's
options by removing constraints which had lost their plausibility.
This was, and continues to be, a desirable process if liberty is one's
objective. It is also a risky process. Not only can it go too far – which
is bearable because it can be corrected by the swing of the pendulum
– it can also inadvertently, if inevitably, lead to the dissolution of
structures which are necessary in order to give options meaning.
Human life opportunities are not just options, but significant options.
If educational expansion destroys the quality of education, or if
democratization discourages initiative and undermines all authority,
or if liberation from oppressive mores leads to disorientation and
vulnerability, then freedom's gain is by the same token freedom's
loss. People are denied the promise of liberty by the very means of its
fulfilment. Fred Hirsch had much to say about this subject in his
Social Limits to Growth. It is the quandary of modernity which the
1960s have left behind.

This is felt particularly acutely in Britain, though perhaps as much
in the 1980s and 1990s as twenty years earlier. The United States has
experienced most social processes earlier than the rest of us; Britain,
on the contrary, has lagged behind. Indeed, the Aristotelian secret of
Britain's political stability throughout the first half of this turbulent
century may well have been the unique combination of old and new,
of pre-industrial values and structures with industrial achievement.
No doubt the former have limited the latter; they account, at least in
part, for Britain's much-quoted relative decline. But others have paid
a high price in stability and liberty – and thus in human happiness –
for their more ruthless progress. Even the 1960s occurred in a much
milder version in Britain compared with other European countries.
The Robbins Report saw to it that educational expansion had its
limits, and older forms of teaching survived the onslaught. 1968
passed the country by almost like the French Revolution did. The
gates at the London School of Economics (LSE) were exciting and
upsetting for those on either side of them, and gave rise to a flurry of
ephemeral books about 'the troubles'; but they were idyllic by comparison with Berkeley and Paris, as were the consequences of six
student members on LSE's 100-strong Court of Governors. Even

value changes remained much attenuated. Class remained a force, as did censorship, the discipline of public schools and the love of all perquisites of status.

Elsewhere, notably in Continental Europe, the 1960s can be described as the great age of social change which has given rise to the problems of the 1970s and 1980s. In Britain, too, many major social changes can be traced to that decade. But it took much longer for them to work their way through British society. Take the dissipation and eventual disappearance of the British working class. In Continental Europe, as in the United States, the dominant social group has long been a diffuse and large middle class with its values of individual advancement and material satisfaction. Britain by contrast had never given its middle class a firm place. 'Scholarship boys' felt embarrassed about having betrayed their working-class origins, and successful businessmen were more likely to emulate upper-class values and attitudes than to develop their own style. The working class (like the upper class perhaps) was as interested in solidarity as in individual advancement; getting on with others was more important than doing better than others. This did not make for a great surge of productivity and growth. It was almost a caste-like attitude dating back to an earlier age. But it did, among other things, make for strong and reliable trade unions, and for a labour movement which was always a force of stability as well as reform.

When the processes which I have here associated with the 1960s hit the British working class, the old order crumbled but there was no new model of a middle-class culture. Such dislocations make organizations and individuals vulnerable to extreme, even absurd, views and leaders. The excesses of trade union behaviour in the 1970s and 1980s are as much a reflection of the dissolution of the old working class and the dislocation of its remnants as they are a result of active subversion by small cadres. They too exist (in part as a consequence of the educational developments described earlier), but they could not have been effective fifty or even twenty years earlier.

The reforms of the 1960s have had important consequences everywhere. Some were desirable; I do not find it difficult, even today, to defend many of the liberal changes of the time. All changes have externalities which you cannot control; they define the new problems. They are very serious in at least one respect, i.e. the loss of what I sometimes call ligatures, or deep bonds. Britain was spared the extreme swings of the pendulum; in an important sense, the 1960s did not swing too far. But how did Gorbachev put it when he saw the

East German politburo in early October 1989? 'Whoever comes late, will be punished by life!' When change came, it took the form of Bennite threats and the reality of Thatcherism. Both ways forced the country into a world for which it was ill-prepared. But that is another matter, outside the remit of this colloquium.

COMMENTS BY ROY JENKINS

I was Home Secretary as well as Chancellor of the Exchequer in the second half of the 1960s, so I open with some thoughts on this transition. Certainly, when I became Chancellor, having been Home Secretary, I regarded it as a major promotion. Being Chancellor was the hardest job that I have ever done. One had a feeling which one did not have in another department, that the fate of the government was in one's hands, and the fate of a significant part of the nation's standard of living as well. But I feel that if I am remembered for anything it will be for what I did as Home Secretary, not as Chancellor. What a Home Secretary does in measures of legislation that last leaves a far greater imprint. A Chancellor of the Exchequer only makes footprints in the sand which are washed away by the tide of his successor.

I was impressed by Terence Higgins's defence of the early 1970s, but not entirely persuaded by it. The handling of the Exchequer was the great weakness of the Heath Government, together with its vulnerability to the miners. It brought me to turn over in my mind the question whether we went down the wrong road by going for trade union reform, rather than concentrating on holding the prices and incomes policy in 1969. I was rather inclined to agree with David Worswick, but became less so as I reflected on it. He is almost certainly right that, had we stuck to prices and incomes policy, we would have had a lower rate of inflation in 1970–1. But when you consider the subsequent position of the trade unions, whose appetites were already whetted by destroying *In Place of Strife*, and then enormously increased when the miners effectively destroyed the Heath Government in 1974; and when you consider how absolutely appallingly they treated Jim Callaghan in 1978–9, in spite of the great claims he had on their loyalty: God knows where one would have got to if trade union power had been left unchallenged. I only regret that we could not deal with it in the 1970s, without leaving it to the unnecessary and highly undesirable excesses of Thatcherism in the 1980s.

As Home Secretary, I had the accolade of having a quotation – or rather, a misquotation – hung around my neck: 'The permissive society is a civilized society'. What in fact I said was, 'I do not like the term "permissive society". What I prefer to ask is whether these changes [referring to those of the 1960s] have made our society more civilized, and I answer "yes".' I still believe the changes were desirable, although it seems a vast exaggeration of my role, or that of Parliament, to believe that either was crucial to the changes in ethos and in standards that took place during that period. These liberalizing measures were both necessary and desirable. You only have to think how extraordinary it would have been had we in Britain decided to remain entirely detached from the rest of the world. It would have meant, for instance, that hardly any foreign films could have been shown in this country; that many serious works of literature could not have been imported; and that there would have had to be a search of every aircraft flight and cross-Channel ferry.

I do not regret what was done then, although I find some of the results mildly offensive. I would prefer rather less sexual explicitness on bookstalls, in novels, sometimes in films. But I do not regard this as the major social evil of the day. I find character assassination by some newspapers to be much more so. I note, with a certain sardonic pleasure, that those who fulminate most against the liberal permissiveness of the 1960s have, in the 1980s, not repealed a single one of the measures on which they claim that the licentiousness has been based, despite their massive parliamentary majorities which could be made to jump through any hoop. In this combination of fulmination and inactivity there is a certain hypocrisy.

There has also been, during that dismal decade of the 1980s, a glaring contrast between the desire to permit the most utmost liberty in anything to do with the making of money, with the despoiling of the countryside, with asset-stripping, the destruction of great enterprises and valued public services, and a restrictive attitude to matters of private conduct. I have not changed my mind about the liberalizing measures of the 1960s, which were both inevitable and desirable.

Sir Ralf Dahrendorf made a number of remarks about universities. In England, even more than in Scotland, there was an extraordinarily small base to university education until recently. Until 1830, there was nothing in England except Oxford and Cambridge. Even by 1914, the great municipal universities – Manchester, Liverpool, Leeds, Bristol, Sheffield and the University of Wales – were educating no more than about 6,000 people between them over a three-year period. Even immediately before the Robbins Report we had only a small core of twenty-three universities in this country. So some expansion was absolutely necessary.

We have not had the uncontrolled expansion of Continental Europe. We have been lucky that that has been so. It is hard to think of any continental university which is really competing in the world league. While we may not have enough students, we look after those we admit much better than in the mass-enrolment, lecture-dominated, city universities of Continental Europe with their sink-or-swim attitude and their heavy fall-out rates. I do not think you should look at the state of universities in this country and be altogether dismal.

DISCUSSION

Lord Callaghan, opening the discussion, said that the comments just made provided the opportunity of looking ahead to the future of the educational system, and especially to the problem raised by Sir Ralf of the conflict between quantity and quality in the universities. How could the big expansion that was clearly desirable in Britain be accomplished without loss of quality?

In Sir Ralf's talk, Lord Callaghan had missed a reference to the impact of the Vietnam War, not just on the idealism of young people but on their efforts to avoid the draft. In other countries there had been similar developments. In France, for example, the strict rules of the universities had helped to provoke student reactions.

Terence Higgins argued that in looking back at the changes that took place in the 1960s on issues such as homosexual law reform, abortion law reform and capital punishment, it was important to stress that they were all effected by private members' bills. But they would not have got through unless they had been given – as they were – indefinite time and so, effectively, government sponsorship. All those measures were way ahead of public opinion – indeed, some of them still are now. If one had relied on referenda, these highly desirable changes would not have come about. Compare them with the attempts of the Thatcher Government to change the law on Sunday trading, using a three-line whip. If that measure had been put to a free vote, the measure would surely not have been defeated.

Sir Alec Cairncross pointed out that the session was a reminder of the way in which economic and social factors always interact. It was not possible to form a view of economic policy without regard to the social climate in which it is operating. The 1960s were a good example of this point. Indeed, the principle tended to work both ways: in the 1960s, the fact that people had more money and could spend it as they pleased encouraged young people to think they should be freer in other ways. Economic freedom of choice gave rise to a desire for freedom of action in other spheres.

In the same way, social factors affect economic growth. The fact that Germany and Japan led the world recovery after the war and had the highest rates of growth surely had some association with military prowess. Their highly ordered societies might make for economic growth – but they also encouraged other kinds of more harmful behaviour.

Trying to forecast how economic and social factors might interact in future, Sir Alec wondered what society would do, if economic growth continued over the next century, with the additional wealth. Surely education would be as important a use as any. Universities might be expanded too quickly: but should it not be an important aspiration for any country to see that its citizens are well educated? That might not mean that everybody should go to university – people could be educated in other ways that might be just as important. He shared with Sir Ralf the conviction that education was not the touchstone of economic success. It was not necessarily true that education paid off, beyond a certain point, in economic prowess. He would not want to double the number of undergraduates purely on the grounds that it would lead to faster growth.

Lord Callaghan, pointing out that he and Lord O'Brien were the only people at the conference without a university education, argued that the hunger for education was no less than it was in the 1920s and the 1930s, when he had grown up. He recalled in the 1930s that the *Daily Herald* had boosted its circulation by offering, for half a crown and then five shillings, the prefaces of Bernard Shaw. The education for young people in ordinary state schools was now much wider, but the hunger for education was still there. He was convinced that it was necessary to educate far more young people to a higher level, but wondered how this was to be done without undermining standards, especially in universities.

He was puzzled by the way that influences on students that might seem peculiar to one country spread abroad. The Vietnam War had an effect, not just on the idealism of young people in America, but through the draft. Why did that have such an impact in other countries too? In France, the strict rules and regulations in the universities had an impact on the attitude of students. But what had stirred students in other countries?

Many people in the United States thought their country now had a comparative advantage in nothing, argued *James Tobin*. In fact, the United States appeared still to have a comparative advantage in higher education, and particularly in graduate education. He had recently visited a tyre factory in South Korea. It had been extremely high-tech, with young Koreans sitting at video screens, directing robotic assembly lines and designing new tyres on computer. They had learned their skills at the university of Akron, in Ohio. Akron used to be the centre of the American tyre industry. Now, not a single tyre is made there.

Americans were often surprised by the fact that university education in Europe was free, and that it was possible to remain a student for a long time, highly subsidized, without disciplined tests of progress. In the United States, even state universities had been charging more. The trend was towards means-tested assistance, rather than universally free or subsidized higher education. In the case of Yale, students were admitted if they were of high enough quality, and anyone who was admitted would be financed, one way or another.

The success of American universities, he thought, was a testimony to the market. That was evident from the sheer range of institutions – private, state, city, municipal – all competing for students and faculty. It worked well, most of the time. America had also always benefited from the brain drain, which had brought it the best scholars from Europe, and now brought it the best graduate-school students from all over the world.

There was now evidence in America that the pay-off in earnings for further education was greater than ever before – first for high-school graduation, and then for further education.

John Williamson wondered what the evidence was for Sir Ralf's remark that the economic case for education was weak. He agreed with Sir Alec that education was a consumer good, as well as an investment good. So even if the economic case were indeed weak, that would not necessarily be an argument against increasing education. He thought the evidence increasingly suggested that education was an important cause of economic growth. He wondered whether the reconciliation of this view with that advanced by Sir Ralf might lie in the two qualifications Sir Ralf put forward: the link did not exist beyond a certain level of education; and vocational training was exempted. Perhaps some of the things taught in American universities, such as learning to make tyres in Akron, might be regarded as vocational training in Continental Europe.

Professor Malinvaud emphasized a unique feature of the events of 1968 in France: the collusion between the students and the working class. The reason was the resentment of a large part of public opinion against the Gaullist Government that elections had maintained. It was true that there had been deficiencies in the way French universities were run at the time; and that a large number of students, including Danny Cohn-Bendit, had arrived at the new campus at Nanterre before it had been finished. But this and other similar deficiencies did not provide the full explanation.

In retrospect, Professor Malinvaud thought that some responsibility for what happened in 1968 had to be given to a failure of parenthood by his generation, because the children of his generation then had incoherent social values. What had the failure been? He did not know, but suspected that it had to do more with the behaviour of his generation than with its ideas. French intellectual society had been dominated by Marxist philosophy, and that had played a role in the special ideology of the student movement; but there remained more to be explained.

Lord Croham drew on his experience as chairman of a committee set up a few years ago to 'Review the University Grants Committee', the machinery for university funding.

He felt that it was not possible, at least in Britain, to separate the scale and nature of tertiary education from the question of how it was financed. He took it as axiomatic that a large part of the cost of higher education had to come from public funds; and that the academic community – teachers and students – would be seen as a large and sometimes annoying vested interest. More important than directing higher education to promote growth was to ensure that students emerged feeling that they had benefited and others in society, who paid but did not go, also felt that they gained.

His report had argued that, because of the problem of suspected vested interest, funding decisions should be taken by a body which had on it some people from outside the academic world, whose advice the government would tend to respect. The government had accepted his report; but what was being put into effect went in entirely a different direction.

He thought that there were benefits to be had from competition between universities provided that competition was based on their

RALF DAHRENDORF

reputation for excellence. He saw great dangers in funding universities in relation to the number of students they attracted, regardless of the reason. It was right that universities should be regarded as in a notional contractual relationship with the rest of the community, in that they were receiving public support in order to produce something of public benefit. But there were tremendous dangers in trying to draw up business-like contracts between universities and the government. It was right to emphasize the training aspect, rather than the educational aspect, of higher education. But it was wrong to look only at training and to think that, because polytechnics provided training more cheaply than universities, the two kinds of institution and their funding bodies should increasingly be merged. It might be right that students should bear some of the cost of their education. But the way the Government had handled student loans did not make one think it would be beneficial to education.

The degeneration that Sir Ralf had described in European higher education was, *Robert Solow* thought, a result more of the speed with which things happened than of the distance which had been covered. It was rather like giving cars to Italians: it took a generation or so before internalization of the necessary institutional restraints occurred. He wondered what Sir Ralf thought of the American system of higher education. It had started larger than the European, and probably still enrolled a larger fraction of the age group. But while it had expanded since the 1960s, that expansion had been smaller. An important difference was the high differentiation of the American system: it had a tremendous variety of institutions. The private colleges included some very low grade and some very high grade institutions; so did the state-financed universities and colleges, which included the universities of California, Wisconsin and Michigan, as well as many small state colleges in Massachusetts and elsewhere which carried out some vocational training.

The main gap in education, as far as economic growth is concerned, is in the transition from school to work, and not in the universities. In the United States, people believed that West Germany handled that much better.

Taking up Lord Callaghan's reference to the Vietnam War, Professor Solow noted that its continuing influence on thinking in the United States had been apparent from President Bush's anxiety to lay its ghost at the time of the Gulf War. The Vietnam War had undermined authority, because people felt that authority was lying. In particular young people, who if they were conscripted would

154

have to fight, felt the Government was not telling them the truth.

Alan Budd thought the greatest victim of the 1960s in England had been education up to the age of 16. As with so much of the decade's legacy, the origins of this damage had often lain in good intentions: in a desire not to label children as failures for life, and in a belief that there should not be a harsh distinction between academic education in grammar schools and an undervalued vocational education in secondary modern schools. The 1960s saw an outpouring of books, such as Ivan Illich's *Deschooling Society*, trying to prove that education was largely indoctrination. The writings of F.R. Leavis tried to convince people that education was largely about moral issues. Such views could be grossly distorted in the wrong hands. The ideas had been excellent, but some of the results, particularly apparent in state education in London, had been tragic.

At the heart of the matter was the vocational nature of education. What appeared to be destroyed in the 1960s was the idea that schools should, among other things, educate people for work. If, as is so often the case in England, education up to 16 is the only education people are going to get, it should unashamedly include preparation for their working lives. Their prosperity and success will depend to a considerable extent on what they are taught up to the age of 16. That aspect of education has been gravely harmed, and will prove extremely difficult to restore.

Robin Matthews thought that education was even worse than economics in the amount of disagreement that it provoked and the lack of understanding involved with it. It was an area where there were big questions but no big answers. A problem is that governments like big answers. The education system is pushed strongly in one direction; five minutes later, for perfectly plausible reasons, it is pushed back in the other.

Another change of the 1960s, partly associated with the name of Roy Jenkins, had been the change to a multicultural society. This was commonly thought of as a main reason for the dynamism of the United States, but not so in France and Germany. In Britain, there were extraordinary differences, which government surely never planned, between different parts of the country: governments did not plan that there would be many Asians in Bradford, but that Glasgow would remain occupied by Scots and Irish.

Christopher Dow, without doubting the usefulness of discussion of these issues, wondered in precisely what way it was useful and by what channels and through whose decisions the lessons could be expected to be put to use. As an economist, interested in growth, he pondered the impact of growth on social stability and the quality of life, which sometimes seemed harmful, or at least to have seriously harmful aspects. But it seemed difficult – perhaps impossible – to provide properly tested answers to such questions. And even if questions about the social effects of economic growth could be answered, what should be done as a result, and who should do it? Sociological discussion is certainly fascinating, but all of it was not necessarily helpful, and it could be misleading. How did one separate the wheat from the chaff? Was not the means of application of socio-logical knowledge as important a question as those usually contained in what sociology discussed?

David Vines pointed out that he was probably the only participant who had been at university at the end of the 1960s, in Australia and Britain. Many of his generation now faced a mid-life crisis of anomy without the moral equipment which an earlier university education might have provided. The teaching of the younger staff had encouraged that demoralization. Those whose teachings might have helped students to resist it had tended to be Victorian figures of an earlier Christian humanist tradition. There were fewer such people in universities now. They had been intellectually undermined by the democratizing passion of the 1960s, numerically swamped by the expansion, and ruthlessly squeezed financially in the 1980s.

In replying to the debate, *Sir Ralf* noted that earlier discussions had raised the question whether it made sense to have growth targets. This also applied to education. The idea of targets, especially quantitative targets, did not make much sense. Manpower planning of this sort is not likely to work.

Having said that, however, more economic growth, and especially more personal wealth, would increase people's demand for something that society was not providing terribly well. In Britain it was bound to increase the demand for better health care, to an extent that few people really understood. That might lead to demands to increase, or even to double, spending on health over a fairly short period. There might also be a considerable demand for increased education – not necessarily just to raise earnings but for many other reasons. Education for the *troisième âge* – the retired – would be a big issue in the coming decade.

People would increasingly demand education, which countries were badly equipped to provide. Sir Ralf felt strongly that the response should be as local as possible. It should come from a particular educational institution, or community, in order to allow differentiation. As the failure of comprehensive schools to live up to early expectations demonstrated, planning educational reforms at a national level would always lead to strong pressure for undifferentiated structures: to give all teachers the same salary, for example, and to make them work the same hours. The only way to achieve differentiation was to allow demand to grow, and free institutions to respond to demand. It was essential to get away from planning.

Second, education mattered not just up to the age of 16, but from 16 to 18 as well. Until recently, education in England and Wales up to the age of 16 had not been intended to provide any qualifications. It was accepted that about half of all children would leave with no qualifications at all. That fundamental mistake was now being corrected. But the reform of education from 16 to 18 remained critical. The British Government ought for the moment to forget about the reform of higher education and concentrate on the very difficult task of persuading employers to co-operate with organizing the transition from school to work in a more sensible way.

REFERENCES

Bell, D. (1973) *The Coming of Post-industrial Society: A Venture in Social Forecasting*, New York: Basic Books (London: Heinemann 1974).

Dahrendorf, R. (1985) *Law and Order* (Hamlyn Lectures), London: Stevens.

Hirsch, F. (1977) *Social Limits to Growth*, Cambridge, Mass. and London: Harvard University Press.

Inglehardt, R. (1977) *The Silent Revolution: Changing Values and Political Styles among Western Publics*, Princeton: Princeton University Press.

6

DID POLICY ERRORS OF THE 1960s SOW THE SEEDS OF TROUBLE IN THE 1970s?

Robert Solow

I am asked whether the policy errors of the 1960s were responsible for the troubles of the 1970s. One has visions of waves of sentences beginning on the one hand ending on the other. There were certainly policy errors in the 1960s, including a huge one in the United States, and they must have left some fingerprints on the 1970s. Inspector Morse's Sergeant Lewis will no doubt find them. But that cannot be the whole story. There was OPEC after all, and the disruptive oil price increases of 1973–4 and 1979 cannot be blamed on the policies of the 1960s, at least not on the kinds of policies we shall be talking about. I will try to avoid the temptation to waffle, but I run the risk of being unsubtle.

My conclusion is going to be that there were several distinguishable kinds of trouble in the 1970s, at least two. One of them probably does have partial roots in the events and policies of the 1960s; the other probably does not, although it helped to make the first problem worse.

The separable problems I have in mind both have names. That they do so may even help to suggest their separability. One of them came to be called stagflation. Its onset is all too visible in the accompanying tables for the United States and the largest European economies. (I shall ignore Japan throughout, on the principle that the inscrutable East does not become more scrutable just by being talked about.)

The story is no less remarkable for being so obvious. Until 1973 or thereabouts it was easy to be an optimist. In West Germany and the United Kingdom, unemployment was very low and inflation tolerable. In the United Kingdom the unemployment rate averaged 1.5–2.0 per cent between 1960 and 1967 (Table 6.1). In Germany the average was under 1 per cent. The price level (consumer price index

158

Table 6.1 Unemployment rates

Year	United States	France	West Germany	Italy	United Kingdom
1961	6.7	1.3	0.8	3.5	1.5
1962	5.5	1.2	0.7	3.0	2.0
1963	5.7	1.4	0.8	2.5	2.4
1964	5.2	1.1	0.7	2.7	1.8
1965	4.5	1.4	0.6	3.6	1.5
1966	3.8	1.4	0.7	3.9	1.5
1967	3.8	1.8	2.1	3.5	2.3
1968	3.6	2.1	1.5	3.5	2.5
1969	3.5	2.3	0.8	3.4	2.5
1970	4.9	2.5	0.7	3.1	2.6
1971	5.9	2.7	0.8	5.4	3.5
1972	5.6	2.8	1.1	6.4	3.8
1973	4.9	2.7	1.2	6.4	2.7
1974	5.6	2.8	2.6	5.4	2.6
1975	8.5	4.0	4.7	5.9	4.1
1976	7.7	4.4	4.6	6.7	5.7
1977	7.0	4.9	4.5	7.2	6.2
1978	6.0	5.2	4.3	7.2	6.1
1979	5.8	5.9	3.8	7.7	5.7
1980	7.1	6.3	3.8	7.6	7.4

Source: OECD, *Historical Statistics*, various numbers

(CPI)) was rising at about 2.7 per cent per year in Germany and 3.4 per cent per year in Britain (Table 6.2). There is a notion currently popular in the United States that the only possible non-cumulative rate of inflation is zero. You would never have guessed it from the record up to the late 1960s.

In France and Italy the experience was not quite so favourable. In France the unemployment rate, though generally quite low, was rising gradually and steadily after 1964; and the events of 1968 – where is Danny Cohn-Bendit now? – led to an immediate acceleration of inflation. Unemployment and inflation were both higher in Italy than elsewhere, but the disparity was not as great as it later became.

There was more turbulence in the United States as usual. Unemployment was falling throughout the 1960s. The decade began with a recession and got better; but by 1966 there was clear over-heating as a result of the Vietnam War and the fiscal policy that financed it. Inflation started low, was still under 3 per cent in 1967, but reached 6 per cent in 1970, and was then damped down again by the recession of 1970–1. So there were signs of trouble in River City.

Table 6.2 Rates of inflation (CPI)

Year	United States	France	West Germany	Italy	United Kingdom
1960	1.6	3.6	1.4	2.2	1.0
1961	1.0	3.2	2.3	3.0	3.4
1962	1.1	4.8	3.1	5.1	4.3
1963	1.2	4.8	3.0	7.4	1.8
1964	1.3	3.4	2.3	6.0	4.0
1965	1.7	2.5	3.5	4.3	4.8
1966	2.9	2.6	3.5	2.0	3.9
1967	2.9	2.8	1.4	2.0	2.5
1968	4.2	4.5	1.5	1.2	4.7
1969	5.5	6.4	2.7	2.6	5.4
1970	5.9	5.2	3.3	4.9	6.4
1971	4.3	5.5	5.4	4.8	9.4
1972	3.3	6.2	5.5	5.8	7.1
1973	6.2	7.3	7.0	10.8	9.1
1974	11.0	13.7	7.0	10.1	16.0
1975	9.1	11.9	5.9	17.0	24.2
1976	5.8	9.6	4.3	16.8	16.5
1977	6.4	9.4	3.7	17.0	15.8
1978	7.6	9.1	2.7	12.1	8.3
1979	11.3	10.8	4.1	14.8	13.4
1980	13.5	13.6	5.5	12.2	18.0

Source: OECD, *Historical Statistics*, various numbers

Something much more fundamental was going on at the same time. The near quarter-century from 1950 to 1973 was a time of unprecedented productivity increase in the industrial world. GDP per hour worked rose at an average rate of 3.2 per cent per year in the United Kingdom; 5.2 per cent annually in France; 5.9 per cent in West Germany; 2.9 per cent in Italy; and 2.5 per cent in the United States. (Here I should make an exception and quote the Japanese figure: 7.8 per cent per year. Keep in mind that a number rising at that average rate goes from 100 to 562 in twenty-three years.) Income per person rose along with output, as it usually does.

This experience of rising incomes was widely shared within each of the industrial economies. Low unemployment saw to that; and continued prosperity made it easier to dissolve social conflicts. A rising tide lifts most of the ships, and makes it easier to float the others. A general air of optimism pervaded the economic and social thought of the period.

In every one of the large countries – and some of the small ones – the fundamental complexion changed, with the watershed coming somewhere around 1974. In the United States the unemployment rate went from 4.9 per cent in 1973 (down from 5.9 per cent in 1971) to 5.6 per cent in 1974 and 8.5 per cent in the recession of 1975. In the United Kingdom the timing was slightly different: 2.7–2.6 per cent in 1973–4; up to 4.1 per cent in 1975; 5.7 per cent in 1976; and 6.2 per cent in 1977. In the Federal Republic of Germany the numbers were 1.1–1.2 per cent in 1972–3; 2.6 per cent in 1974; and 4.7 per cent in 1975. In France the unemployment rate was level at 2.7–2.8 per cent in 1971–4; rose to 4.0 per cent in 1975; 4.4 per cent in 1976; 4.9 per cent in 1977, and kept on rising. In Italy the pattern was different again: the first jump, from 3.1 to 5.4 per cent, came in 1971, another jump in 1972–3, a small dip in 1974 and then an increase to 5.9 per cent in 1975; 6.7 per cent in 1976; 7.2 per cent in 1977, and then on from there. In every large country except the United States the pattern of high unemployment rates persisted well into the 1980s and has only recently turned around. The reasons for the continued high unemployment and long-term unemployment in the 1980s have been much discussed and I am not going to trespass into that decade here.

So much for 'stag' in the 1970s; now for the 'flation'. The rate of inflation began to accelerate before the persistent rise in unemployment. Beyond that, national patterns show some diversity. In the United States the recession of 1970–1 knocked the CPI inflation rate down from 5.9 per cent in 1970 to 3.3 per cent in 1972. But the CPI rose to 6.2 per cent in 1973; 11.0 per cent (the dreaded double-digit) in 1974; back down to 5.8 per cent in 1976; up to 7.6 per cent in 1978 and then back into double digits in 1979 and after. The pattern in the United Kingdom was qualitatively similar but at a higher level; acceleration began in 1973; inflation peaked at 24.2 per cent in 1974; down to 8.3 per cent in 1978 and then up again in 1979 and 1980. In West Germany the trend in the inflation rate was upward after 1967–8 (1.4–1.5 per cent) to 5.5 per cent in 1971–2; 7.0 per cent in 1973–4; back down to 2.7 per cent in 1978 and then up beyond 6 per cent in 1981. In France acceleration dates from 1968, with a peak at 13.7 per cent in 1974, down only to 9.1 per cent in 1978 and then up to 13.5 per cent in 1980–1. Finally, in Italy, acceleration begins in 1969, with big steps upward in 1973 and 1974, when CPI inflation reached 19 per cent annually, followed by very slow deceleration to 1978 and another small jump in 1979 followed by a big one in 1980 (to 21.2 per cent).

I do not want to dwell on differences between countries. The important generalization, I think, is that an inflationary situation was already visible by the end of the 1960s. The first oil shock fell on pretty dry tinder. The recession of 1975 damped down the flames noticeably, but even so every country had faster inflation in 1978 than at any time in the 1960s. So the second oil shock in 1979 caused every large country to end the decade with another dose of accelerating inflation.

Like nearly everyone else I have taken it for granted that the two OPEC oil-price increases played a central role in the inflation of the 1970s. The timing of events makes that inference irresistible, whatever the purest monetarism might suggest to the contrary. But there is still a paradox lurking here. Oil and energy are important commodities. They figure in the cost of just about everything. Even so, they account for relatively small proportions of GDP in modern industrial economies: something like 5 per cent is the right order of magnitude. Is it reasonable that an event as large and as pervasive as the stagflation of the 1970s could be *just* the consequence of even larger exogenous increases in the price of 5 per cent of GDP? I suppose it is that consideration that tempts us to implicate the policy errors of the 1960s: OPEC is not enough. But neither is OPEC nothing; the timing alone is enough to arouse the suspicion that the excesses of the 1960s are not by themselves sufficient to account for the troubles of the 1970s.

This story gets even more complex when we turn to the productivity numbers. I pointed out earlier that the 1960s (or the longer period 1950–73) were a dream for increasing productivity and incomes. The dream came to an end in 1973. Between 1973 and 1984 GDP per hour rose at annual rates of 2.4 per cent in the United Kingdom; 3.5 per cent in France; 3.0 per cent in West Germany; 1.0 per cent in Italy; and 1.0 per cent in the United States. (The figure for Japan was 3.2 per cent per year.) In every case there was a dramatic deterioration compared with the earlier period. The rate of productivity increase fell by a third or more in each of the large countries, by 60 per cent in Japan.

Here, too, the timing is such as to point the finger inevitably at higher-priced energy. It is not hard to make up plausible stories in which the causation runs exactly that way. Nevertheless I think it has to be said that – although there has been a considerable amount of expert research attempting to go beyond the mere timing, to find a smoking gun or a fingerprint that would confirm those stories – it has always come up short. It is possible to piece together enough growth-accounting details to account for perhaps half of the productivity slowdown. Energy is only a fraction of that half; and the other half is not identifiable with any confidence.

Now what about those excesses of policy in the 1960s? The egregious case, about which there is hardly room for argument, is the financing of the Vietnam War by the Johnson administration in the United States. At the end of 1965 the unemployment rate came down to 4 per cent. That was the figure that had been identified as a target at the beginning of the Kennedy administration, a limit to what could be achieved by demand-side expansion without moving into inflationary territory. Later research has tended to conclude that 4 per cent was half a percentage point (or maybe a bit more) too low. That may be so; my current feeling is that such talk smacks of more precision than the data or the behaviour of the economy will allow. However that may be, the economists of the time, including President Johnson's own advisers, would have recommended – did recommend – that any further net expansionary impulse from fiscal and monetary policy would be dangerously inflationary, a 'policy excess' you might say.

We shall never know what the 1970s would have been like had those warnings been heeded. Instead, the prosecution of the war in Vietnam was allowed to drive the unemployment rate to 3.8 per cent in 1966 and 1967, and then down to 3.5 per cent in 1969. This was not a result of miscalculation or inattention. It was straight politics. The war was becoming unpopular; protests and demonstrations were frequent and visible. Those who favoured the active prosecution of the war feared that a decision to finance the war by taxation would merely emphasize its costs and bring normally conservative elements of the population into opposition. Congress might have substituted cutbacks in Mr Johnson's domestic programmes. Inflation seemed the preferable alternative.

In those ancient days we used to measure the macroeconomic stance of fiscal policy by the 'full-employment surplus', although some of the weaknesses of that indicator were well known to economists. (Others, like its neglect of the whole issue of 'sustainability' of deficits, came to the surface much later.) There has been a recent revival of interest in the definition and measurement of an appropriate index of fiscal stance. Much of it has been carried by the OECD, whose calculations I will be using later on. For the United States in the 1960s, however, I will cite two sources. The first is the McCracken Report, whose measure of fiscal impact did not attempt to standardize for the level of economic activity and thus did not try to separate induced from autonomous changes in budget items. The second is a series produced by Darrel Cohen of the Federal Reserve Board; it gives a discretionary measure, standardized in each year at the initial level of activity and measured as a percentage of the budget (not of GNP) (Table 6.3).

Table 6.3 A measure of discretionary fiscal policy in the United States

Year	$ billion (1982)	Year	$ billion (1982)	Year	$ billion (1982)
1960	– 5.8	1970	– 8.7	1980	5.0
1961	14.2	1971	– 8.1	1981	– 11.6
1962	16.1	1972	15.8	1982	28.0
1963	– 2.3	1973	– 17.5	1983	32.0
1964	14.1	1974	– 2.8	1984	19.5
1965	6.0	1975	14.7	1985	10.7
1966	33.3	1976	1.7		
1967	28.2	1977	4.3		
1968	5.3	1978	8.9		
1969	– 18.0	1979	6.8		

Source: Cohen 1987: 39

The two measures tell slightly different stories; where they differ the Cohen series is to be preferred. It shows the initial expansionary policies of the Kennedy administration, including the tax reduction of 1964. It then exhibits with great clarity the massive fiscal impulse that came from the intensification of the war in 1966 and 1967, *after* the achievement of the 4 per cent target for unemployment. That episode is also clearly visible in the McCracken Report. This clearly inflationary stance was reversed in 1969 with the late passage of a tax increase, and then briefly renewed in 1972, presumably with the Presidential Election in mind. According to the calculations of Blinder and Goldfeld (1976) the fiscal expansion of 1966–7 was accompanied by a further stimulus from monetary policy and then another, considerably sharper, dose of monetary expansion in 1970 and 1971. The later combined fiscal–monetary expansion undid whatever damping of inflation had been accomplished by the 1970 recession. Inflation was accelerating in 1973 before OPEC took a hand.

It is hard to escape the conclusion that this piece of policy perversion stored up a lot of trouble for the United States economy – and for the world economy – in the 1970s. There was a certain amount of bad luck too. It was probably not the fault of deficient policy that a worldwide boom in food and raw material prices supervened at almost the same time as OPEC acted, though better macroeconomic management might have lessened, if not forestalled, that difficulty too. In any case, the first oil shock struck an economy that had already experienced the onset of some policy-induced inflation. Had the timing been different, it is at least possible that the world could have ridden out a brief excursion into supply-side-induced inflation, or perhaps would have been able to reverse it by brief demand contraction. That opportunity never arose.

Whether it was coincidence, destiny or punishment, the fact is that some demand-side inflation was already in the works when OPEC came. The consequences may have lasted well beyond the 1970s. Both casual observation and the behaviour of statistical wage and price' equations suggest that there was a major intensification of inflationary expectations in the 1970s. We still do not know whether the recession and high unemployment of the 1980s has reversed that change. The collapse of the Phillips curve, after its apparent stability in the 1950s and 1960s, might have been postponed or avoided had the supply shock of 1973–4 not supervened on an economy that had been deliberately overheated by the perverse financing of the war in Vietnam.

There was another piece of mistaken policy that originated in the United States in the 1960s and found its way very directly into the European economies. This was the prolonged attempt to maintain the parity of the dollar at what can now pretty clearly be seen to have been an overvalued exchange rate. The main trading partners of the United States were cajoled into holding large quantities of dollars. The liquidity thus created was an embarrassment, to put it mildly, in the inflationary 1970s. The policy error here, although it originated in the deteriorating competitiveness of the US economy, was not the sole property of the US Government. The recipients of all those dollars could have revalued their own currencies and some of them did, although probably too little and too late. Alternatively they could have gone further in sterilizing their incremental holdings of dollars. That they did not do so was not for lack of economic understanding. Political reasons overrode the simple claims of economic policy here too.

It is worth taking a look at the stance of fiscal policy in the large European economies during this same period. Tables 6.4. and 6.5 (which I owe to the kindness of J.–C. Chouraqui of the OECD) show the level and the percentage change of the cyclically adjusted budget balance as a fraction of trend GNP in Germany, France, Italy and the

Table 6.4 General government budget balances, cyclically adjusted

Year	% Level of trend GDP/GNP				
	United States	*Germany*	*France*	*Italy*	*United Kingdom*
1965	—	− 1.4	0.1	− 4.0	− 0.7
1966	—	− 0.5	− 0.2	− 4.0	0.1
1967	—	− 0.1	− 0.3	− 2.6	− 3.8
1968	—	0.0	− 0.7	− 3.5	− 0.6
1969	—	0.6	0.8	− 3.9	2.2
1970	− 0.7	− 0.5	0.3	− 4.2	3.3
1971	− 1.3	− 0.4	0.1	− 5.5	1.9
1972	− 0.5	− 0.7	0.4	− 7.8	− 0.8
1973	− 0.5	0.8	0.3	− 8.3	− 3.6
1974	− 0.4	− 1.0	0.7	− 8.7	− 4.1
1975	− 2.8	− 3.7	− 1.0	− 11.7	− 3.9
1976	− 1.4	− 3.4	− 0.2	− 9.8	− 4.8
1977	− 1.0	− 2.9	− 0.8	− 8.5	− 3.6
1978	− 1.0	− 3.7	− 2.7	− 10.5	− 5.7
1979	− 0.6	− 4.9	− 2.0	− 11.2	− 5.3
1980	− 1.5	− 4.8	− 0.9	− 9.9	− 3.8

Source: OECD, *Historical Statistics*

Table 6.5 General government budget balances, cyclically adjusted

Year	% Change of trend GDP/GNP				
	United States	*Germany*	*France*	*Italy*	*United Kingdom*
1965	—	—	—	—	—
1966	—	0.9	− 0.3	0.0	0.7
1967	—	0.5	− 0.1	1.4	− 0.8
1968	—	0.0	− 0.4	− 0.8	0.2
1969	—	0.6	1.5	− 0.5	2.8
1970	—	− 1.2	− 0.6	− 0.3	1.0
1971	− 0.6	0.1	− 0.2	− 1.3	− 1.3
1972	0.8	− 0.3	0.3	− 2.3	− 2.8
1973	0.0	1.5	− 0.1	− 0.5	− 2.8
1974	0.0	− 1.8	0.5	− 0.4	− 0.5
1975	− 2.3	− 2.7	− 1.7	− 3.0	0.2
1976	1.4	0.3	0.8	1.9	− 1.0
1977	0.4	0.5	− 0.7	1.2	1.3
1978	0.0	− 0.8	− 1.8	− 1.9	− 2.1
1979	0.4	− 1.3	0.7	− 0.7	0.4
1980	− 0.9	0.2	1.1	1.3	1.5

Source: OECD, *Historical Statistics*

Table 6.6 Primary balances, cyclically adjusted

Year	% Level of trend GDP/GNP				
	United States	Germany	France	Italy	United Kingdom
1970	0.5	1.1	0.7	− 4.2	5.5
1971	− 0.2	1.2	0.5	− 5.5	3.8
1972	0.6	0.8	0.6	− 7.8	0.9
1973	0.7	2.6	0.4	− 8.3	− 1.8
1974	0.6	0.8	0.8	− 8.7	− 1.9
1975	− 1.7	− 2.2	− 0.5	− 11.7	− 1.9
1976	− 0.2	− 1.9	0.3	− 9.8	− 2.6
1977	0.2	− 1.4	− 0.4	− 8.5	− 1.0
1978	0.2	− 2.3	− 2.1	− 10.5	− 3.0
1979	0.6	− 3.6	− 1.2	− 11.2	− 2.4
1980	− 0.2	− 3.5	− 0.1	− 5.1	− 0.7
1981	0.8	− 2.7	− 1.1	− 6.7	1.8
1982	0.0	− 0.3	− 2.0	− 4.5	2.4
1983	− 0.2	1.0	− 1.1	− 2.9	1.3
1984	− 0.3	1.3	0.0	− 3.4	1.0
1985	− 1.1	2.3	0.4	− 4.4	1.7

Source: OECD, *Historical Statistics*

Table 6.7 Primary balances, cyclically adjusted

Year	% Change of trend GDP/GNP				
	United States	Germany	France	Italy	United Kingdom
1970	—	—	—	—	—
1971	− 0.7	0.1	− 0.2	− 1.3	− 1.7
1972	0.7	− 0.4	0.2	− 2.3	− 2.9
1973	0.1	1.7	− 0.3	− 0.5	− 2.7
1974	− 0.1	− 1.8	0.5	− 0.4	− 0.2
1975	− 2.3	− 3.0	− 1.3	− 3.0	0.0
1976	1.5	0.4	0.8	1.9	− 0.6
1977	0.4	0.5	− 0.6	1.2	1.5
1978	0.0	− 0.9	− 1.7	− 1.9	− 2.0
1979	0.4	− 1.3	0.9	− 0.7	0.6
1980	− 0.8	0.1	1.1	6.1	1.7
1981	1.0	0.7	− 1.0	− 1.7	2.5
1982	− 0.7	2.5	− 0.9	2.2	0.6
1983	− 0.3	1.3	0.9	1.6	− 1.2
1984	0.0	0.3	1.1	− 0.5	− 0.2
1985	− 0.8	1.0	0.3	− 1.1	0.6

Source: OECD, *Historical Statistics*

United Kingdom. I shall pay attention mainly to the full cyclically adjusted balance; for completeness I cite also the cyclically adjusted primary balances (i.e. net of interest payments on publicly held government debt) (Tables 6.6 and 6.7). These provide a better indication of the long-run sustainability of fiscal policy, and they may have some relevance for the short run as well if the marginal propensity to save out of interest payments on government debt is very high.

The record in the late 1960s is quite varied, but not extreme. In 1964–5, although the tables do not cover those years, there was an electioneering episode of fiscal stimulus in Germany. In turn, German expansion spilled over into other European economies. Between 1965 and 1969 the cyclically adjusted deficit was diminishing in Germany, i.e. fiscal policy was mildly contractionary by this rough measure. In France there was a net expansionary impulse in 1966, 1967 and 1968, which was reversed in 1969. Italy recorded a shift toward tightening in 1967, but then successive expansionary moves in every subsequent year until 1976. In the United Kingdom, fiscal policy was on the whole contractionary until 1971, though not consistently; then, presumably in response to the rise in unemployment in 1971 and 1972 and despite the inflation of those years, fiscal policy turned expansionary more or less until the end of the decade.

Fine-tuning is much easier after the fact than before, by virtue of what Walter Heller used to call 20–20 hindsight. One should keep firmly in mind that this is the beginning of the era of stagflation. That is precisely why we are so interested in it. In 1975 the CPI rose by 9 per cent in the United States, 12 per cent in France, 6 per cent in Germany, 17 per cent in Italy and 24 per cent in the United Kingdom. Why, then, did the cyclically adjusted deficit rise in the United States, France, Germany and Italy and remain essentially neutral in the United Kingdom? Because the unemployment rate was at or near a historic peak in every one of those countries (not quite in Italy until 1976). The first lesson we have learned from those years is that, in the face of an adverse supply shock, aggregate-demand-oriented policy is not enough. And the second lesson is that there is a grave shortage of aggregate-supply-oriented policies. One does not have to be very cynical to observe that the closest we have come to a supply-side policy is to blame the victim and learn to live with high unemployment.

The original question can be asked in two ways. (1) Would the policy mistakes of the 1960s have made a mess of the 1970s even without the oil-price increases of 1973–4 and 1979? (2) Would the oil shocks have made a mess of the 1970s even without the inflationary legacy of the 1960s? My suggested answer is that the combination of the two was, so to speak, worse than the sum of the parts. There was no getting away from the aftermath of the Vietnam War; some inflation had to be squeezed out of the North American and European economies. But the oil shocks did more than just add to the disinflationary need. They did at least two things more. The less important was that they confronted the policy-making machinery with the novel and intrinsically more difficult problem of dealing with a supply-induced inflation. The more important, I guess, is that the drawn-out sequence of events led to the deeper embedding of inflationary expectations. Had OPEC never happened, the policy errors of the 1960s would have exacted a much smaller price.

For much the same reasons, dealing with the oil shocks was much more difficult because they impinged on an already potentially inflationary situation. Had Vietnam never happened, a shorter disinflationary episode might have done the job. Even so I would emphasize that there is still no good way to deal with supply-side-induced inflation. It is quite true that the history of incomes policies is not exactly a string of triumphs. That the idea does not die is an indicator that there are no better ideas.

Now I would like to push the argument one step further. There was another sort of problem associated with the 1970s (and after) that goes under the name 'productivity slowdown'. All over the industrial world, productivity rose much less rapidly in the 1970s and 1980s than in the 1950s and 1960s. I have already cited some figures on labour productivity to that effect. The watershed is often placed at 1973 or thereabouts, but 1969 is another candidate for the change in the United States. (I do not know about elsewhere. In the nature of the case such an event cannot seriously be said to have occurred at a given instant.)

Table 6.8 contains figures on the growth of total factor productivity in three intervals. This is likely to be a better indicator of exogenous

Table 6.8 Rates of growth of total factor productivity

Period	United States	France	Germany	United Kingdom	Japan
1913–50	1.99	1.42	0.86	1.15	1.10
1950–73	1.85	4.02	4.32	2.14	5.79
1973–84	0.52	1.84	1.55	1.22	1.21

Source: OECD, *Historical Statistics*

productivity growth than output per unit of labour. The main generalizations are obvious from the figures. First, the 1950s and 1960s were a special period. Neither before nor after those decades did productivity surge so strongly. It is hard to resist the notion that the 1970s and 1980s marked a return to 'normal' after an exceptional episode. One can even invent plausible explanations: for instance, the delayed exploitation of technological innovations created in the 1930s and 1940s but placed in cold storage during the Great Depression and the Second World War. Nevertheless, I think that temptation should be resisted. There is no strong reason to believe that total factor productivity has a 'normal' rate of change. Anyway, that is an altogether different issue.

The second obvious generalization is that the pattern of acceleration followed by deceleration is common to all the major countries, including Japan. (My source did not provide figures for Italy.) That suggests, although it does not ensure, that the pattern was not the consequence of macroeconomic policy choices.

The argument I want to make is that the productivity slowdown was itself a contributor to the macroeconomic troubles of the 1970s. It made the problem of stagflation harder to deal with. The point I have in mind is easiest to see in connection with the adverse supply shocks. One way or another the consequent loss of real income had to be shared out. Attempts to maintain real wages or real property incomes tend to be resolved – or rather dissipated – by price increases. The process can, of course, be resisted or reversed by the monetary and fiscal authorities, but there is no comfort in that sage remark. The difficulty just translates itself: a deeper recession, with higher unemployment, is needed to achieve any given amount of disinflation. The productivity slowdown makes the job of macroeconomic policy that much harder. It must enforce not only the transfer of real income to oil producers, but also the inability of the economic system to dispense the normal productivity gains to income recipients. All this will appear in the *ex post* econometrics as wage inertia (or as disappointed expectations – thus demonstrating, in fact, how hard it is to distinguish between the two).

This mechanism is not tied to oil shocks or similar events. Any model of inflation that has a place for the competing-claims mechanism is likely to conclude that a productivity slowdown is stagflationary until normal expectations of income gains are revised downward. Revision will be a slow process because the deceleration of productivity only emerges slowly, in a piecemeal way.

I mentioned earlier that the timing of the slowdown led to the natural inference that it was somehow a by-product of the rise in the world price of oil and energy generally. On the whole that inference has not stood up. It is just as likely, maybe more so, that the preceding period of rapid productivity growth was the exceptional event, as illustrated earlier. Growth-accounting studies have led to some important insights, for example a failure of capital formation to keep up with accelerating growth of the labour force in the 1970s, or a very small diversion of investment into pollution control that provides unmeasured benefits, and so on. Some of these sources of slower measured growth might have been offset by proper policy (and some should not have been). In that sense one may say that policy errors in the 1960s led to problems in the 1970s. But it must be understood that the relevant policy errors are not the ones we usually have in mind in making the connection. Besides, it should be remembered that a good chunk of the slowdown remains mysterious in origin. There was no apparent task for policy.

This story is too simple to need summarizing. The policies that led to avoidable overheating and excess liquidity in the 1960s were guilty of manslaughter but not first-degree murder. Events of the 1970s – OPEC, the productivity slowdown and a little mischief at the time of the 1972 elections – were an important part of the plot.

What sort of strategy of rehabilitation is suggested by this tale of criminal conspiracy? It is pure naivety to complain that the demands of political advantage should not be allowed to mess up the economy. They have and they will. Perhaps the main conclusion to be drawn is not so different from the McCracken Committee's. There is a safe zone that lies between overstressing the economy on one side and self-reinforcing slack on the other. That zone is not infinitely wide, but it is not a thin line either. The fundamental goal of demand management is to keep the economy inside that safe zone. To say that fine-tuning is beyond us is not to say that policy can wait until the economy is on the edge before taking preventive action. The alternative to fine-tuning is not large discrete policy shifts; it is, to resurrect a phrase, a leaning against the wind.

That is fine as far as it goes. But there is a loose end. Part of the problem of the 1970s was that trouble came in the form of adverse supply shocks. In those circumstances demand management is not enough, and there appears to be nothing else. (Nothing is to be expected from the mere absence of demand management, either.) The McCracken Committee's passage on incomes policies strikes what may be, alas, the right note. They walk around the idea that it can apparently not be done well, wish that it could be done at all, and end up neither here nor there. Wishful thinking offers only the possibility that the dismal record of incomes policies comes from the fact that governments have resorted to them in the vain hope of rescuing the economy from ill-judged demand-side policies. That will never work. Can one imagine demand management and incomes policies working together and not in opposition? I suppose the answer is yes. With some effort one can imagine that.

AMPLIFICATION

In introducing his paper, Professor Solow said that if the question was whether the policy-makers and their advisers in the 1960s had much to feel guilty about his answers would be 'a little'. There was always plenty of guilt to go around and he doubted whether one could blame much on the policy errors of the 1960s.

Had the conference taken place in the United States it would have been more impersonal, partly because Cabinet Ministers there were drawn from a different social spectrum and partly because power was shared with Congress in a way not paralleled in Britain. John F. Kennedy felt that he was barely President of the United States and although he had a formal majority in Congress it retained a large degree of independence or even hostility towards him. There would also be a different view of the substance of policy in the 1960s in the United States. For example, the nostalgia for incomes policy apparent in the conference would be entirely foreign to American economists under 50, who would regard the very idea as laughable.

Inflation had begun to accelerate in the United States at the end of 1965 or early in 1966 – well before it did in Europe – but it was not until about 1974 that there was a broad semi-permanent increase in unemployment. This was characterized by some economists as a rise in the natural rate of unemployment – a description Professor Solow found unenlightening since it attributed the acceleration in inflation to this rise but at the same time pointed to the acceleration as the sole evidence that there had been such a rise.

Governments and economists had been lulled by the successes of the 1960s into underestimating the force of inflationary expectations by the end of the decade. Contractionary measures should have been taken earlier. No doubt if there had been no rise in oil prices and no commodity boom, inflation might have been reversed in the usual way by a relatively mild contraction. To that extent there was bad luck. But the biggest error had nothing to do with lack of economic understanding. It arose from President Johnson's failure to raise taxes in spite of strong warnings from his advisers of the consequences. He no doubt feared that this revelation of the cost of an unpopular war would have made it impossible to continue it or, as Professor Tobin had suggested, that it would have given Congress an opportunity to cut social expenditure at the expense of the Great Society programme.

A second policy error was to prolong the overvaluation of the dollar and cajole creditor countries into holding dollars they did not want. Some blame here, however, attached also to other countries for failing to appreciate their currencies or sterilize the inflow of dollars.

Professor Solow concluded by emphasizing the effect on inflation of the slowing down of productivity growth in the 1970s described in his paper. He warned against reliance on incomes policy to offset a too expansionary policy. It was, he thought, just conceivable that incomes policy might work differently if used in conjunction with appropriate demand management in ways to which younger economists gave no thought.

COMMENTS BY ALEC CAIRNCROSS

Whatever errors of policy were committed in the 1960s, it was a highly successful decade from the economic point of view. In Britain, the growth in GDP was about 45 per cent more than in the 1950s and compared favourably with growth in the 1970s.

The question remains whether this had involved acquiescing in situations and policies that had undesirable consequences in the 1970s. Were there forces working away unsuppressed that came to the surface later and might have been brought under control by earlier action? Were there tolerance and encouragement of attitudes and expectations likely to create problems sooner or later and that might be increasingly difficult to cope with?

Of the troubles in the 1970s the main one was unquestionably more rapid inflation, and the need to curb it had superseded unemployment as top priority. Inflation had been accompanied by a slower growth or even a fall in employment and production. Simultaneously productivity growth had slackened. As Professor Solow had pointed out, this slackening threw a greater burden on anti-inflationary policy by raising costs per unit of output. In Sir Alec's view, the falling-off in productivity growth was intimately connected with the slower growth in output. It had always been recognized that there was a short-term relationship between the two but there was also a longer-term association. If the more rapid growth in the 1950s owed something to the postponement of improvements set aside in the 1930s until conditions were more propitious, the less rapid growth from the mid-1970s illustrated the process in reverse. Innovations were more readily introduced with the prospect of a rapidly expanding market, especially if heavy investment was involved, and were deferred when the business outlook was less reassuring. When markets again expanded rapidly in the late 1980s, productivity growth recovered too, and in the United Kingdom had apparently regained the rates achieved in the 1960s.

The alternative view was that the rapid growth in productivity up to the 1970s reflected a convergence of productivity levels on what had already been achieved in the United States; and that, once the catching-up process was complete and industry in the laggard countries was closer to the frontier of technology, there were inevitably fewer opportunities of improving industrial practice. While there was force in this explanation, the abrupt change in the business outlook and in the rate of market expansion after 1974 had also had an important influence.

In the 1960s there had been no thought of this change in trend. Full employment was more or less taken for granted and policy in Britain was directed to *accelerating* growth. It was believed that such acceleration was within the power of governments, as indeed was obviously true where the necessary infrastructure had yet to be created. But in the United Kingdom the consequence of pursuing faster growth had been overexpansion and inflation just when the government was anxious to restore competitive power. The British economy had been at full stretch since 1945, without the slack available on the continent that allowed the domestic market to expand rapidly. Growth was slower and, from the 1960s, inflation was faster.

In the 1960s the struggle with inflation took the form of an exchange-rate struggle aimed at improving competitive power. But just as the US government failed to check demand by raising taxes, so the British government failed to use stop–go in 1964, as it had done previously, and let demand increase when the best hope of avoiding devaluation was to reduce the pressure and increase the margin of spare capacity. By the time an incomes policy could be introduced earnings were rising at 10 per cent per annum and devaluation had become almost unavoidable. Governments could intervene too much but they could also do too little and too late. If inflation was not scotched as it occurred, more violent adjustments, including devaluation, would be necessary later. A ratchet effect was liable to come into play and 2 per cent inflation might rise to 4 per cent, 6 per cent or more with no fresh stimulus to demand.

Each session of the conference had had a bearing on the responsibility for the troubles of the 1970s. Looking back to the first session, Sir Alec said that no explanation had been given of the duration of the Golden Age. The move to a higher level of employment after the war had called for a corresponding enlargement of the capital stock and had generated high investment demand. Marshall Aid had provided a bridge across what might have been a post-war depression and given time for the conviction to grow that governments would act to maintain full employment. Some of the expansionary forces were exhaustible but governments had never had to exert themselves to drum up demand before the mid-1970s. The question was why later years were so different.

Reviewing the second session, Sir Alec suggested that the more moderate inflation of the 1950s and 1960s reflected recollections of earlier decades. We were living on the exhaustible asset of past memories that slowed down reactions to price increases. The bursts of inflation that occurred were usually set going by a rise in import prices and a swing in the terms of trade, as in 1951 and 1973, with wages reacting to price increases. But by the end of the 1960s there was some acceleration in wage increases without much prompting from international prices. This was important because a rise in commodity prices was less likely to be self-perpetuating than a rise in money wages. There was no 'annual round' of commodity price increases.

The difference between domestic and international influences was also important in the third session. Swings in the terms of trade imposed a tax on the community that somebody had to bear; and quite apart from the inflationary stuggle to which this gave rise, it required time to effect the necessary adjustments. For this purpose larger reserves were an important instrument that had not been mentioned. So far as domestic influences in the inflationary process were concerned it was important to recognize the role of public opinion. Had enough been done in the 1960s to generate public alarm and detestation of higher inflation? In Germany it was not so much the policies of the Bundesbank as the concern of the public that kept inflation in check and an appreciation by wage earners and their representatives of the dangers of excessive increases in wages.

DISCUSSION

Lord Callaghan, commenting on Sir Alec's concluding observation, pointed out that trade union officials in Britain had sometimes found employers willing to concede wage increases that the officials had regarded as unrealistic and had put forward only under pressure from their members.

Before inviting discussion of the paper, he then warned the group of his intention to take a vote at the end of the session. He was told that academics preferred discussion to decisions whereas decisions were the business of Cabinets. So he proposed to embarrass the group by insisting that they should make up their minds and vote on the issue under debate without amendment. Abstentions would be allowed but discouraged!

David Worswick said that there had been a clear slowdown in productivity in the United States before 1973 at the end of a period of rising demand, while in Europe the slowdown came after 1973. In the United Kingdom production and productivity moved together and it was natural in the 1970s to start by attributing the fall in both to a slackening of demand. When asked by Professor Matthews at a conference whether productivity gained from high demand he concluded that on balance it did. He held to this view until the mid-1980s but accepted that the sustained expansion of the 1980s went against the proposition.

Professor Kloten cited German experience after 1969. Long-run economic growth at 4–5 per cent had been taken for granted and policy had aimed at the stabilization of aggregate demand by anti-cyclical demand management combined with a moderate incomes policy and the use of monetary policy. This was intended to reconcile the views of the liberals and the neo-Keynesians. But it became increasingly clear in 1971–3 that neither the private sector nor the public sector (nor the politicians) was conforming to the assumed pattern of behaviour. In 1973 the Council of Economic Experts (chaired by himself) had proposed a new policy assignment, with a medium-term orientation of monetary policy, that focused primarily on productive potential and aimed to keep inflation to a low but unavoidable rate. Fiscal policy would be neutral in relation to the business cycle while monetary policy would take the lead. This new approach to stabilization policy was accepted but overruled in 1973 by the oil price shock and the subsequent clash in 1974 between monetary policy and wage policy. This was one of the main reasons for the rise in the rate of unemployment and the lower growth in productive potential, accompanied by a large expansion in public-sector spending (from 39 per cent to almost 50 per cent of GNP between 1970 and 1980), leading to signs of stagflation. The response to these events was that stabilization policy must include encouragement of investment by means of regulatory policy, and so embrace short-term, medium-term and long-term features, the latter being given increasing emphasis in the second half of the decade. The composition of this German version of a supply-side policy – different from the American version – should vary with circumstances, with priority given to medium-term considerations through appropriate monetary and fiscal targets supported by short-term measures and, in special cases, by incomes policy.

Andrea Boltho accepted that there had been both policy mistakes and accidents. After the shock of 1973 Europe had done much, much worse than either the United States or Japan. Instead of catching up, as in the years before 1973, Europe fell back in relation to the United States. Recovery came only in the late 1980s after the counter-oil shock. This might be due to policy mistakes in the 1980s when a tight policy stance was maintained for too long. But perhaps also there had been one or two policy trends from the 1960s that made European adaptation, as opposed to Japanese and American, more difficult. For example, it was argued by Herbert Giersch and Assar Lindbeck that Europe overdid the development of the welfare state so that when growth broke down large budget deficits were inevitably generated through loss of revenue. These were in some countries much larger than any American deficit and might account for Europe's greater difficulties. A second factor was a spate of trade union inspired legislation on the continent in the late 1960s and early 1970s, which legalized what might be called the permanent employment of the labour force. This impeded large redundancies, made the discharge of workers much more difficult and reduced freedom to change the disposition of the labour force within the factory or office. In Italy in 1970, for example, legislation required management to obtain trade union agreement when firms sought to re-tool or improve productive performance. All this legislation could hardly fail to slow down productivity growth and contributed to the difficulties of the 1970s.

Terence Higgins thought that the seeds of trouble had been thrown out of the window by the incoming government in 1970. Incomes policy had been abandoned. Indirect taxation had been overhauled and purchase tax replaced by value added tax (VAT). Devaluation had already occurred.

Robin Matthews had no doubt that the 1960s contributed to more rapid inflation in the 1970s but, if he were given two votes, would be agnostic about the slowdown in productivity. When he co-operated in a study of growth in different countries with Professor Malinvaud, the latter, by finishing earlier, was exposed to a greater risk of error over trends. The first study to be completed, by Rosovsky and Ohkawa on Japan, was entitled, ironically enough, 'trend acceleration', which they wrongly expected to continue.

Samuel Brittan proposed to vote 'yes'. He retracted a view he had expressed thirty years ago that demand should be expanded more rapidly in the interests of accelerating growth. There had been too much demand management, not too little. In his view, there were too many accidents in Professor Solow's paper. The rise in international commodity prices in 1972–3 had not been an accident but followed too rapid an expansion in international demand. There had been a wrong theory of demand management in 1970 and some economists he would not dare to mention had been nearer the truth. If policy assumed that demand management could influence real, not just nominal, variables, there would sooner or later be an inflationary explosion.

Andrew Crockett said that the central problem of the 1970s had been inflation: how to get it under control and out of the system. Although there were important extenuating circumstances, the seeds of that inflation were sown in the 1960s. There was evidence suggesting that the kind of overheating experienced in the 1960s could have been corrected more quickly and at less cost than eventually was necessary. However, the public support to combat inflation at the kind of levels that seemed to be imaginable – 2, 3, 4 or 5 per cent – was simply not there. He agreed with Sir Alec that, however convinced a government or central bank might be of the need to curb inflation, it could not be done in the absence of public support. He also agreed that high commodity prices in 1973 were not just an accident. Nobody had mentioned the role of the Club of Rome. At that time there had been a public feeling that we were running out of resources and this added to the monetary influences in creating a commodity price boom that tipped things over.

John Williamson said there were three basic parameters relevant to the orientation of demand management policy. There was first the potential rate of growth given by the supply side, about which there was little to be done in the short run. Then there was the fundamental equilibrium rate of exchange. Third, there was the NAIRU, or the natural rate of unemployment. He was sad to hear this dismissed by Professor Solow as an 'unenlightening' concept. But it was fundamental to know whether the natural rate had risen. If so it was not just the interaction between inflationary expectations and commodity price increases that produced the trouble, but something needing a more fundamental long-lasting solution.

Sir Donald MacDougall proposed to vote 'no'. He thought that there was a bad start to the 1960s in the failure to devalue and the 'Christine Keeler boom'. But by 1970 the economy was in reasonable shape. There had been a massive transfer of resources to benefit the balance of payments and investment while containing inflation to 5 per cent. What really caused the trouble was the first oil shock and the excessive expansion of demand in 1972–3.

Lord Callaghan said that, in his view, incomes policy was not a long-term instrument. He was doubtful whether it could be made to work with demand management as Professor Solow had suggested. It formalized wage differentials far too much at the start and introduced too many distortions of relationships and too much rigidity as time went on. A short-term instrument – yes. A long-term instrument – no.

As to how a healthy balance could be maintained between growth, low inflation, high employment, balance of payments etc. he was much in favour of self-enforcing rules, if the right rules could be found, as opposed to better co-ordination. If this was not possible, then it was better to have the system of surveillance developed in the 1980s by Nigel Lawson and others: critical analysis in group discussion by one's peers from other countries. This could affect informed opinion very much. The system should be continued and developed with even more intensity.

CONCLUDING COMMENTS
BY ROBERT SOLOW

I will respond only to a few of the questions raised in the discussion, primarily the ones that touch on issues of principle rather than particular events.

First of all there is the point, made by Alec Cairncross and David Worswick, that productivity may respond to the expansion of demand, as against the alternative that productivity change is autonomous and merely widens or narrows the scope available for demand expansion. It is common ground that there is a normal business-cycle pattern to measured productivity growth, and we understand the mechanisms – labour hoarding, overhead costs – that give rise to it. That is not the issue here: if demand expansion in the 1970s would have brought forth further increases in productivity, they would have come not from improved capacity utilization but from induced innovation. That is an attractive hypothesis; it must sometimes happen that way. But I do not read the historical record as suggesting that this is a reliable mechanism. Look at the long upswing of the 1980s in the United States, accompanied by persistent slow growth of productivity and correspondingly rapid growth of employment. The productivity slowdown of the 1970s and 1980s was so nearly universal across countries as to preclude any strong relations to individual demand experience.

Second, I had better explain to John Williamson why I find the 'natural rate of unemployment' an unenlightening concept. I have no problem with the notion that there is at any time in any economy an 'equilibrium' rate of unemployment. Whatever one means by equilibrium, an unemployment rate will be part of the constellation. There could indeed be several equilibria, several states in which the economy could stay once it was there, and an unemployment rate attached to each one. The notion that an even slightly higher or lower unemployment rate would be accompanied inevitably by accelerating deflation or inflation has only the flimsiest theoretical and empirical foundation. And to use the behaviour of the price level to *measure* the natural rate is to empty the notion of all explanatory value. To be useful, the natural rate would have to be a slowly moving structural characteristic of each economy and there would have to be some independent way of estimating and forecasting it. It does not seem that way.

I agree with Lord Callaghan that incomes policy is at best a short-run instrument and surely not a long-run instrument. What I meant by my remark is that it is futile to run an over-expansionary demand policy and hope to restrain wages and prices by incomes policy. But when a disinflation is necessary, say, there might be something to be said for simultaneously restraining demand and operating an incomes policy. US experience is that wage differentials move slowly anyway,

180

and little would be lost if they were briefly frozen by a temporary incomes policy. I hope Lord Callaghan would go along with that view.

Finally, introductory remarks already state my agreement with those participants who think that policy moved too slowly against inflation in the late 1960s. Mr Brittan will some day explain to me why the debt-financed purchase of a car by a private citizen has real effects while a debt-financed purchase of a car by the Post Office does not.

REFERENCES

Blinder, A.S. and Goldfeld, S.M. (1976) 'New measures of fiscal and monetary policy, 1958–73', *American Economic Review* 66, no. 5, pp. 780–97.

Cohen, D. (1987) 'Models and measures of fiscal policy', Working Paper 70, Board of Governors of the Federal Reserve System, March.

CONCLUSION OF THE CONFERENCE

Concluding the conference, Lord Callaghan took a vote on the questions just debated. The score was nine in favour, eight against – a verdict described by the Chairman as 'not proven'.

CALENDAR OF MAIN EVENTS IN THE 1960s

Readers may find it useful to have a brief calendar of events in the 1960s as a source of reference for events discussed in the text. What follows is essentially a much abbreviated version of the series of calendars included annually in the first quarterly number of the *National Institute Economic Review*.

Reference to the full calendar brings home the enormous number of official reports issued every year: on prices and incomes (170 reports from the National Board for Prices and Incomes between 1965 and 1970, apart from the succession of White Papers issued by the government); on mergers, monopolies and restrictive practices; on strikes; and on all the government's own business. The items included below are heavily concentrated on macroeconomic policy and on the affairs of the United Kingdom. But they include a selection of important political and other events to convey something of the background to the development of economic policy.

1960

4 January	End of eight months' steel strike in the United States
13 March	Development Assistance Group set up
28 April	First call in the United Kingdom for Special Deposits
2 May	European Free Trade Area begins to operate
13 May	Commonwealth Prime Ministers' Conference ends
3 June	Bank rate raised to 6 per cent
12 August	Federal Reserve discount rate reduced to 3 per cent
30 August	Abandonment of over 1,000 restrictive agreements announced in the United Kingdom
14 September	Foundation of OPEC
22 September	West Germany budgets for a 6 per cent increase in GNP in 1961

| 8 November | Election of John F. Kennedy as President of the United States |

1961

15 February	Ten European countries move to convertibility under Article 8
5 March	Deutschmark revalued by 5 per cent
17 April	UK budget introduces two tax 'regulators' and reduces surtax on earned incomes
31 May	South Africa leaves the Commonwealth
20 July	Plowden Report on Control of Public Expenditure (Cmnd 1432)
25 July	UK mini-budget imposes indirect tax regulator, raises bank rate to 7 per cent and announces 'pay pause' in the public sector
31 July	Fourth and final report of Council on Prices, Productivity and Incomes recommending a long-term study of economic growth and a national policy on wages and profits
4 August	The United Kingdom raises $2 billion from IMF
10 August	The United Kingdom applies for membership of the EEC
30 September	OEEC becomes OECD with the United States and Canada as full members
16 November	Electricity Council breaks the 'pay pause': rebuked by the Prime Minister
17 November	OECD members accept target of 50 per cent growth in output between 1960 and 1970
18 December	First Director of National Economic Development Council appointed (Sir Robert Shone)

1962

1 January	IMF obtains drawing rights of $6,000 million from ten member countries under the General Agreement to Borrow (GAB)
2 February	Publication of *Incomes Policy: the Next Step* (Cmnd 1626) proposing a limit to the average increase in wages of 2–2.5 per cent per annum
31 March	End of 'pay pause'
17 April	Talks on European political treaty broken off indefinitely

4 May	Canada reverts to fixed exchange rate
9 May	NEDC to examine implications of 4 per cent growth from 1961 to 1966
3 July	3 per cent wage increase accepted by engineering and shipyard workers
13 July	Seven Ministers leave the UK Cabinet, including the Chancellor (Selwyn Lloyd)
26 July	National Incomes Commission to be set up; opposed by trade unions
31 July	All debts to IMF discharged
1 August	First stage of Common Agricultural Policy
19 September	UK proposal of Mutual Currency Account in IMF to increase international liquidity: opposed by the United States
11 October	President Kennedy signs Trade Expansion Act
23–8 October	Cuban missile crisis

1963

1 January	Cold spell for over two months causes big rise in unemployment in the United Kingdom
14 January	De Gaulle vetoes UK membership of EEC; offers associate membership
14 February	Harold Wilson becomes Leader of the Labour party in succession to Hugh Gaitskell (died 18 January)
3 April	Expansionary budget in the United Kingdom: new 'guiding light' of 3.5 per cent
15 April	NEDC publishes *Conditions Favourable to Faster Growth*
18 July	Kennedy announces new balance-of-payments measures including 15 per cent tax on purchases of foreign securities
26 July	Japan joins OECD
14 August	Kennedy tax cuts pass Ways and Means Committee of Congress
29 September	IMF agrees to set up two enquiries into world liquidity requirements
19 October	Lord Home succeeds Harold Macmillan as Prime Minister of the United Kingdom
23 October	Robbins Report on Higher Education in the United Kingdom
14 November	Industrial Training Bill sets up seven new training boards

22 November	Assassination of President Kennedy
18 December	UK public spending to increase by 4.1 per cent a year over the next four years

1964

27 January	UK school leaving age to be raised to 16 in 1970
5 February	TUC rejects NEDC draft of a prices and incomes policy statement
25 February	Resale Price Maintenance Bill introduced: becomes law on 16 July
3 March	Ministry of Transport agrees to Beeching proposals for railway closures
15 March	Italy to receive credits for £1,000 million from US and European banks
16 March	President Johnson submits $1,000 million 'attack on poverty' bill to Congress
23 March	UN Conference on Trade and Development opens (closes 16 June)
14 April	UK budget raises taxes; aims to reduce rate of growth from 5.6 to 4 per cent
4 May	Kennedy Round opens in Geneva
28 July	IMF renews stand-by credit of $1,000 million to the United Kingdom
10 September	Governors of IMF agree to 25 per cent increase in quotas
15 October	Labour party wins General Election with overall majority of five
16 October	Brezhnev succeeds Kruschev as First Secretary of Soviet Communist Party
16 October	China explodes her first nuclear device
26 October	UK government announces measures to reduce external deficit estimated at £700–£800 million; surcharge of 15 per cent on all manufactured imports and system of export rebates
3 November	Lyndon Johnson elected President of the United States
11 November	UK budget raises taxes and national insurance contributions and announces increase in pensions in 1965
19 November	EFTA Council not satisfied of need for surcharge without consultation

23 November	UK bank rate raised to 7 per cent
25 November	Bank of England announces credits of $3000 million from banks of sixteen countries and the Bank of International Settlements (BIS)
16 December	Joint 'Statement of Intent' on prices and incomes policy signed by Government, CBI and TUC
18 December	GATT Council declares UK import surcharge a violation of the Treaty
28 December	Signor Saragat elected President of Italy after twenty-one ballots

1965

5 January	French government to convert dollar holdings into gold
25 January	Biggest increase in US social expenditure since the New Deal
4 February	General de Gaulle demands abandonment of reserve currencies and return to gold standard
10 February	President Johnson announces plan for reducing US balance-of-payments deficit
17 February	India imposes 10 per cent import surcharge
18 February	Board of Trade orders end of all resale price maintenance
22 February	UK import surcharge to be cut in April to 10 per cent
22 February	UK public expenditure to be limited to increase of 4.25 per cent per annum
26 February	IMF quotas to be raised by 25 per cent (more for larger countries)
17 March	TUC agrees to 3–3.5 norm for wage increases
6 April	UK budget introduces (long-term) capital gains tax and corporation tax
30 April	Publication of steel nationalization White Paper
6 May	London clearing banks to limit increase in lending to 5 per cent in 1965–6
6 May	First meeting of National Board for Prices and Incomes
12 May	The United Kingdom draws $1.4 billion from IMF
1 July	France decides to block further progress on Common Market
27 July	Restrictive financial measures in the United Kingdom

9 September	General de Gaulle calls for revision of Treaty of Rome, repudiating supra-national provisions
16 September	Publication of *The National Plan*
22 September	TUC to set up 'early warning system' for wage claims

1966

15 January	US budget puts emphasis on Great Society and Vietnam War: tax cuts to be balanced by quicker collection of taxes due in 1966–7
25 January	UK government to set up Industrial Reorganization Corporation to encourage mergers
1 February	London clearing banks asked to limit advances to 105 per cent of March 1965 level
10 March	France withdraws from NATO
31 March	UK General Election gives Labour increased majority of ninety-seven
3 May	UK budget introduces Selective Employment Tax and seeks voluntary restraints on investment in developed sterling area countries
13 June	£2,000 million credits to the United Kingdom arranged at BIS annual meeting
8 July	France and the United Kingdom announce decision to build Channel tunnel
20 July	Harold Wilson announces measures to reduce home demand by £500 million and overseas spending by £150 million: voluntary wage freeze
25 August	Group of Ten issue *Report on International Liquidity*
4 October	Compulsory provisions of Prices and Incomes Act are actuated
22 November	White Paper on wages and prices policy during period of severe restraint (Cmnd 3150)
30 November	Import surcharge removed
31 December	Final reduction to zero in EFTA of internal tariffs on industrial goods

1967

11 January	President Johnson asks Congress for $4,500 million in new taxes for Vietnam War
20 January	Finance Ministers of the United States and four main European countries agree at Chequers to co-operate in keeping interest rates down

16 February	UK government spending to be £660 million higher in 1967–8
21 March	White Paper on Prices and Incomes Policy (Cmnd 3235). Voluntary vetting system by TUC and CBI to replace compulsory notification
11 April	Neutral UK budget aiming at 3 per cent growth in 1967–8
11 May	The United Kingdom applies to join EEC
5 June	Yom Kippur War between Israel and neighbours; fighting ends 12 June
9 June	White Paper on Regional Employment Premium (Cmnd 3310), to be operative 4 September
30 June	End of period of severe (wage) restraint; period of moderation to follow
30 June	Kennedy Round tariff agreements signed
19 July	Large natural gas strike off Norfolk coast
24 July	Cutback in UK government spending to 3 per cent average over next three years
23 August	Race riots in Detroit; damage of $1 billion
29 August	The United Kingdom relaxes hire-purchase restrictions
1 September	Arabs restore full oil supplies to West
11 September	Group of Ten agree to create SDRs to supplement reserves
2 November	Test rate of discount for nationalized industries fixed at 8 per cent (Cmnd 3437)
18 November	Devaluation of pound sterling from $2.80 to $2.40; bank rate increased to 8 per cent; target of £500 million improvement in balance of payments
29 November	James Callaghan (Chancellor) and Roy Jenkins (Home Secretary) exchange places; IMF agrees to standby credit of £1,400 million; Letter of Intent next day fixes limits for government borrowing and 'domestic credit creation'
29 November	Federal Reserve Bank of New York announces increase in swap facilities to $6,780 million after pressure on dollar
12 December	Informal central bank agreement to limit demands for gold from gold pool countries
19 December	France vetoes discussions by EEC of applications to join by the United Kingdom, Eire, Denmark and Norway

189

| 21 December | Fiftieth Report from Prices and Incomes Board |

1968

1 January	President Johnson announces restrictions on foreign spending designed to save $3,000 million in 1968
16 January	UK Prime Minister announces cuts in government spending to save £700 million in 1968–9
16 January	Industrial Expansion Bill to provide aid for industrial modernization (Cmnd 3509)
12 February	Basle credits renewed for a further year
29 February	OECD calls for 5.5 per cent economic growth in 1968 in France, Germany and Italy to offset US restrictions
7 March	OECD Working Party 3 urges cut in the United Kingdom official target from 4 to 3 per cent growth
15 March	London Stock Exchange, foreign exchange and gold market closed; George Brown resigns as Foreign Secretary
18 March	After meeting in Washington, two-tier gold system is established
19 March	Stringent UK budget to raise £923 million in new taxation in 1968–9; legislation to follow enforcing maximum increase in wages and dividends of 3.5 per cent in year from end July
25 March	Chancellor rejects TUC Economic Committee's call for 6 per cent growth target
1 April	London gold market re-opens
3 April	White Paper on Productivity, Prices and Incomes Policy in 1968 and 1969 (Cmnd 3590) announces legislation to freeze wages for twelve months, enforce price reductions and control rents and dividends
11 April	Restrictive Trade Practices Bill
6 May	Demonstrations by Sorbonne students in Paris; general strike on 14 May; riots continuing on 24 May
29 May	Pompidou announces agreement with French trade unions and employers
5 June	Senator Robert Kennedy assassinated in Los Angeles
7 June	Douglas Jay calls for withdrawal of application to join EEC

26 June	France announces temporary import quotas, export aids and price controls for second half of June; GATT accepts quota restrictions
1 July	Kennedy Round tariff cuts implemented
8 July	'Basle facilities' of $2 billion agreed to help the United Kingdom offset sterling balance fluctuations
9 July	Monopolies Commission rejects merger between Lloyds, Barclays and Martins by six votes to four; Martins accept takeover bid from Barclays on 25 July
13 August	French budget aims at 7 per cent growth in 1969
21 August	Invasion of Czechoslovakia by Warsaw Pact
30 September	Labour Party Conference votes by large majority for repeal of Prices and Incomes Act
16 October	Seminar at UK Treasury with IMF on monetary policy
1 November	New restrictions on hire-purchase in the United Kingdom
6 November	Richard Nixon elected President of the United States
16 November	Deutschmark exceeds dollar ceiling in Zurich
20 November	Flight from the franc: Group of Ten Finance and Economic Ministers meet with central bankers in Bonn, extend $2,000 million standby credits to France on 22 November; France devalues by 10 per cent on 24 November
22 November	UK Chancellor announces import deposit scheme; use of tax regulator; reduced ceiling on bank lending
15 December	NEDC accepts 3 per cent growth target for 1969 but TUC reasserts its 6 per cent target next day
21 December	The United States launches Apollo spacecraft with crew of three to circle the moon

1969

17 January	White Paper on *In Place of Strife: a Policy for Industrial Relations* (Cmnd 3888)
29 January	100th Report of Prices and Incomes Board
10 February	Labour Party Executive rejects provisions of *In Place of Strife*
14 February	Government to encourage nationalized industries to raise capital abroad
2 March	Concorde's maiden flight in France; 9 April in the United Kingdom

4 April	US bank rate raised to 6 per cent: highest for forty years
15 April	UK budget raises additional £345 million in new taxation
28 April	Resignation of de Gaulle
12 May	Danish bank rate at 9 per cent
12 June	British exports reported under-recorded by £10 million per month
18 June	British government drops Industrial Relations Bill
19–20 June	Six National Board for Prices and Incomes reports issued
23 June	New Letter of Intent to IMF giving targets for balance-of-payments surplus, public expenditure and domestic credit creation
17 July	Germany increases minimum reserve ratios of commercial banks by 10 per cent
21 July	Armstrong steps onto the moon
22 July	The United Kingdom imposes tariffs on Commonwealth imports of textiles
8 August	France devalues franc by 11.1 per cent
19 August	Test rate of discount raised to 10 per cent
3 September	TUC votes for complete repeal of Prices and Incomes Act
11 September	West German bank rate raised to 6 per cent
21 September	IMF Annual Report opposes floating rates of exchange
28 September	Deutschmark floats temporarily
5 October	Department of Economic Affairs abolished
8 October	French bank rate reaches 8 per cent
17 October	Arthur Burns succeeds William McChesney Martin at Federal Reserve Board
21 October	Willy Brandt becomes West German Chancellor
24 October	Deutschmark revalued by 9.29 per cent
6 November	Expansionary monetary measures in Germany
2 December	EEC Summit Conference on agricultural finance, monetary co-operation and applications for membership from the United Kingdom and others
12 December	Monopolies Commission and National Board for Prices and Incomes to be merged
30 December	Increase in IMF quotas of 35 per cent or over

BIOGRAPHIES OF PARTICIPANTS

Artis, Michael
b. 1938   Professor of Economics, University of Manchester, since 1975; Editor, *National Institute of Economic and Social Research Review*, 1967–72; Professor of Applied Economics, Swansea University College, 1972–5.

Atkinson, Sir Fred
b. 1919   Chief Economic Adviser, HM Treasury, and Head of Government Economic Service, 1977–9; Member of the Economic Section, Cabinet Office, later Treasury, 1949–69; Chief Economic Adviser, Department of Trade and Industry, 1970–3; Assistant Secretary-General, OECD, 1973–5; Chief Economic Adviser, Department of Energy, 1975–7.

Boltho, Andrea
b. 1939   Fellow of Magdalen College, Oxford; Japan Foundation Fellow 1973–4.

Brittan, Samuel
b. 1933   Principal Economic Commentator, *The Financial Times*, since 1966; Economics Editor, *The Observer*, 1961–4; Adviser, Department of Economic Affairs, 1965.

Budd, Alan
b. 1937   Group Economic Adviser, Barclays Bank, since 1988; Professor of Economics, London Business School, 1981–8 (and part-time 1988–); Senior Economic Adviser, HM Treasury, 1970–4.

Cairncross, Sir Alec
b. 1911   Chancellor, University of Glasgow, since 1972; Economic Adviser to H.M. Government 1961–4; Head of Government Economic Service 1964–9; Master of St Peter's College, Oxford, 1969–78.

Callaghan, Lord
b. 1912   Prime Minister, 1976–9; Chancellor of the Exchequer, 1964–7; Home Secretary, 1967–70; Foreign Secretary, 1974–6; President, University College, Swansea, since 1986.

Crockett, Andrew
b. 1943   Executive Director, Bank of England, since 1989; Bank of England, 1966–72; International Monetary Fund, 1972–89.

Croham, Lord
b. 1917   Chairman, British National Oil Corporation, 1982–5; Deputy Under Secretary of State, Department of Economic Affairs, 1964–6; Permanent Under Secretary of State, 1966–8; Permanent Secretary, HM Treasury, 1968–74; Deputy Chairman, British National Oil Corporation, 1978–82.

Dahrendorf, Sir Ralf
b. 1929   Warden, St Antony's College, Oxford, since 1987; Director, London School of Economics, 1974–84; Professor of Sociology, Hamburg, 1958–60; Tubingen, 1960–4; Konstanz, 1966–9; Parliamentary Secretary of State, Foreign Office, West Germany, 1969–70; Commissioner, EEC, 1970–4.

Dow, Christopher
b. 1916   Executive Director, Bank of England, 1973–81; Assistant Secretary General, OECD, Paris, 1963–73; Treasury, 1945–54, 1962–3; Deputy Director, National Institute of Economic and Social Research, 1954–62.

Higgins, Terence
b. 1928   Chairman, Select Committee on the Treasury, since 1983; Opposition spokesman on Treasury and Economic Affairs, 1966–70, 1974; Minister of State, the Treasury, 1970–2; Financial Secretary to the Treasury, 1972–4.

Hunter, Laurence
b. 1934   Professor of Applied Economics, University of Glasgow, since 1970; Vice Principal, 1982–6.

Jenkins, Lord
b. 1920   Chancellor, University of Oxford, since 1987; Home Secretary, 1965–7, 1974–6; Chancellor of the Exchequer, 1967–70; Deputy Leader, Labour Party, 1970–2; President, the European Commission, 1977–81.

Katz, Sam
b. 1916   Professor of Economics, Georgetown University, since 1975; Economic Adviser in International Finance Division, Federal Reserve Board, 1948–74; Editor, *Finance and Development*, IMF/IBRD, 1977–82.

Kindleberger, Charles P.
b. 1910   Professor of Economics, Massachusetts Institute of Technology, 1948–81; Winner of Harms Prize, 1987.

Kloten, Norbert
b. 1926   President of the Landeszentralbank of Baden Württemberg since 1976; Member of the Central Bank Board of the Deutsche Bundesbank; Professor of Economics at the University of Tubingen, 1960–76; Member of the Council of Economic Experts, 1969–76; Chairman, since 1970.

MacDougall, Sir Donald
b. 1912   Chief Economic Adviser, Confederation of British Industry, 1973–84; Economic Director, National Economic Development Office, 1962–4; Director General, Department of Economic Affairs, 1964–8; Chief Economic Adviser to the Treasury and Head of Government Economic Service, 1969–73.

Malinvaud, Edmond
b. 1923   Professor of Economics, Collège de France; Institut National de la Statistique et des Etudes Economiques, 1948–74; Director General, 1974–87; President of the Econometric Society, 1963; Directeur de la Prévision du Ministère de l'Economie et des Finances, 1972–4; President of the International Economic Association, 1974–7.

Matthews, Robin
b. 1927   Professor of Political Economy, Cambridge University, since 1980; Master of Clare College, Cambridge, since 1975; Drummond Professor of Political Economy, University of Oxford, and Fellow of All Souls College, 1965–75; President, Royal Economic Society, 1984–6.

Meade, James
b. 1907   Nobel Laureate, 1977; Professor of Commerce, London School of Economics, 1947–57; Professor of Political Economy, Cambridge, 1957–68; Fellow, Christ's College, Cambridge, 1957–74.

O'Brien, Lord
b. 1908   Deputy Governor, Bank of England, 1964–6; Governor, 1966–73; President, British Bankers' Association, 1973–80.

Skinner, Andrew
b. 1935   Daniel Jack Professor of Political Economy, University of Glasgow, since 1985.

Solow, Robert M.
b. 1924   Nobel Laureate, 1987; Professor of Economics, Massachusetts Institute of Technology, since 1974; Senior Economist, Council of Economic Advisers, 1961–2; President, American Economic Association, 1976.

Tobin, James
b. 1918   Nobel Laureate, 1981; Sterling Professor of Economics, Yale University, 1957–88; Member of the Council of Economic Advisers, 1961–2; Director, Cowles Foundation for Research in Economics, 1955–61.

Vines, David
b. 1949   Adam Smith Professor of Political Economy, University of Glasgow, since 1985; Fellow, Pembroke College, Cambridge, 1976–85.

Williamson, John
b. 1937   Senior Fellow, Institute for International Economics, Washington, DC; former member of the Economic Section, H.M. Treasury.

Worswick, David
b. 1916   Director, National Institute of Economic and Social Research, 1965–82; Fellow, Magdalen College, Oxford, 1945–65.

GENERAL BIBLIOGRAPHY

Beckerman, W. (ed.) (1972) *The Labour Government's Economic Record, 1964–70*, London: Duckworth.

Benn, A.N.W. (1987) *Out of the Wilderness: Diaries 1963–67*, London: Hutchinson.

—— (1988) *Office without Power: Diaries 1968–72*, London: Hutchinson.

Blackaby, F. (ed.) (1975) *British Economic Policy 1960–74*, Cambridge: Cambridge University Press.

Castle, B. (1984) *The Castle Diaries 1964–70*, London: Weidenfeld & Nicolson.

Cohen, C.D. (1971) *British Economic Policy 1960–69*, London: Butterworth.

McKie, D. and Cook, C. (1972) *The Decade of Disillusion: British Politics in the Sixties*, London: Macmillan.

Wilson, J.H. (1971) *The Labour Government 1964–70: A Personal Record*, London: Weidenfeld & Nicolson and Michael Joseph.

INDEX

Aberrations 30–1
Abramovitz, M. 20–1, 25, 106
Abs, H. 34
Acceleration of growth 7, 35, 58, 106, 174; of prices 7, 9, 13, 39, 54, 60–1, 65, 69, 74–5, 102, 121, 159, 161; of wages 6–7, 13, 45, 47, 52, 58–63, 66, 75
Accelerationist theory of inflation 116, 121, 128–9
Accord de Grenelle 28
Adenauer, Konrad 34, 38
Adjustment process 112–13, 119, 134–5
Allen, Douglas *see* Croham, Lord
American loan of 1946 107
Anomy 145, 156
Armstrong, William 97
Artis, Michael 72–3, 94–6, 100, 104–5
Assignment rules 118–19
Atkinson, Fred 108
Australia 48, 107
Austria 18, 48, 107
Authority, paralysis of 144; undermined by Vietnam war 154

Balance of payments 1, 3, 8, 12, 81–2, 88, 90, 105, 118–19; crises 2, 88, 104; deficits 17, 28, 55, 69, 83–4, 95, 111; medium-term 112
Ball, R.J. 69
Balogh, Thomas 101
Bancor 112, 113

Bank advances 54, 82
Bank Charter Act 128
Bank deutscher Länder 34
Barber, Anthony 55, 60, 69, 73, 98
Barro, R.J. 69, 73
Basle Agreement (of 1968) 127
Beckerman, Wilfred 17
Belgium 24, 48
Bell, Daniel 145
Benign neglect 28, 121
Beveridge, William 86
Bevin Ernest 75; boys 26
Blackaby, Frank 10
Blinder, A.S. 164
Boltho, Andrea 129–30, 177–8
Bonn Summit 132
Boom 17, 20, 22–3, 27, 76, 130; Barber 98; commodity of 1972–3 129–30, 173, 178; post-war 53
Brandt, W. 139
Bretton Woods 10–12, 20, 25, 37, 40, 55, 59–60, 63, 69, 110–20, 127, 132; breakdown of 28, 115, 130, 133
Brittan, Samuel 77, 101–2, 179, 182
Brookings Report of 1968 86–7, 93
Brown, A.J. 57–62, 64
Brown, George 9, 72, 92, 104
Brown, Henry Phelps 6, 10, 58, 64, 68, 73
Budd, Alan 73–4, 155
Budget 22, 55, 84, 121, 126, 164–8; balanced-multiplier 22–3 *see also* Fiscal policy

26, 42; investment-led 66; social
effects of 156; theories of 68-9,
105 *see also* Productivity
'Guest workers' 25, 32, 38
Gulf War 154
Gutt, Camille 107

Hall, Robert 87
Harrod, Roy 87, 91
Hattersley, Roy 98
Hayek, Friedrich von 101
Heath, Edward 60, 69, 73, 99, 148
Heller, Walter 20, 22, 168
Higgins, Terence 98-100, 148,
150, 179
'Hinge' 58-9, 64, 68, 73
Hire purchase controls 54, 82, 94
Hirsch, Fred 146
Home, Alec Douglas 103
Hopkins, Richard 16
Howe, Geoffrey 74, 126
Hunter, Lawrence 194
Hysteresis 70, 73

Illich, Ivan 155
IMF 33, 34, 53, 85, 107, 120, 126,
127, 132, 134, 135
Import control 82-4, 87, 91; prices
6, 56, 58, 59, 62, 65; surcharge
1, 84-5, 92; surpluses 25
Incomes policy 1, 2, 7-9, 27,
58-62, 65, 71, 73, 77, 83-8,
91-3, 95, 98, 115, 120, 160, 172,
179-80; statutory 13, 85
Industrial Development Certificates
(IDCs) 94
Industrial Reconstruction
Corporation (IRC) 1, 84
Inflation Introduction, *passim*; 23,
28, 36, 39, 41, 45, 54-8, 60-4,
67-70, 72-4, 81, 92-3, 95, 102,
104, 115, 119-20, 125, 148, 158,
161-2; spiral 57, 74; divergent
rates of 123, 128; structural 55-6
Inglehart, Robert 145
Innovation 1, 3-5, 27, 69
In Place of Strife 9, 62, 65, 70-1,
75, 148
Instruments of economic policy

Ch. 3, *passim*, 11, 62, 81, 85,
115, 120
Interest rates 18, 28, 37, 67, 82,
131; negative real 112-13
Investment boom 22-3, 25, 53;
currency 1; grants 1; industrial
19, 90; international 3

J curve 103
Jacobsson, Per 33, 34
Jenkins, Roy 2, 9, 36, 41, 70-1,
148-50, 155
Johnson, Harry 23
Johnston, President L.B. 16, 22,
163
Jones, Fred 72
Jones, Jack 64, 75
Joseph, Keith 100

Kahn, Richard 84
Kaldor, Nicholas 5, 100, 121
Katz, Sam 33-4, 37, 41, 133-7
Keeler, Christine 103, 180
Kennedy, President John F. 2, 64,
164, 165, 173
Kennedy Round 12
Kessler matrices 111
Keynes, J.M./Keynesian 22, 23,
36, 37, 39, 40, 67, 84, 110-11,
112, 118, 124, 131, 132, 135
Kindleberger, Charles 11, 15-30,
30-2, 33-8, 68-70, 72, 120,
127-8
Kloten, Norbert 10, 38-9, 76-7,
177-8
Kondratieff cycles 4, 16, 18-19, 29,
38
Korean War 13, 38, 59, 60, 114
Kredit Anstalt 107
Krugman, Paul 69

Labour supply 25, 27, 70, 72;
skilled 26
Lags 100
Lamfalussy, Alexandre 20
Lawrence, Robert 114
Lawson, Nigel 69, 97, 179
Layard, Richard 67, 70
Leavis, F.R. 155

For Product Safety Concerns and Information please contact our EU
representative GPSR@taylorandfrancis.com
Taylor & Francis Verlag GmbH, Kaufingerstraße 24, 80331 München, Germany

www.ingramcontent.com/pod-product-compliance
Ingram Content Group UK Ltd.
Pitfield, Milton Keynes, MK11 3LW, UK
UKHW042159240425
457818UK00005B/26